JEWISH MARRIAGE:
A Halakhic Ethic

THE LIBRARY OF JEWISH LAW AND ETHICS
VOLUME XII
EDITED BY NORMAN LAMM

Jakob and Erna Michael professor of Jewish philosophy
Yeshiva University

YESHIVA
UNIVERSITY
1886-1986
תרמ"ו-תשמ"ו

JEWISH MARRIAGE:
A Halakhic Ethic

By

Reuven P. Bulka

KTAV PUBLISHING HOUSE, INC.
YESHIVA UNIVERSITY PRESS
NEW YORK AND HOBOKEN

marriage -religious aspects- Jewish
marriage - Jewish law

© 1986 REUVEN P. BULKA

Library of Congress Cataloging in Publication Data
Bulka, Reuven P.
　Jewish marriage.

　(The Library of Jewish law and ethics; v. 12)
　Bibliography: p.
　1. Marriage—Religious aspects—Judaism. 2. Marriage
(Jewish law) I. Title. II. Series.
BM713.B76　1986　　　296.3'85　　　85-8094
ISBN 0-88125-077-5
ISBN 0-88125-078-3 (pbk.)

MANUFACTURED IN THE UNITED STATES OF AMERICA

To my
dear wife
Naomi,

Who made this
and so much else
possible.

Your deeds will effect closeness; your deeds will effect distance.

—*Ediyot* 5:7

One should enjoy the extension of proliferating goodness to another as one does for the self, and should place no limits on love.

—Ramban, Leviticus 19:17

In all unions, one receives the other, and both receive from each other.

—Maharal, *Netivot Olam, Netiv HaAvodah* 16

The true bond between husband and wife evolves when both actualize the virtue of giving.

—*Mikhtav M'Eliyahu, Kuntrus HaHesed*

Contents

Editor's Preface

"One must not marry a woman", the Talmud instructed an earlier generation, "until he has seen her first, lest he find her uncomely and thus violate the commandment, 'love thy neighbor as thyself.' "

Our contemporaries, of course, are not particularly in need of this caution. But there is a timeless teaching here: love of humanity is expressed, in the first instance, by love of one's spouse.

Marriage is the paradigm of all human relations; society is the family writ large. Whether contemporary societal ills are the cause or the effect of the hard times upon which marriage has fallen is a question worthy of study. Influences probably go in both directions. But clearly marriage, so problematical in our times, deserves to be illuminated by the insights of Halakhah.

Rabbi Reuven P. Bulka performs this task with intelligence and sensitivity. He brings to bear upon it the imposing advantage of his training as a professional psychologist, his learning as a Talmudic scholar, and his counselling experience as a pulpit Rabbi.

Our author's elaboration of a halakhic ethic of marriage is of special importance, of course, for those who seek instruction in Jewish marriage from the sources of Judaism. But his work will prove enlightening as well on a more universal plane. Three thousand years of history, thinking, and experience have much wisdom to teach men and women of all commitments in this most human of all institutions—marriage.

August 10, 1985

NORMAN LAMM
Editor

Acknowledgments

This book was written during a family sabbatical in Israel, 5744 (1983–84). My spending the year in Israel had a distinct impact on the book. The very air of Israel was an inspiration, as was the manifest scholarship everywhere in evidence, and the vast number of Judaic texts readily available. That the subject of marriage is of immediate moment was driven home to me quite forcefully in the first few months of our stay. Every week of those initial months, a new volume concerned with marriage appeared on the bookstalls. Some of these texts are quoted from in this presentation, and even those which are not quoted from directly made some impression, for better or for worse.

This presentation reflects the efforts of many who helped in so many different ways. Dr. Norman Lamm, the overall editor of this series, was the ideal editor, concerned and involved in developing the work, yet not overbearing or imposing in offering timely and always insightful comments. His influence is felt not only editorially, but also through his important book *A Hedge of Roses*, whose ethos and essence have had a significant impact on this volume. Dr. Lamm's approach to marriage, first presented in 1965, remains instructive today.

Mr. Bernard Scharfstein, of Ktav, made some very useful suggestions which have enhanced the volume aside from being his usual helpful self. I am also appreciative of the very proficient copy editing supplied by Mr. Robert Milch.

Thanks are due to the Rabbinical Council of America for granting permission to quote liberally from the *Family and Marriage Newsletter*, and also from an article originally written for *Tradition*. I am privileged to write and edit for them. Thanks, too, to Chief Rabbi Sir Immanuel Jakobovits, for permission to quote from a piece which appeared in *L'Eylah*.

As I mentioned at the outset, this book was written during a sabbatical. This was made possible by the understanding and cooperation of the shul I have been privileged to serve as rabbi for the past seventeen years (sabbatical included), Congregation Machzikei Hadas in Ottawa. To all those involved in making the sabbatical possible goes my grateful appreciation.

The Hebrew University, specially the Givat Ram Library, was almost home for quite a while. The staff there and at the Mount Scopus Library were always gracious and helpful. In all the research done there, only one Judaic text that was needed could not be found, and that, fortunately, was available in the library of Mosad HaRav Kook. To Hebrew University and its library staff go my profound thanks.

In Israel I had the advantage of many conversations with a recent *oleh*, Rabbi Shubert Spero, himself an author in this series. His penetrating insights always gave new dimensions to evolving ideas. The areas covered in the full gamut of marriage involve sensitive topics, and I learned to admire those authors who had the courage to address some vital issues where others had feared to tread, issues where direction and help are most desperately needed. They and their works appear frequently in the notes to the text of this book.

The book was written in Jerusalem but it was typed in Ottawa. I greatly value the special care in delivery of various parts of the manuscript by Paul Litwack, Molly Borenstein, Doris Bronstein, and Sol and Molly Sherman. The typist herself, my secretary at Congregation Machzikei Hadas, Blanche Osterer, did a superb job of making this a coherent manuscript, overcoming many obstacles, not the least of which was deciphering my less than elegant handwriting. Hers is a real achievement.

Jean Naemark was particularly helpful in trying to locate source material. I am grateful for all her assistance.

To my dear parents, Rabbi and Mrs. Hayyim Yaakov Bulka, whose home and library in Israel were graciously shared, and whose example and encouragement were always salient, a special expression of thanks for so much is made with the awareness that words are inadequate to describe what they have meant to me and to our family.

To my dear children, Yocheved, Shmuel, Rena, Eliezer, and Binyomin, who thought they were going to Israel so that the family could be together, only to find their father wrapped up in writing a book, goes my appreciation for their understanding and good humor.

Finally, I come to the one to whom this book is dedicated, my dear wife, Naomi. Consistent with a theme developed in the text, I am indebted to my parents-in-law, Mr. and Mrs. George Jakobovits, for their part in my wife's being what she is, and for all they continue to do for her, and her family. It was my wife's idea to come to Israel for a sabbatical, and then it was her perseverance and courage that carried the family through a very difficult time, what with the many trips back to Ottawa that I made during the course of the year. My wife not only read and improved the manuscript, she also inspired it.

I conclude these acknowledgments with the wish that all who had a hand in this work will gain fulfillment from the positive contribution to Jewish marriage and Jewish marriages that this volume will hopefully make.

Reuven P. Bulka

Jerusalem and Ottawa

Introduction

Jewish law regarding the family, and most specifically husband-wife relations, is all-encompassing and all embracing. More than mere legalities are involved, for Halakhah (Jewish law applied to life) programs the structure of the family, and at once urges the distinct, individual, humane response of each partner, of each couple, to thus live out the sublime beauty of the Jewish home as was envisaged by the Torah.*

The halakhic structure remains essentially the same today as in the past generations, but the individual response within the halakhic context must perforce incorporate the different social realities of the day. This is not to legitimize a compromise of Halakhah; on the contrary, it is to ennoble Halakhah by applying its principles, in dignity, resoluteness, and profound understanding, to the unique situation confronting Jews today.

In the process of formulating a marriage ethic, it will become patently clear that within the context of Halakhah, much has been adapted and continues to be adapted. Contemporary sages, aware of the different position of women today, their superior intellectual development and their closing of the gap separating them from men, argue that this should be incorporated into the marital context. To cite another example, the frequency of *onah* has not gone unaffected by present contingencies. These and other points will become clear in the course of the volume. Thankfully, unlike the Karaites' approach, Halakhah is structure, not stricture. It is the framework for the way to go (*halikhah*), a framework which is at once uncompromising around the borders and yearning for majestic expression within, or inside, the halakhic context.

---

*For further discussion of how Halakhah functions in Jewish life, see Appendix 1.

The ways of the Torah are the ways of pleasantness (Prov.
3:17). The Torah, properly applied, is an expression of life which
is pleasing and pleasant. That the realities of Jewish family life
today are far from pleasing and pleasant is in most instances a
case either of the Torah not being applied or of its being applied
improperly.*

A Halakhic Marriage Ethic

What follows is the formulation of a halakhic ethic which will
attempt to project the pleasing and the pleasant in marriage from
a theoretical view. But theories only work if they are properly
applied. Hopefully, what is herein proposed will reinvigorate
Jewish marriage and make it the foundation of the Jewish family
of today and the cornerstone of the Jewish community of tomorrow.

Before embarking on this rather imposing task, a word is in
order to explain what is meant by "a halakhic ethic." A halakhic
ethic is not *the* halakhic ethic. Judaism is not, and never has been,
a monolith. One approaches the formulation of a halakhic
approach or position with trepidation, praying and hoping not to
distort through selective use of sources or biased interpretation.
This volume is a proposal, a firm proposal, but certainly not the
only possible proposal.

The book itself is presented almost as two books. The basic
text is written for a general audience, with footnote markings
appearing only at the end of paragraphs. The notes in the back
are almost a text in itself, providing the sources for the proposi-
tions in the text.

A *halakhic* ethic is one which is rooted in the primary sources
of Jewish tradition, namely the Torah, the Talmud, and the
authentic explications of these sources in ensuing generations.
Modern thinking about marriage, psychological or sociological,
however much in vogue, must be judged in the light of time-
proven Jewish traditions, rather than the reverse. This halakhic
ethic, whilst it focuses on marriage, is essentially an ethic of

---

*For further discussion of the Jewish family today, see Appendix 2.

personal existence escalated onto the marital platform. It is decency, *mentshlichkeit*, with all that this implies, socially and religiously, for the individual, plus the unique *mentshlichkeit* imperatives that must operate in marriage.

A halakhic *ethic* is not a superimposed code of behavior tacked onto the Halakhah. A halakhic ethic should be nothing more or less than the all-embracing Halakhah of how marriage is to unfold. If ethics is the Halakhah lived to its full in time and space, then a halakhic ethic for marriage should be precisely that for the couple united in matrimony.

In a sense, what is herein presented is a variation of *Pirkey Avot*, "Chapters of the Elders," which may be termed, with apologies, *Pirkey Ishut*, "Chapters of the Married Couple."

JEWISH MARRIAGE

1

The Prelude to Marriage

Why Marry?

To be or not to be married is the question for many in contemporary society. With all the discouraging findings related to the traditional family, many people are opting out of traditional marriage, and into new forms of relationship. In fact, a recent major study of American couples gave equal time and treatment to lifestyles that had until recently been considered bizarre.[1]

The trouble people have experienced in marriage has doubtless caused a significant number to think twice about getting married. We hear talk of trial marriage, open marriage, relationship without marriage, and other alternatives that steer clear of marriage pure and simple. Plainly, marriage pure and simple is neither pure nor simple anymore. It is complex, complicating, and not a guarantee of bliss or happiness. And, at the same time that we are preoccupied with the pursuit of happiness, indications are that society itself is far from being happy. Loneliness is a pervasive condition, mental hospitals are full, psychologists and psychiatrists are solidly booked, and generally one is hard-pressed to see even a segment of society that is reasonably happy.[2]

With traditions crumbling and society at loose ends, there is another alternative, other than searching for a "new" lifestyle, a more rewarding alternative that may offer hope to contemporary society. That alternative is to take a second look at tradition itself. For society at large, it is to ask: Why should the patterns of yesterday be rejected simply becaue they are not modern?

1

For the Jewish community, it is to ask: What is the deeper meaning of the traditions that have served us so well in the past? What was it about the Jewish family of yesteryear that made it, as a general rule, a happy, inspiring, spiritually uplifting entity? What has been left out of the modern family that has led to the uneasy, even precarious state of the modern Jewish family?

We know that we are here today because of the Jewish family of yesterday. We do not know what will be tomorrow, because of the disarray in the Jewish family of today. But we do know that we can go a long way toward ensuring a viable future if we stabilize the family, and infuse it with the spiritually uplifting and inspiring ingredients that are essential to growth and continuity.

The way toward infusing the family in this manner begins with the husband-wife relationship. When that relationship is not merely good, but transcendingly good, the effects are felt in the environment of the home. The children are happy and fulfilled, and more likely to continue the parental pattern in their own lives.

But this very continuity is in jeopardy because of the domino effect in the family. The parents are unhappy, the children are therefore also unhappy, and grow up hating their formative years, resolving to distance themselves from their heritage at the first opportunity. That the intermarriage rate in North America is alarmingly high is a well-established fact. But we would be indulging in self-delusion if we attributed that high rate merely to assimilationist forces in society at large. A significant part of the problem is the unhappiness of the Jewish home, which for many has ceased to be a haven, or even a desirable place to be. In saying goodbye to their past, too many eagerly say goodbye at the same time to the Jewishness in their past.[3]

Granted that one can point to relatively happy families which still are forced to confront intermarriage situations; nevertheless, a significant percentage of those who intermarry have a negative attitude to their childhood, their formative years, and resolve to start afresh, unencumbered by the past.

There is thus a twofold concern. The first is that Jews are marrying less; the second, that so many, when they actually do marry, marry outside the faith. From the Judaic perspective, that type of marriage is not recognized as binding, so it is really another form of not being married.[4]

The question "Why marry?" relates to a marriage that is binding and valid according to Jewish law, or Halakhah. In broad, communal terms, the answer to the question "Why marry?" is simply that without marriage, there is no prospect for a future Jewish community.

There is, at the same time, a very personal side to the question "Why marry?" The Talmud is very blunt on the matter. It asserts without equivocation that anyone who is unmarried is a deficient person, an incomplete being. The unmarried person lives by the self, for the self, and knows only the self. But extending outward to embrace another is a fundamental component of being human.[5]

The creation configuration figures prominently in the matter of "Why marry?" The original human being, Adam, was of two forms, the one male, the other female. These two components were separated in God's surgical procedure, and the two, male and female, in coming together, in effect return to the oneness that is their pristine state. Marriage is thus projected, from creation itself, as the natural condition of man and woman.[6]

Marriage is an ideal which has no age limit. One should marry even in the twilight years. In the later stages of life, childbearing may be impossible, but procreation in the form of enhanced value-sharing is still very much a possibility. Living out elemental decency and extending outward toward another being is the firmament for *hesed,* for kindness, concern, empathy, and warmth.[7]

We do not worry that through concern for the other we may possibly lose our individuality, our sense of who we are. Since the highest goal in Judaism is to emulate God, and that emulation expresses itself primarily in the kind deeds we do for others, marriage, and the preoccupation with the partner in marriage rather than with the self, is the way that we get in touch with our true selves, and uncover our spiritual essence, that which makes us human beings created in the Divine Image. The creation model of man as combining the male and female sides presses forward this notion that neither male nor female is really complete without the other, and we achieve completeness not by turning inward but by focusing outward.[8]

Recent studies which link marriage with longer life expectancy and less depression only serve to confirm what has been a Judaic truism for centuries.[9]

Perspective on Dating

According to the Talmud, we begin expounding the laws of a festival thirty days prior to the festival. Obviously, celebrating the festival properly demands adequate preparation. Extrapolating this concept to marriage, which ideally lasts an entire lifetime, not merely seven or eight days, it is only logical to assume that much preparation is imperative, certainly more than thirty days. Indeed, all one's formative years are, or at least should be viewed as, preparation for marriage. The education, training, value orientation, and character development which form one's personality are what one brings to the marriage, and to the next generation. Parents and teachers are obliged to approach their charges not as mere kids, but as children who are adults in the making, and thus they must raise and educate them to carry the mantle of responsibility with all the skills and sensitivity this awesome task demands.[10]

Having been reared into adulthood in this sensitive manner, the aspiring husband or wife is ready to search for a fitting partner. Whilst the locus of search will usually depend on family tradition or established group patterns, the ultimate responsibility for choosing rests with the prospective partners. They must, after meaningful personal encounter, decide whether they complement each other in all the dimensions that fuse marital partners into a harmonious unit. To an extent which varies with each individual, such elements as value compatibility, character type, and physical attractiveness, among other factors, will enter into the decision-making process.[11]

The term "dating" is used to describe the male-female encounters that precede the decision to marry. With the marital context as the focus, the dating procedure itself takes on a very specific coloration. Rather than being an opportunity for a good time, it is instead a serious time, serious so that future good times, in a good and fulfilling life, will be realized. And, even before embarking on the process of completing oneself by finding a partner, it is vital to know oneself, one's strengths and weaknesses, for only thus can one have a clear idea of which "other" will complement and complete the union.

Going places may be a good way to overcome initial hesitancies, but the process of "getting to know" the other is better achieved in meaningful conversation. It is obviously impossible to mandate precise guidelines for how many times a prospective couple should meet before deciding whether they will share the future together. At the same time, it can be stated that frequent dating in and of itself is not a panacea. More important than the number of hours spent together is the quality of the time spent together.[12]

Of utmost importance is that those who are dating be absolutely honest with each other. Honesty here refers to more than simply not telling lies, which is prohibited anyway, under normal circumstances. Honesty here includes telling the entire truth; not conveying false impressions, or projecting false images. When the encounter reaches beyond the formal and into the critical, each of the couple who are "dating" must be able to form a true picture of the other. It is in no one's interest to pull off an immediate coup when the price that will be paid is future disappointment, disillusionment, even potential breakup of the engagement or marriage. This may seem obvious, even simplistic, but the matter is so vital that it demands special mention and attentiveness.[13]

In some circles, the first impulse may be to decorate oneself excessively in order to impress. As an initial gesture of respectfulness, this is certainly not objectionable. But it should not be used as a device to mask reality. At some juncture the natural self, untarnished by the available camouflages, must come to the fore.[14]

One approaches the dating encounter with some measure of behavioral control, mindful of protocol, aware of and sensitive to common niceties, and careful not to utter untoward remarks. If this is a true reflection of how one really is, then there is no problem. But if it is merely a temporary repression which will be

followed by explosion after the finalization of the union, then it is
deception at its worst, and unfair to everyone involved. It is
incumbent on each one of the couple to ensure that the other
should not eventually say, "The person I was engaged to is not the
person I married."[15]

Generally, people are on their best behavior when in the
company of strangers, and less inhibited, to say the least, among
intimates. This pattern, when applied to the period prior to
marriage and the period following marriage, points to an almost
unavoidable trap, the trap of familiarity and the "taking for
granted" syndrome it engenders. Before marriage, one is trying
to "catch," after marriage the other is "caught," or so the subcon-
scious talks. It is therefore advisable to see the dating period not
as a time frame in which one behaves differently, but as that time
frame in which the postwedding behavior pattern is established.
With due allowance for human frailty, it helps immeasurably to
think in terms of continually winning over one's mate, even after
the mate is legally won over.[16]

However much precision is employed in the decision-making
process, the decision to marry still involves a calculated risk. The
partners may be sure of their resolve at the moment, but they
cannot be sure that present and future reality are one and the
same. Future developments, such as economic crisis or the addition of children to the family network, may bring out problems
almost impossible to anticipate in the period prior to marriage.
However, attendant to this unavoidable risk is the simple human
fact that if the partners are unconditionally committed to each
other and to their union, they can usually meet and overcome
almost any crisis together.[17]

One more observation concerning the period prior to the
wedding is in order. Using as a paradigm the union effected
between God and the Israelite community on Mount Sinai via the
Torah, it is worthwhile to keep in mind that the first set of
commandments, given amidst great pomp and fanfare, did not
endure. The second set, transmitted in a more sober setting, have
remained with us to the present.[18]

In the marital context, overexuberance at having found the
perfect partner may be contagiously exciting, but is not necessar-

ily indicative of a superior partnership. Often the euphoria at having found one who can do no wrong is a bad sign, a sign that one has placed passion before reason, and has not approached the process of finding a life's partner with the sober seriousness demanded. Rather than falling in love and then marrying, it is probably better to marry and then rise in love. As such, marriage, instead of being the apex, is merely a significant plateau on the way up. The end goal being an enduring, meaningful union, it is folly to let temporary infatuation obscure what is of ultimate significance.[19]

As with the giving of the commandments, not pomp and fanfare, but sober seriousness, conduces to a union which is of enduring quality.

Who Is The Right One?

Having spelled out some cursory guidelines for choosing a mate, the question "Who is the right one?" still remains. Does one search for *the* right one, or does one search for *a* right one? Is there a predetermined other waiting to be found, or are there many possibilities from which we choose, and then proceed to make it the right choice? In other words, is finding a match as simple as following a heavenly voice, or as complex as the splitting of the Reed Sea?[20]

Ideally, we would like the correct choice to fall into our lap like manna from heaven, but often it is difficult to discern whether the prospective mate is a heavenly gift or a human choice. We look for signs, for the Divine imprimatur to confirm that this is indeed a marriage made in Heaven. But we do not really know; we hope and pray, but we are not sure. What is quite clear is that we are matched with the mates we deserve, and the quality of married life is directly related to deservedness. The type of person one is dictates which other person will be one's life's partner; the type of person one evolves into after marriage greatly affects how one's partner will develop and how the marriage will grow.[21]

Though it is generally true that we get out of marriage what we put into it, yet there are some basic ingredients which, if present, increase the chances of the marriage working. Physical attractiveness is one such ingredient. To be attracted rather than repelled by the other's physical being is important enough that one must take this dimension into account in choosing a mate, and even protracted contemplation of this feature is permitted. Misrepresentation concerning physical condition is prohibited. There is also the matter of physical compatibility. Such factors as the prospective partner's height and age must be taken into account when contemplating marriage.[22]

However important the physical component may be, it is not of overriding importance, for however beautiful the prospective partner may be, if the person is characterologically unfit, the marriage should not proceed. For ultimately, the person's inner beauty is much more crucial to the marriage and its offspring than is external attractiveness.[23]

Inner beauty, of course, refers to character. That one's mate should be of noble character is considered to be of paramount, even overriding, importance. Having sensitivity, a sense of responsibility, and the inclination to act kindly is of critical importance in this regard. Brazenness, intemperate attitude, and inconsiderate behavior are not part of a noble character, and those who manifest these traits are to be avoided when choosing a life partner. What are those of deficient character to do? Are they to remain single? If they persist in their aberrations, they really have no business marrying and thereby locking someone else into a life of misery. The insistence on marrying only one of decent character is a form of genetic engineering which seeks to weed out from the community and its posterity those characteristics which are inconsistent with the humane ethos of Judaism. Insisting on proper character should serve to orient communal educational priorities and hopefully induce those affected to improve.[24]

Since the family is the breeding ground for one's values, much emphasis is placed on the family from which one's prospective partner comes. There is no guarantee that good parents have only good children, but it is more likely. Family stature, or yiḥus (pedigree), is thus important, but only up to a point. The more important factor in choosing a spouse is the stature of the potential partner. It is possible for a child to transcend and surpass the parents in commitment and character, and thus be a more than fitting candidate for marriage.[25]

The Torah scholarship of the family from which one emanates is considered vital, but ultimately it is not intellectual ability as much as the character and good deeds of the family which are crucial. Scholarship which does not translate into deeds is not true scholarship. This is true not only of the parents, but of the potential mate as well. Being the best in the class is not a comment on one's personality. And it is personality more than pure intellectual ability that is basic to marriage.[26]

Specifically but not exclusively when dating is done through arrangement by the parents, who screen the prospective partner before any meeting of the prospective couple takes place, there may be times when the proffered choice of a marriage candidate may seem imposing. In such instances it is preferable to link with a partner with whom one feels more at ease. There are other times when parents may venture a feeling regarding who the child should or should not marry. Parents usually know better than most what is good for their children, and their advice should not be underestimated. Imposing a choice upon the child or vetoing the child's choice is another matter. The child has the right to choose over parental objections, or to refuse a parental choice. But it is equally absurd to reject parental opinion merely because it comes from the parents. Under normal circumstances, and there are exceptions, parents want what is best for their children. The quest for autonomy should not come at the expense of those who are so unconditionally committed to the child's welfare.[27]

Because of the relative disarray in the marriage situation today, there are those who argue for the return of arranged marriages. The traditional *shadkhan* (matchmaker) or the contemporary counterpart, the computer, may be useful in making positive proposals, but decisions must be made by those directly involved, with the aid of family and friends vitally concerned with their well-being. In the end, not burning passion but sober realism should carry the day.[28]

It is possible that even after protracted search one may not find the right one. That is not a matter over which one has direct control. However, it helps to work on oneself, to perfect oneself, to be the right one for someone else who is also looking for the right one.[29]

Readiness for Marriage

Although for most commandments the fulfillment obligation commences on entry into Bar Mitzvah for males and Bat Mitzvah for females, this does not apply to the marriage situation. Here, "Eighteen years for entry into the nuptial canopy" is the operating principle, although in actual practice marriage does not take place that early and is deferred to a later time. Since it takes two who agree for a marriage to be finalized, the idea of eighteen years is more to program readiness than to mandate an unconditional obligation.[30]

There are enough circumstances which justify putting off marriage until one is ready. However, given the proper conditions, there is much reason to argue in favor of marrying the right one early. Two mature individuals with the capacity to adapt may be better able to grow together at an early stage in life than later on when they have molded their personalities more definitively and may be less likely to adjust and accommodate. In spite of the possible advantages, much care must be exercised to prevent jumping into marriage prematurely. Parents should not push their children, for whatever self-serving reasons, before the children are ready, nor should children rush into marriage as an escape from whatever predicament they feel they may be in. The end result may be an even greater predicament from which escape is excruciatingly painful.[31]

Maturity upon entry into marriage is essential. Maturity implies an awareness that life is more than pleasure and luxury, that it includes responsibility to a partner and to ensuing offspring, hard work to ensure that the marriage develops properly, and crises of varying degrees which must be confronted together. But maturity is more than abstract awareness; it is also capacity, the capacity to translate this awareness into effective action. This maturity is often a function of age, but not necessarily. Some are mature in their late teens, others are immature in their thirties. To avoid future complications, it is vital that individuals be honest with themselves and confront their limitations before extending out to others.[32]

Having found the right one does not, or at least should not, automatically translate into immediate marriage. A mature readiness to marry must perforce include the capacity to sustain the marriage with adequate means. It matters little who of the couple is to be the provider, or whether both together will provide. What matters is that a measure of financial stability should accompany the decision to marry. Marriage hardly ever solves one's personal problems. Marriage is even more shaky if the actual coming together creates problems, and adequate income is one of the most likely difficulties to be created by marriage. To leave the matter of income provision to chance is to be irresponsible to oneself and to the other.[33]

There is another side to financial considerations, where instead of finances being ignored, they are overemphasized. Marrying merely for financial gain is a contemptible abuse. This does not mean that it is sinful to marry one who is rich, only that wealth should be more tangential a factor in the marriage decision.[34]

In a situation where mature readiness in all aspects is evident, there is little reason to delay marriage if the decision to marry has been made. However, the mature individual or couple may at times harbor doubts even when everything seems to fit. Here maturity implies taking a bit more time, or taking other steps to resolve one's doubts. The individual or couple should not be coerced by persuasion either subtle or blunt, and others involved should be careful to respect the doubts and patiently await their explication in whatever direction. Additionally, the officiating rabbi who feels the couple are not compatible, or at least not ready, should feel free to tactfully express these views rather than be party to an event in which he feels ill at ease. Officiating at a wedding is a sacred responsibility rather than mere rubber-stamping.[35]

Readiness for marriage, the maturity with which one approaches marriage, is reflected in the priorities in evidence prior to the wedding. Too often the couple is bogged down by trivial matters, at the expense of the ability to focus on how to most responsibly face the future together. It is preferable that the couple detach themselves from the prewedding excitement and concentrate on their goals in life, the values they cherish, and how they propose to implement these values and actualize these goals.

Serious soul-searching by the bride and groom, and study of outstanding Judaic tracts on ethical perfection, is the more superior way to prepare for the marriage. Additionally, knowing fluently one's direct responsibilities in marriage, as spelled out in the Code of Jewish Law (*Shulḥan Arukh*), is essential.[36]

Equipped with the proper knowledge and attitude, one is then able to enter the marriage compact and become a source of joy and fulfillment for one's partner, an inspiration to the community, and a foundation for Jewish continuity.

2

Man and Woman

Respect for Woman

Marriage is, in simple terms, the physical, emotional, valuational union of a man with a woman. Marriage is more than friendship, although it is also friendship. Marriage is intimacy, a fusion of souls, a partnership in the totality of life.

In this partnership, the husband comes into his own thanks to his wife, and the wife comes into her own thanks to her husband. One without the other is incomplete. It is thus wrong to think of man and woman, husband and wife, in terms of being anything other than true equals.[1]

Guidelines which may be offered for the way that husband and wife interact should not be seen as a means of putting the woman in her place, even if that place is a pedestal. Instead, these guidelines should be seen as the suggested manner in which marital life can evolve in the framework of mutual respect and cooperation. What is proposed by Jewish law is not to be imposed by husband on wife or by wife on husband; it is to be put into practice in the true spirit of marital harmony and interdependence.

The Talmud's variant statements concerning women are not necessarily normative. Disparaging remarks may reflect personal experience or relate to specific circumstance, but can in no way diminish from the respect, admiration, and honor accorded to the woman in Jewish tradition from biblical times onward. This, and what follows, is posited without any resort to apologetics. Granted

13

that there are conditions where Jewish law poses difficulties for women. Granted that there are chauvinists in all spheres of Jewish life who enjoy putting women into a subservient position. With all this, one must maintain perspective. Jewish law, on balance, does infinitely more to protect women than to hound them. If the law sometimes creates difficulties for women, it creates plenty more difficulties for men. And where difficulties exist, sensitive rabbinic leadership will not allow the situation to go uncorrected.[2]

Concerning the chauvinists, we may say categorically that they do not represent authentic Judaism, and if imposed subservience is defended with arguments from tradition, these are little more than self-serving rationalizations. For, in the final analysis, there is nothing that can or should diminish the interdependence of man and woman in Jewish life. Witness the fact that so many essentials of Judaism, ranging from norms of prayer to resurrection to *olam haba* (the world-to-come), are all explicated via women.[3]

We speak of man and woman as equals because each, in a unique way, contributes toward the fulfillments that man and woman gain from being together. We do not grade the respective contributions, even as we do not allocate points for the specific commandments. Each is vital because it is part of the totality.

The relationship of man with woman is one of interdependence, each receiving from the other what could not be gained alone. Interdependence most assuredly points away from sameness and toward uniqueness. Uniqueness is not relegation, or denigrative stereotyping; it is the elicitation of one's unique, inimitable capacities. It is in this context that one must view the guidelines and formulations of Jewish tradition regarding husband and wife in marriage.

Foremost among these formulations is the general principle that women are exempt from all positive-command fulfillments that are linked to a specific time. Many reasons have been suggested to explain this principle.[4]

In addition to, and quite apart from, some of the suggestions, this principle serves to establish the radical otherness of male and female, in that, though they are alike in what they cannot do, they are different in what they are obliged to do. The specific exemptive quality within the Halakhah serves to program what Halakhah considers as healthy reality. Based on the proposition that the precepts were given to Israel in order to shape humankind, then those who have been legislated to fulfill more commandments, the men, are in need of more shaping, and women, who have fewer commandments, are in better shape than men. If the Divine will is to bring humankind to the highest level of spiritual excellence, then the fact that men have more commandments merely indicates that they need these commands in order to reach that level. It is thus eminently logical to take seriously the fact that women do not need all the positive commandments. And this is not simply to placate women, but to direct women to the greater challenges that are by definition timeless.[5]

This exemption as ordained in Jewish law, if extended with logical consistency to the home, translates into a healthy reality. If the Torah refuses to tie the woman down to time-related commands, then it stands to reason that no Jewish husband should impose upon his wife what the Torah refuses to impose. This means that the husband should not bind his wife to tasks or obligations that must be done at specific times. The wife must be free to be true to her calling in life. She must not be reduced to time-bound enslavement by the husband.[6]

What seems to be a mere theological formulation is thus transmuted into a vital principle of husband-wife relations, or part of the healthy reality that should prevail in the home, a reality based on profound mutual respect.

Women Today

It is not a distortion or diminution of Halakhah to say that sometimes changes in situations bring about a different application of Jewish law. Halakhah itself relates to circumstance and thus says different things for different circumstances. Throughout the generations, as circumstances changed, the masters of Halakhah, working within the halakhic framework, strove to extrapolate the Halakhah for the new conditions. Even if at times the conclusion reached was that the Halakhah remained the same, this in itself was an extension of the Halakhah, as was the premise that new conditions legitimized the halakhic investigation.

Changing conditions have had their effect on the laws regarding women. Their position, relative both to their husbands and to society, has undergone change. Such changes are not a bandwagoning trendiness, be it of the liberal or the conservative stripe. The changes reflect the reality, and halakhic sensitivity to the real world.[7]

It is acknowledged that women are today much more capable, in general, than ever before. The knowledge gap between men and women has for all intents and purposes been erased; in certain respects women have even superseded men.[8]

Additionally, tasks which originally were considered the province of women have been taken over by technology. Must women be relegated to being at home and making meals when these are readily available in the stores, or can be made in bulk at home and then stored in the freezer? To answer yes to this question is to relegate women to being locked into the home to twiddle their collective thumbs. Not only is this unrealistic and unfair, it is also against basic Jewish law, which has long ago categorically rejected wasteful, idle, purposeless behavior and the mental and emotional destructiveness such behavior engenders. Because the consequences of idleness are potentially so devastating, Jewish law has granted the husband the right to coerce his wife to do trivial work if the alternative is no work and potential atrophy.[9]

It is not the normal way of women, or of men for that matter, to do nothing, and to mandate doing nothing when meaningful and educational work is available goes against the halakhic grain.[10]

But entry into the workplace should be in addition to, not instead of, home responsibilities. And this statement applies equally to men and women. If anything, more men than women have been guilty of neglecting primary home responsibilities to spouse and family in favor of more time at work, or more energy and concentration expended on work.

Ultimately, what really matters in the marital and family context is not who works but why. If the work is an escape from home obligations, then it bodes ill for the home, whether it is the husband or the wife who is escaping. If it is work motivated by a balanced perspective, and in conjunction with home responsibilities, then the fulfillment it brings can enhance one's ability and desire to embrace marital life. Jewish women in the past have more than proven that they are equal to the twin tasks of work and home. For this twin commitment to continue today, not much needs to be modified, perhaps only the capacity of husbands to understand, support, and encourage their wives when they seek to give meaning to their lives in differing domains.[11]

This approach is not intended to destroy stereotypes any more than it is intended to obliterate the differences between men and women. The intent is to see the issue in its proper focus. If the stereotype suffers, then maybe it is a welcome casualty, for we demean not only women but humanity as a whole by subjugating equals into a hemmed-in life which closes off meaningful opportunity.[12]

On the other hand, if this approach erases the differences between men and women, it would be equally a distortion of its intent and a disservice to women and men, both of whom come into their own through the feelings, emotions, and strengths gleaned from each other.[13]

Specifically concerning women, they were always perceived to be the strength and emotional support of the family. Whatever her outside interests, woman's mastery of *inner space*, the inner space we refer to as the home, was an inspiration and model for her husband and family. If this is today taken for granted, or not appreciated as it should be, then perhaps the soul-searching taking place regarding women's position is a timely message to men that they must once again come to grips with their own values, and put their priorities in proper order. Failing that, it is in the natural order of things that what is not appreciated and reinforced eventually disintegrates. For society at large, this places in peril the values of sensitivity, nurturance, and love. For the Jewish community, it verily jeopardizes the coherence of its future.[14]

In Jewish law, women, unlike men, do not have to marry. How, then, do the twain meet? They meet at the junction where respective need-fulfillments correlate, where authentic appreciation of the other prevails. In societal terms, this speaks of a positive climate between men and women. In personal terms, this speaks of a precise instance when the right man comes along, the one who will add meaningful dimension to a woman's life and thus inspire her to do that which, according to Jewish law, she is not obligated to do, namely to marry.[15]

One of the consequences of the trend in society to place the building of a home at a low point on the priority list is that a new repression has evolved, the repression of the procreative urge. It is, of course, not suggested that one have children merely to satisfy the procreative urge; however, repression of the vital urge to have children can have damaging effects on the person or society concerned.[16]

To reject, in one sweeping motion, every "male" idea (read stereotype) regarding women is an unfortunate instance of throwing out the baby with the bathwater. That some are willing, even eager, to do this is an extreme that is lamentable. That others are affected by this supposed trend is even more painful. Suffice it to observe that Judaism does not ride the crest of trends, and could not have survived if it had done so in the past. Its stance regarding women has never been the societal trend. In past generations and in different cultures, it was vastly more liberal. Today, many may see it as much more conservative. But in reality it is neither. In reality, the Halakhah for women and their relation to men is no different today than yesteryear. It is the Halakhah which unabashedly seeks the best for women in the framework of what is conceived to be the best for the community.[17]

Equality or Equitability?

It has already been pointed out that the ideal relationship between man and woman is one of interdependence, an interdependence implying uniqueness rather than sameness. But are men and women equal? The answer, in general terms, is yes and no. There is a measure of equality in the male-female equation, but at the same time there are also pointed and programmed differences between male and female which Jewish tradition projects, and continues to argue for even if there are pressures against that proposition. *Biologically,* man and woman are different; *dialogically,* or how they interact with one another, they do so as equals.

That men and women are equal in those laws which apply to both is a well-established fact. Where a previously justifiable legal norm becomes a case of inequity because of changing circumstances, Halakhah steps in to effect equality. That men and women are dialogically equal is firmly rooted in the Torah, and reflected in the similar names for the male (*ish*) and female (*ishah*).[18]

This equality is fundamentally equality of importance and equality relative to fair treatment. It is not equality of essence, for men and women are not the same, else they would not be men and women, but persons, and their physical structures would be indistinguishable. Biologically, a man cannot give birth, but he can cause many births in a short period. On the other hand, women can give birth, but only to one child at a time, or at least only from one man at a time. Dialogically, true encounter of man and woman, in which each is fulfilled by the other, could not really unfold if they were both the same. The *ḥesed* (kindness) of marriage, in which each gives what the other lacks, is predicated on fundamental difference.[19]

But Jewish tradition refuses to leave such a vital matter as the interaction between husband and wife to chance, or to arbitrary, easily made, easily broken agreements. Within a framework that allows freedom to negotiate in some areas of the marriage compact, there remain certain spheres where responsibilities are specifically delineated. One may choose to call these specifically delineated responsibilities "roles." What these specific roles are will become clear in the ensuing chapters. For the present it is enough to state that Jewish tradition takes a dim view of sacrificing role coherence on the altar of equality. Equality may make it to the top as a banner or slogan, but as an operative equation in marriage, it invites failure, accusation, argumentiveness, disintegration. Such matters as the customs to be followed by the married couple cannot be reduced to personal negotiation. Where husband and wife come from different traditions, for example, each would want to push to the fore the family practice to which he or she is accustomed. The law governing such a situation is clear, and thus helps to avoid argument, or at least it should help to avoid argument.[20]

The law on delineated responsibilities is not geared to serving the interests of the husband alone or the wife alone. It is geared to creating the proper conditions for *shalom bayit* (domestic bliss) to flourish. *Shalom bayit,* the conquest of the "inner space" of the home, is more important than personal vested interests. And true *shalom bayit,* in the end, is in the best interests of husband and wife.[21]

On balance, then, one would describe husband and wife as true equals, but their specific responsibilities in marriage as unique. They are equal, the rules governing their dialectical relationship are equitable.[22]

Marriage and Procreation

There are many creative values in marriage, including the enhanced meaning of life for each of the partners through the love and devotion shared between them. But there is no greater creative value, or creativity, than that of a couple combining their respective beings and bringing new creations into the world. This is extending beyond the self, sharing with the next generation one's home, one's love and commitment, one's knowledge and insight, one's very being. All that is good in God's world comes to the fore in having children and raising them.[23]

In Jewish law, there is an anomaly regarding the *mitzvah* (command) to "be fruitful and multiply" (Gen. 1:28) somewhat akin to the anomaly concerning marriage, but more pronounced. Concerning marriage, women are not under a direct imperative. Similarly, concerning childbirth, although it involves carrying the child in her own body for nine months, it is not the woman who is obliged to "be fruitful and multiply." When a child is born, the *mitzvah* fulfillment (*kiyum hamitzvah*) accrues to the husband-father, not to the wife-mother. She is more than a mere helper in the birth process, and as such is not dissociated from the *mitzvah* fulfillment; but the *mitzvah,* in the main, is his, not hers.[24]

Though at first glance this seems unfair, there is a profound logic at work. Raising children is a challenge which has its difficulties, but giving birth is more than merely difficult; it is painful and potentially dangerous for the woman. The Torah therefore refused to place this burden of pain and danger on the woman. If she wants children on her own, fine; but to be burdened with a "must" would be unfair. Where pain and danger are clear and present, the Torah, as a way of "life," in its declining to place an obligation on the woman, makes a telling statement about the sanctity of existent life, in matter and in kind, even if the issue at hand is creating more life.[25]

As with getting married, the man must seek out a woman who, through her love and commitment to him, will on her own want to marry, and on her own will want to have children. This is a compound illustration of the Torah's sensitivity to the delicate situation of the woman, and needs to be fully appreciated by any man who approaches marriage.

Another offshoot of the fact that women are not obliged to bear children is that there are less holdbacks for women resorting to birth control than there are for men. There is a flip side to this, in that where birth control is an issue for the couple, it is the woman who, because less restricted since not obliged to propagate, has the primary responsibility to employ contraceptives. To claim this is unfair is to look at matters through a distorted lens. The woman's position regarding birth control emanates directly from the extreme sensitivity of the Torah to her own personal reality.

Moreover, if her health is in jeopardy, she can resort to birth control without her husband's consent. Conjugal relations, and the husband's responsibility in this sphere of married life, are quite apart from the procreation imperative. Even if, for whatever reason, birth control must be employed, marital conjugality should not be adversely affected. However, once his procreative obligation has been fulfilled, some leeway is given to the husband regarding conjugal obligations.[26]

An irony in the childbirth situation is that the edict of Rabbenu Gershom, which forbade the taking of more than one wife at a time, and simultaneously virtually eliminated the right of the husband to divorce his wife against her will, places some burden on the wife. If previously the man whose wife refused to have children could marry an additional wife, in the post–Rabbenu Gershom era this is not possible, so that a meeting of the minds and hearts of the couple concerning their obligation to have children is crucial.

Aside from the *mitzvah* to "be fruitful and multiply," there is another category at work pertaining to childbirth. This category, based on the passage "He did not create it waste, but formed it for habitation" (Isa. 45:18), is the obligation to "inhabit" the world, rather than leave it in desolation, as a waste. Here, women are fully obligated, charged with the responsibility to add more inhabitants to God's world. To leave the world with an obvious void, to fail to make a significant contribution to "inhabit," is to be a receiver only, not a giver. It is to live a thankless existence, without any gratitude for having been part of God's world. This is not the Jewish way.[27]

There are situations where, try as they may, a couple is unable to have children. There are also situations where one partner is unwilling to cooperate with the other in having children. If one member of a couple desires children but is prevented because of the other's physical condition or outright refusal to cooperate, he or she may leave the marriage. But a couple who have each other are not compelled to divorce because they cannot together have children. The marital harmony which thrives between the couple is so precious that it may not be forced to collapse.[28]

The love that exists between husband and wife is independent of procreation and is an exalted human expression. Such love is a compound blessing if children grow up in that loving atmosphere. But the failure of this compound blessing to materialize need not diminish from the ennobling relationship that is unique to a couple very much devoted to one another.[29]

3

The Legal Framework of Marriage

The Need for a Legal Framework

If a couple love each other, and are committed to spending their lives together, that in itself, it may be argued, should be enough to bind their union and ensure that it is free of difficulties. Why, then, is there a need for a legal framework to marriage, a framework which is quite comprehensive in its attentiveness to the many nuances of married life?

The answer, in blunt terms, is that love and commitment are not enough, and for more than one reason. There is no guarantee that today's love will not go sour. Nor is there a necessary connection between love and the capacity to protect oneself and one's future partner from the many contingencies and exigencies of life. And finally, life together, even though obviously in need of some measure of spontaneity, also demands a structure, even a relatively rigid framework, which will allow the relationship to prosper.

The marriage ceremony itself projects the primacy of the legal framework in Jewish tradition. The ceremony contains no affirmation of love by the couple. Love cannot be legislated. But legitimate responsibilities can be, and are, legislated. The marriage ceremony is primarily a legal act, and a legal undertaking. In the framework clearly set up in the legal compact, areas of responsibility are coherently delineated, with room for maneuvering where the specific situation allows, or even calls for, adjustment. The structure and detail of the marital covenant fre

23

the couple from entering into the union as if it were a business, and allows their full attention to be directed to each other.[1]

The legal document which binds the marriage is known as the *ketuvah*. The *ketuvah*, in the legal dimension, underlines the relationship and spells out the husband's obligations to his wife both during and after marriage. So important is the *ketuvah* to the marriage that it is prohibited for the relationship to continue for the smallest time period without the wife having the *ketuvah*. When it comes to maintaining the legal integrity of the union, and to ensuring that the wife, even for the slightest period, cannot be exploited, there is no room for compromise. Today, most *ketuvah* documents have a postmarital settlement in the sum of 200 *zuz* (silver coins). This is constant even though the economic status of each wife is different, because in any event the wife cannot be divorced against her will, so that her being adequately cared for after termination of the marriage, should that occur, is not compromised.[2]

It should also be noted that aside from the basic *ketuvah* and conjugal obligations, as well as aspects of inheritance, the couple can negotiate, both before and after the wedding, the other responsibilities in marriage. As with the other commandments, the tradition affords a delicate balance, providing the structure, and also providing the freedom of the couple to respond to each other, in the context of the structure, in their own unique way.[3]

The Legal Obligations of the Husband

The husband has ten essential obligations. Briefly, they are as follows: (1) to sustain his wife; (2) to provide adequate clothing; (3) to provide conjugal visitation; (4) to fulfill the essential *ketuvah* obligations; (5) to pay her medical bills; (6) to redeem her if she is kidnapped; (7) upon her death, to ensure her proper burial, assuming the expenses for same; (8) to ensure that she will be sustained from his estate and live in his dwelling should he predecease her; (9) to provide for the maintenance of her daughters, in the event of his death, until they reach maturity or marry; and (10) to ensure the right of her sons to her *ketuvah* settlement, after her passing, over and above the inheritance they would share with brothers from the husband's subsequent marriage.[4]

These obligations cover a wide range of contingencies, and are obviously intended not only to materially protect the wife but also to ensure her peace of mind about eventualities which may ensue following the death of her husband and even her own demise. It is a tribute to the halakhic process that it concerns itself not only with legal basics; its concerns stretch to putting the wife at ease so that she can enjoy her married years with reasonable tranquility and minimal anxiety. Human frailty and greed may sometimes distort the intentions of the Halakhah, but this should not detract from recognition that there is a humane ethos at work in it.

Working backwards from the last four of the husband's ten obligations, which deal with the postmarital period—the period following the death of either the husband or the wife—the sixth of the ten previously listed obligations, to redeem a kidnapped wife, is absolute, and applicable even if the wife waives the privilege. Her dignity is so vital that even she cannot vitiate her husband's obligation. Even if the redemption problem is caused by her own negligence, the husband's obligation is not eliminated.[5]

Likewise concerning medical expenses, the fifth of the listed obligations, the husband is duty bound to take care of his wife's incurred expenses, and that duty is not waived if her medical problems are due to her own negligence, though the bindingness of the duty in such instances is weakened. Even should the medical expenses, in normal (non-negligence) circumstances, be substantial, the duty remains, since the husband's care of his wife cannot be subject to price limits.[6]

Should the marriage terminate, either through divorce or through the death of the husband, the wife receives a settlement as specified in the *ketuvah,* together with whatever additions to the basic *ketuvah* are due through her husband's adding to the *ketuvah* and/or the differing types of material substance that she contributed to the marital partnership. This is the fourth obligation. The third obligation, conjugal visitation, one of the essential obligations in marriage, is a simple duty with complex and wide-ranging ramifications. Suffice it at this point to observe that it signifies the bodily and spiritual union of the husband and wife as one corpus, and its importance for the vitality of the marriage can hardly be overestimated.[7]

The second and first obligations, those of clothing and sustenance, are also essential to the marriage, and speak of the husband's sacred duty to ensure that his wife lives in dignity and comfort, free from worries about where her bread will come from, and adequately clothed and housed. Personal needs are also included in this obligation, for to properly sustain one's wife is to satisfy her legitimate needs. The needs can vary depending on the living standard to which the wife was accustomed prior to marriage. The operating principle is that marriage should not lower her living standard, and, if the husband can afford it, should raise her living standard. Even if the wife has funds of her own, the husband must sustain her. Never must the granting of adequate sustenance be used as a weapon with which to threaten or control the wife. Such behavior eats away at the union both emotionally and legally.[8]

In fairness, the wife cannot expect to be sustained even if her behavior is less than exemplary. Her leaving her husband compromises her claim to sustenance, unless it can be shown that her leaving was precipitated by understandable concerns. Included in the category of understandable concerns are her discomfort because she is harassed by the neighbors, or because she cannot countenance living in proximity to her in-laws. The house may legally belong to the husband, but it is equally the wife's home.[9]

This understandable concern is not reduced to arbitrariness. The wife's claim that her in-laws cause her unbearable discomfort needs to be substantiated to ensure that her claim is not an unwarranted act of spite.[10]

The husband's leaving the house does not exempt him from sustaining his wife. In fact, failing such circumstances as his being sick or unable to find a job, the husband, even at great pains, must find the means to sustain his wife; not only for minimal sustenance, but also to maintain the standard to which his wife is accustomed.[11]

As with conjugal relations, one does not properly fulfill the obligation to sustain simply by placing the provisions in his wife's lap. This concept is best reflected in the ideal that the husband must endeavor to eat together with his wife, to provide emotionally as well as materially. Thus is the wife's dignity and self-respect assured.[12]

The Legal Obligations of the Wife

In the absence of any special arrangements reflecting a unique situation, the wife's earnings during marriage accrue to the husband. This is a tradeoff for the husband's being obliged to sustain his wife. Any items she may find or win in a sweepstakes, and the earnings from the material substance she brings with her to the marriage, go to the husband, who also is the beneficiary should his wife predecease him.[13]

The wife, if she so desires, can maintain her economic independence and insist on keeping her earnings. If she does, this absolves the husband from having to provide for her sustenance. In general, the wife has the upper hand in the matter of sustenance, and can make the decision that she feels is in her own best interests, and hopefully the best interests of the marriage.[14]

If, in the course of events, the wife becomes ill and cannot work, the husband is obliged to maintain her. His claim that she is not fulfilling her part of the arrangement is discounted.[15]

At no time can the wife be placed in the position of being obliged to sustain her husband. If perchance she is gainfully employed and he unemployed and out of funds, she can be urged to sustain her husband, but as an act of charity, not as a legal marital obligation.[16]

The types of work that are basic to the household are the wife's obligation. To whatever extent the husband can afford to pay for household help, to that extent is the wife discharged from having to take care of these duties. To this there is a limit, in that those types of work which are personal and expressive of the intimate bond between husband and wife should not be done by a substitute, even where the wife assumes her own sustenance and maintenance, in which case she is exempt from normal household work. Though definite leeway to choose the home's economic balance is given the wife, she is always linked with some meaningful work in the home which binds her to her husband. This serves to prevent the estrangement which may arise if husband and wife have little or nothing which reinforces their relationship on an active level.[17]

If, in the course of taking care of the home, the wife breaks utensils, she is not obliged to compensate the husband. Were she obliged to pay, she would constantly be full of anxiety lest something break, and the relationship, rather than being of a "give-and-take" nature, would reduce itself to petty concerns and arguments. When something does break, the wife can always remind her husband that he was the first to break something in their marriage.[18]

The Husband's Right to Divorce

Long before modern society came up with the idea, no-fault divorce was already a possibility in Jewish marriage. The husband and wife could, by mutual consent, agree to terminate their marriage without having to contrive evidence to back up untrue claims of grounds for divorce. Yet although the escape from marriage was available, the Jewish marital-stability record was admirable. Marriage was seen as an exalted way of life, bringing happiness, contentedness, and meaning. It was natural for people to desire marriage, and no artificial protections were needed to maintain the marriage institution. If a marriage did not work, there was no sense in imposing permanent misery on the couple. Rather, the logic went, let them disentangle and try finding themselves with more suitable partners.[19]

Divorce, though unfortunate, is nevertheless relatively straightforward when husband and wife are in agreement. It is when only one of the two wants or demands a divorce that the complications arise. Halakhah has forged a precise inventory of the circumstances when either husband or wife has the right to a divorce and the other is compelled to cooperate. Problems abound mostly when the husband refuses to cooperate, and to a lesser degree when the wife, who should not be divorced against her will, refuses to cooperate. Rabbinic courts can use all the force their moral standing will generate, but the courts lack the real muscle of threatened excommunication, as in yesteryear.[20]

The husband may demand a divorce (*get*) if his wife denies him the benefits of conjugal visitation (*onah*). This is a fundamental marital expression which, if refused, destroys the marriage compact. This, and her desertion without just cause, which is also grounds for his gaining a divorce, also carries the penalty of her forfeiting the *ketuvah* settlement. Since she precipitated the break, she is not allowed to gain materially from her causing the marriage to disintegrate.[21]

Where there is eyewitness testimony to the wife's adultery, the law leaves the husband no choice but to divorce his wife. In the face of the wife's brazen contempt for the sanctity of marriage, failure to protect the integrity of the marriage institution eats away at the very fabric of Jewish life. The community, in the final analysis, is larger and more vital than a single individual.[22]

Suspicion of adultery, where direct proof is lacking but legitimate suspicion is present, is a more complicated situation. Here the husband has the right to divorce his wife, but he is not constrained to exercise that right.[23]

Other types of aberrant behavior by the wife, including immodest conduct, cursing or insulting her husband, or in his presence insulting the children or his parents, or hitting him, give the husband the right to divorce. Here, however, the husband must show bad intentions on the wife's part, that her behavior was not isolated, provoked, or a tantrum, but was a calculated and spiteful verbal or physical assault.[24]

The husband similarly can pursue divorce if the wife perverts him regarding matters of Jewish law, such as if she feeds him unkosher food or induces marital relations when she is in a menstrual state. The husband, for his part, must be able to show that his wife intentionally resorted to religious subversion, and also that he really cares about these matters more than merely as a front to gain a divorce.[25]

The husband may press for divorce if a physical blemish of his wife impedes their union. This he can do only if he was unaware and could not be aware of the blemish prior to the marriage. A blemish which evolves only after the wedding is not sufficient grounds for the husband to press for divorce.[26]

Included in the possibilities of just cause for divorce is the situation where the wife spoils the husband's food. The language of the Talmud seems to incline toward the element of spite; that is, her meal was okay, but his was spoiled. She deliberately sets out to ruin things for him, making for an untenable situation. The rate of divorce would be astronomical and married life unbearable if every burned supper could be manipulated into a divorce.[27]

The Wife's Right to Divorce

The most primary mention of right to a divorce concerns a woman whose basic marital needs were neglected. Even though in physical fact it is the husband who gives the *get* (divorce) to his wife, still this does not preclude the wife's arguing that she has a right to the divorce. When the wife is within her rights, and there are a host of such situations, the rabbinical court takes up her cause and elicits the divorce from the husband. In most instances of this nature, the wife also is entitled to the *ketuvah* settlement.[28]

The husband who is derelict regarding his obligation to sustain his wife, or to provide conjugal visitation, has violated the primary articles of the marriage covenant, and the wife has a right to divorce. These elements of marriage are so vital that their being used to emotionally and physically deprive the wife are a breach of a sacred agreement.[29]

The wife whose husband is philandering with other women likewise has a right to divorce. Even his causing her a bad name through his actions can precipitate a legitimate divorce action by the wife.[30]

The husband's failure to annul vows made by the wife that affect the marriage is seen as a desire on his part to sever the relationship, and the wife may demand a divorce. Should the husband forbid the wife, by means of a vow, to engage in work, this too is reason enough for the wife to be granted a divorce.

Imposed idleness has adverse personal consequences, and no wife can be expected to endure such adversity.[31]

The husband who hits, curses, ridicules, or insults his wife, or insults his wife's parents in her presence, or forbids his wife from visiting her parents or family, or whose communication with his wife is generally temperamental and disrespectful, cannot expect his wife to live with this behavior, and she can assuredly argue for divorce. Here the wife must be able to show that it was not a once-in-a-lifetime, isolated event, but that it is indicative of the husband's usual behavior. The burden of proof is on the husband if he tries to counterclaim that she instigates his repulsive behavior.[32]

The wife whose freedom is removed by the husband, as, for example, through his insistence that the mother-in-law move into the house, may demand a divorce. The wife who is forced into conjugal relations by her husband during her menstrual period likewise may demand a divorce, even if she is not scrupulous in observing the laws concerning menstruation. The common denominator in the aforementioned instances is the failure or refusal of the husband to accord the wife the dignity and respect to which she is unquestionably entitled.[33]

If the husband is impotent, the wife may ask for a divorce, provided that this demand is coupled with her statement that she desires children. Where the husband disputes the wife's claim of his impotence, her direct statement to the contrary is considered the more powerful argument, as long as the claim is made by her directly, and not by her lawyer.[34]

The husband who develops a repulsive blemish or adopts a malodorous habit or an offensive trade may thus make life so unbearable for the wife that she can demand a divorce. The wife can do so even if this situation existed prior to the marriage and she was aware of it but now claims that it is in fact much worse than she envisaged it would be.[35]

The land of Israel comes into the picture relative to divorce. Save in circumstances where moving to Israel would make the couple dependent on charity, whichever of the couple desires to move to Israel has the upper hand over the reluctant spouse, and can ask for a divorce because of that refusal. Interestingly, the same equation applies relative to living in Jerusalem versus living in any other city in Israel. Here too the one arguing for Jerusalem has the upper hand. Since Israel is pivotal to one's spiritual growth, and marriage is designed to facilitate rather than obstruct this growth, the Halakhah allows for exit from marriage when the marriage runs contrary to its perceived purpose.[36]

The Mored and Moredet

Of special interest in the realm of claims to divorce is the unique title and attendant rules given to one specific situation. Refusal of conjugal relations by either the husband or the wife, as previously elaborated, is grounds for the injured party to demand divorce. The instigator of this refusal is legally termed a "rebel," *mored* (masc.) in the case of the husband, and *moredet* (fem.) if it is the wife.

This term is generally perceived to apply only to conjugal visitation, and speaks volumes about the seriousness with which deviation from conjugal responsibility is viewed. Pejorative labels are not the usual Judaic way of expressing displeasure with behavior, so that the use of such a label here must be seen as a comment on the extreme gravity of the offense. Using one's body as a weapon to punish one's partner prostitutes the marriage compact.[37]

The *mored* husband must give the divorce and marriage settlement (*ketuvah*), the *moredet* wife is divorced and forfeits her *ketuvah* settlement. When the husband is *mored* (rebels), the wife has a right to divorce, but she is not compelled to exercise that right, since such compulsion would contravene the basic notion that a wife cannot be divorced against her will.[38]

The husband is considered a *mored* even if he just swears off conjugal relations for a short time, even if that period coincides with the wife's menstruation, when conjugal visitation is anyway enjoined. The point here is that one's body, one's very being, should never be used as a device to punish, deprive, or threaten.[39]

The husband who insists on engaging in conjugal relations with his clothes on, even though motivated by considerations of modesty, is likewise a *mored*. This may not be spiteful deprivation, but it is deprivation nevertheless.[40]

The wife who denies herself to her husband is a *moredet* even if she claims that her lockout is because of the husband's debts to her. She does not, however, have an obligation to submit to conjugal relations beyond the prescribed amount. She is not his chattel to be used at his whim. She is not a *moredet* if she leaves him because he fails to keep up his maintenance responsibilities. On the contrary, he is here the instigator. If she leaves for other reasons, such as neighborhood or in-law difficulties, then again she is not a *moredet* if she is still willing to engage in conjugal relations with the husband.[41]

The main intent of the edict of Rabbenu Gershom was to make the power of the woman equal to the man concerning divorce. Concerning *mored* and *moredet,* they are likewise equal, in that whatever would take the one out of the category of rebel would accomplish the same for the other, and vice versa.[42]

This, in broad outline, is the general legal framework for Jewish marriage. The context presented here may not cover all possibilities, and the varying nuances within the possibilities, but the intent of the legal framework is clear. It is to set up a strong legal foundation for marriage, protecting the dignity of the partners, taking care of their needs and interests, and making it possible for the couple to grow meaningfully together and achieve their aims and responsibilities. How the couple succeed in this depends on how they apply not only the letter but also the spirit of the Halakhah.

4

The Essence of Marriage

The Marriage Ideal

There is much in the rich expanse of Judaic literature which projects the Jewish marriage ideal. This projection of the marriage ideal is not intended as merely a theoretical formulation; it is intended as a practical guide for how marriage is ideally to be approached and lived out to the full. What is that ideal?

Marriage is not simply living the same as before, but with someone else. Nor is it simply a change of lifestyle with added benefits and duties. Marriage is, and should be lived as, a higher dimension of existence. All that goes on prior to marriage ideally prepares for marriage, but marriage itself is a fresh start in the way life was meant to be. The ritual immersion, the Yom Kippur–like atonement for iniquity, and different customs prior to and during the ceremony all converge on this point.[1]

What is one to make of this fresh start? It is a fresh start, but toward what? In a word, toward connectedness-cum-completeness. In creation, everything came in pairs, from the human being down; and the pairs comprised male and female.[2]

With the human, it was two forms in one corpus, originally fused, then parted, only to be brought back together in a spiritual fusion that was to reinforce their primordial oneness. Unlike animals, whose togetherness is primarily for copulation, human togetherness, whilst incorporating copulation, is much more than that. It is a togetherness that has no time limitations, a togetherness which is to be a oneness and a completeness. The idea of man (*adam*) in Judaic terms is that of man and woman together.[3]

Oneness is more than partnership; it is connectedness without barriers, unity of mind, body, and purpose. To be interconnected is to be friends, confidants, and intimates in the most noble sense. For alone, man and woman are exposed and spiritually wanting. Together, man and woman complete themselves by each completing the other. To be united in mind, body, and purpose is to forge life together in total devotion, with utmost awareness of the other, alertness to the other's needs, and commitment to common ideals and values, in thought and practice. It is to be able to say, "My wife's foot hurts us," and to mean it. In a word, it is to be as God wanted us to be.[4]

Marriage, then, is infinitely more than simply adjusting one's outer appearance. In the abstract, it may even appear as an unreachable ideal. And maybe it is, for at no point in life should the human being ever be able to claim that all has been achieved, that the summit has been reached, or that perfection has been attained.[5]

There is probably no marriage which reaches the ultimate ideal. What separates the bad from the good marriage, or the good from the better, is that the one is mired in or satisfied with the status quo, while the other strives to improve toward the ideal. To make things better, to strive toward the ideal, is what energizes marriage and assures its durability.

The Marriage Reality

Having spoken of the marriage ideal, and the importance of maintaining an awareness of the ideal, it is now appropriate to shift focus to the reality, and how to deal with it, to live with it and improve it.

A matter of prime concern is the attitude one takes to marriage and what one expects from marriage. Given that there are more than enough situations where divorce is possible, it is nevertheless extremely important that one not enter marriage with divorce in mind. This means more than not planning to divorce after a prescribed number of years, or when better opportunities present themselves. It means that one must throw oneself into the marriage wholeheartedly and unconditionally, rather than half-enthusiastically or too philosophically and with the fallback notion that divorce is always possible if the marriage does not succeed. Such distancing almost invites the conclusion incorporated in the thinking.[6]

Once having made the marital choice, it is counterproductive to look at other potential mates and ask whether they would not have been better partners. Such continued speculation will do little else but make the actual choice the wrong one, by neglect, self-centeredness, and dissatisfaction. It is better to see the choice made as ideal simply because it was you, the husband or wife, who made the decision. And, rather than looking to see if there are better options, it is wiser to make your own choice better by accepting it, working within the context of the choice to do all that is possible for the spouse and to thus enhance the marriage.[7]

This message is conveyed in Abraham's being unaware of the true beauty of his wife, Sarah, until faced with a potential emergency. That he did not stare even at his own wife implies that he accepted her unconditionally, for what she was, her exterior beauty being less relevant than her essence as a person. The husband who did not notice a glaring physical deficiency in his wife is in the Abrahamic model. For him, there was no thought given to getting a better deal. And precisely because of this was his married life so rewarding.[8]

Unconditional acceptance of one's spouse makes devotion to one's spouse an almost natural expression. And devotion to spouse is one of the ingredients that makes marriage succeed. The spirit of devotion is also the salient ingredient which enables the couple to survive the crises that will assuredly confront one or the other or both during the marriage. Devotional concern contributes toward giving each member of the marital union the strength and will to help the other, to lighten burdens.[9]

For husband and wife to reach the stage where they not only live for each other but are also willing to die for each other, a stage of devotion that is less than likely to prevail at the outset of their relationship, they both need to embark on life together in the spirit of unconditional acceptance. That spirit carries with it all that is meaningful in marriage.[10]

Shared Destiny

One of the more intriguing customs in the Jewish wedding ceremony is the breaking of the glass, which, coming at the conclusion, is the ceremony's climactic act. It is following this act of apparent destruction that the participating audience erupts with the spontaneous cry *Mazal Tov* ("Good luck"). Among the reasons advanced for this custom is that we should, in the moment of supreme joy, recall the destruction of the Holy Temple by destroying a glass. This is done by the *ḥatan* (groom) himself, and this act of recollection brings with it the good wishes of the assemblage, as if prior to the breaking no *Mazal Tov* were merited. One could say that the *Mazal Tov* comes not because of the breaking of the glass, but because the ceremony concludes with the breaking of the glass. There is another possible explanation aside from dismissing the connection as coincidence. It relates to why we marry. A marriage that is simply for mutual gain hardly merits communal approbation. A marriage in which the couple express an awareness of and commitment to Jewish continuity is another matter. This merits communal congratulations, since it is the community itself whose continued growth is ensured by such marriages.[11]

There is hardly a better way to express the link with Jewish continuity than by recalling the event that had the most devastating effect on the Jewish community, the consequences of which are still being felt. The Temple's destruction, and the exile, physical and spiritual, which came in its wake, reverberates with lingering impact and calls for massive communal effort to restore spiritual autonomy. This restoration is accelerated if more people are devoted to it. The breaking of the glass is thus more than a symbolic act; it is the step that launches a spiritually meaningful and communally significant marriage. We shatter, we thus recall the shattering experience, and we resolve, in our limited way, to put the pieces together. Hence, the communal *Mazal Tov* at the breaking of the glass.[12]

A truly Jewish marriage is another link in the chain of tradition. The couple is here Jewishly because of a heritage that is alive and well despite endless trials and tribulations. Though it is hoped that trials and tribulations will not come in the couple's way, if they do appear the couple will be able to respond inspired by the countless examples of Jewish history. Trials or no trials, they should be able to contribute to strengthening the community and making the heritage they acquired available to the next generation.

The couple are united in an intensely personal relationship, but they also are deeply involved in a shared destiny to which they are committed. This shared destiny gives their life direction and purpose, and effectively reinforces the bond uniting the couple. A shared destiny in marriage means that the marriage is much more than a union of enlightened self-interest with immediate recompense. It means that if the immediate experience in marriage does not yield the normal pleasures or contentment, one can more readily accept this and live with it. After all, the couple are in marriage together, in space and time, as one. Each would no more think of leaving the other than contemplate amputation of an arm simply because it is sore.[13]

An admittedly radical example of shared destiny as an essential component of marriage is manifest in an episode related of the famous eighteenth-century Ḥasidic sage, Rabbi Schneur Zalman of Liadi, who was once approached by an unhappy husband seeking to divorce his wife. His complaint was that he was constantly badgered, pestered, and reviled by his wife, to the extent that it was impossible for him to persevere.

Rabbi Schneur Zalman sat the husband down and explained to him that he had to see his situation in a wider perspective. He at the same time introduced the husband to the concept of the perfection of souls, a notion which has great currency in Jewish mystical tradition. This notion suggests that individual souls go through various stages (transmigrations) until they reach a state of perfection, at which time they unite with the primordial soul. Transmigration is necessary in order to achieve a higher degree of perfection than had been realized in a previous body.

Rabbi Schneur Zalman then went on to explain to his oppressed visitor that his soul was, in fact, a very wicked one, and that were it to go through its natural pattern of transmigration, it could never reach the state of perfection in time for the messianic redemption; never, that is, unless it went through an inordinate number of deaths. Every time that you feel as if you cannot take it from your wife any longer, the husband was told, it is like a death, so that, in reality, your wife's miserable treatment of you accelerates your transmigration process, such that you will be part of the messianic redemption.[14]

This approach totally ignored the normal contentedness of the present in favor of a future destiny, beyond even the duration of the marriage. There was no talk of persevering till matters improved; perhaps this was an unrealistic hope. The husband and wife, as partners in the present and toward an ultimate future, may endure what is seemingly senseless agony; but faith in an eventual, even otherworldly explication makes the present pain bearable. Faith, authentic integration of the belief in *olam haba* (the future, post-messianic world), affords the capacity to resist sacrificing the marriage on the altar of instant gratification.

The traditional marriage-preservation arguments, such as (1) try to be happy even in the depressing circumstances; (2) pray to God that your spouse improves; (3) try to accept your fate with equanimity; or (4) there is great benefit in a bad spouse in that you are guaranteed of not having to go through hell (*gehinnom*), all, in differing degrees, fly in the face of modern marital-therapy techniques. They also run counter to our own logic, and our conception of the marriage ideal.[15]

However, it is still useful to keep these arguments in mind, even if we are not likely to apply them directly. Shared destiny as a concept in Jewish marriage appears to be significant by its absence. The increasing frequency of breakdowns of marriages within the Jewish community is partly attributable to the reality that marriage is too often entered into with no commitment to remain in the union and work it out if problems arise. Couples seem to be sharing less in a destiny, and more in an experiment.[16]

In this climate of a rather facile attitude to quitting an unhappy marriage, the example of Rabbi Schneur Zalman and the four traditional marriage-preservation arguments should be seen as welcome counterattitudes. The counterattitude to "quit when problems arise" is "never quit, no matter what problems arise." Obviously, neither extreme is a welcome proposition, but both approaches, pulling against each other, may restore a more balanced perspective to marriage preservation. This perspective argues that both members of the couple should do all in their capacity to make things work, and should be patient and charitable in judging whether the efforts are bringing the positive results anticipated. Only when everything has been done and the situation is hopeless should quitting become an option.

The guess is that in a majority of cases, if this perspective were maintained, the marriage would be preserved and the agony of separation avoided.

5

The Way to *Shalom Bayit*

What Is Shalom Bayit?

Shalom, as the word which is used to describe "peace," relates in a fundamental sense to the word *shlemut*, or "completeness." *Shalom* disconnected from *shlemut*, peace disconnected from completeness, is a peace which manifests itself as mutual nonaggression, peace as the absence of war. *Shalom* with *shlemut* is peace with harmony, peace with cooperativeness, peace which moves toward completeness. It is this higher level of peace which is so exalted, and should be the everpresent goal of our personal and communal strivings.[1]

The ultimate goal, of course, is a true peace which permeates the entire world, but that is too massive a task to be thrust upon any single individual. However, each individual can make a contribution toward this all-encompassing goal by working to create peace in his or her immediate environment. Having done all that is within one's power to effect peace is thus seen to have much more than local implications.[2]

The home is the primary locus where one's obligation to effect peace unfolds. Here is where one is able to have significant input, if not control, over the peace of the world, the world of one's home. *Shalom bayit*, the peace of one's home, in its true sense as desired in marriage, is best translated as "domestic bliss." *Shalom bayit* is not the peace of sameness or absence of conflict. It is the completeness of opposites, the translation of differences into

41

more effective action and greater love, incorporating the wisdom gained from shared opinions and give-and-take.[3]

To be conversant in the ways of *shalom bayit* is to be conversant in the ways of local-cum-global peace. It is to have an exemplary home which is a model for other homes, eventually all homes. It is lamentable that not enough attention is given to the mastery of *shalom bayit* formulations upon entry into marriage.[4]

Whose is the obligation to create *shalom bayit*, domestic bliss? Simply stated, it is the obligation of both husband and wife. That the home should be fortunate enough to enjoy such tranquility and harmony is ultimately a Godly blessing, but it is a blessing which comes only after the couple work to be eligible for and worthy of that blessing. To be worthy, each of the couple must see *shalom bayit* as an obligation directed not at the other, but at the self. Precious little is contributed toward *shalom bayit* when each member of the marital team demands that the other do something for *shalom bayit*. *Shalom bayit* is a personal responsibility that beckons each of the partners to make demands on their own selves toward improving the home atmosphere. It is generally a good practice, in areas related to living a life of responsibleness, to be very demanding on one's own self. It is a practice which makes for better marriages. Rather than waiting for the other to change, or to make a move, one should take the initiative; the other will likely follow. Waiting for the other is standoffish, leads to frustration, and builds up abundant hostility. It can ruin what could have been blissful.[5]

This is the active side of *shalom bayit*. There is another side to *shalom bayit*, the preventive side. In this, the most appropriate advice is: Do not provoke, do not become provoked. Do not provoke, do not introduce strife or contentiousness into the home vocabulary, and go out of your way to prevent strife situations from developing.[6]

Do not become provoked if situations arise in which expectations have not been realized, requests have not been heeded, or the normal household pattern has been upset; do not react with anger to your spouse, to whom you may attribute this unwarranted situation. Instead, assume that understandable circumstances have caused the problem, rather than bad intentions. Again, one should not stand on one's rights or be touchy concerning the honor that is due. Rather than demand what you are convinced belongs to you by right, be flexible and forgiving, not rigid and unforgiving.[7]

If possible, try to anticipate what to you may be anger-provoking situations and have second options, so that "no-escape" situations are avoided. Accept that dishes may break, or that important items may be misplaced, but ensure that the true perspective is never distorted.[8]

Domestic bliss is such a vital ingredient of life that it neutralizes what under normal circumstances are positive obligations. In a case of either-or, where the choice is either lights for the home to have a bright rather than a depressed atmosphere (*shalom bayit*) or wine for sanctification of the Sabbath, the lights for the home come first. The same is true if the other alternative is lighting matter for the Hanukkah *menorah*. Great sages allowed themselves to be humiliated if that humiliation preserved the peacefulness of a home. This was reason enough to forgo accepted protocols, even to turn a blind eye to obviously contemptible disrespect. These sages did not want to be associated, however indirectly, with a marriage breakdown. They saw each union as personally and communally significant, and were perhaps fearful that one marriage collapse would pave the way for more, making it acceptable, then maybe even trendy.[9]

The sages were working in the background of an even more astounding precedent. Manipulating the truth in order to preserve peace is permitted. In order to preserve the *shalom bayit* of Abraham and Sarah, God personally manipulated the truth. Even that, however, is not the astounding precedent.[10]

The astounding precedent relates to the very severe transgression of erasing God's name. If such erasure could possibly restore the *shalom bayit* of an estranged husband and wife, the erasure is mandated.[11]

The aforementioned rabbis were singularly aware of the extent to which the law withdraws temporarily to preserve the traditional home. One may suspend the usually sacred commitment to the truth, one may violate what is normally a most violent attack on the holiness of God. Surely, then, it is within the bounds of acceptability, even desirability, to swallow personal insult.

The rabbis' example, in the background of illuminating precedent, brings the *shalom bayit* factor to the fore as a communal obligation. Husband and wife have the primary responsibility, but others who may affect the couple are not outside the pale of obligation.

That God's name is erased to possibly bring harmony back into a troubled home, even though associated with a procedure no longer in practice, nevertheless has practical contemporary applications. If God allows sacred Godly principles to be compromised, this means that God is effectively declaring that not even God and God's honor will be allowed to stand in the way of husband-wife harmony. Duty to God should thus not be used as an excuse to deny one's domestic responsibilities. Insisting that one's learning and talmudic scholarship are too important and that therefore one need not help with the dishes, or other housecleaning, is a claim that uses God in a way that God refused to be used, and is thus an abuse.[12]

Shalom bayit, it is patently clear, is a priority item par excellence in the Jewish home.

To Honor One's Wife

Shalom bayit is more likely to be realized if each of the marriage partners lives up to the letter and spirit of their obligation to the other. The legal framework of obligation has already been delineated. The attitude with which one approaches the legal compact is itself a legal construct, broadly subsumed under the category of honor. To honor one's mate is obligatory. It is achieved through tangible manifestations of honor. The true purpose of the obligation is best achieved through integrating into one's being the feeling that one's partner is deserving and should always be honored, in all situations and circumstances. Respect and dignity, appreciation and gentleness, are expressions that should be forthcoming without compromise.

The husband is duty bound to honor his wife. This is not

optional and extra-legal; it is obligatory. Honor is more than the absence of disrespect; it is the according of salient, deferring respect to the one who is the main cause for true blessing residing in the home. The husband, by working out in his own mind the essentiality of his wife in his own life, will make it more likely that the honor imperative remains everpresent in his thinking process, never allowing for a laxity which not only may presage a regressive pattern but also reflects that the honor he bestows is perfunctory and conditional, when in fact the honor should be authentic and constant.[13]

The husband who honors his wife appreciates and values her dignity as a person. He respects what she considers vital to her own self, and to her sense of self-worth, and cooperates fully with her in attaining and maintaining self-worth. He does not take his wife's contributions to the marriage and the home as a matter of course, to be expected. Instead, he continually voices his appreciation for all things, large and small.[14]

The husband who honors his wife talks in gentle tones and is exceedingly careful not to embarrass his wife or cause her to feel as if she is not keeping up her part of the marital responsibilities. The honoring husband conveys his respect, but he does not employ the formal language of a royal palace. His is more the language of an intimate.[15]

The honoring husband will take great care not to make excessive or unrealistic demands of his wife. In fact, he will not demand; he will gently ask. He will be sure that he is asking at a proper time, and that what he asks for is not a triviality which betrays disrespect or something excessive which betrays insensitivity. If for whatever reason the trivial or the excessive is requested, it should be preceded with an appropriate preamble assuring the wife that no disrespect or insensitivity is involved, and that she is greatly appreciated no matter. The husband will use this approach not as an effective technique to get what he wants, but because this is the way that his wife should be acknowledged.[16]

The husband who honors his wife, upon seeing that she is too busy to attend to him as she normally does, will not sit and sulk. He will get up and take care of matters on his own. With this and other components of honor due to the wife, the wife should not use the husband's obligations as a device to demand from him, or to refuse to do her part. The obligation to honor is his responsibility, not her weapon.

The honor given by the husband to his wife is dimensionally different from the generally respectful demeanor with which one must conduct oneself. For example, there is a general prohibition against causing pain or anguish to anyone. It applies to everyone, but specifically and mainly to one's wife. She is much more vulnerable, and thus must be treated with greater care. Pain can mean either direct action causing pain or failure to act properly and thus causing pain. The husband must be ever aware that he is a vital, integral part of his wife's world and that this places upon him a heavy burden, an onus to be sensitive to what pains her. This includes that which under normal circumstances would not cause pain to others. Failure to praise strangers or friends may not be a serious matter, but the wife is likely to seek the approbation and appreciation of her husband to reinforce her dedication to him. The husband must thusly honor his wife, and should never take advantage of her vulnerability; he must always be sensitive to her delicate situation.[17]

The other dimensional difference in the honor incumbent upon the husband is that he must honor the wife more than he honors himself. One normally does not place excessive demands on oneself; that same respect must be extended to one's wife. And more. The husband may have ascetic tendencies, or lean toward being frugal. He may be content with less to eat, and comfortable with old, worn-out clothes, but he must not impose these predilections on his wife. She must be maintained in dignity and honor, even more honor than the husband accords to himself. Honor to one's wife is not relative to or contingent upon the honor one gives to oneself. Self-respect is no doubt important, and proper care of oneself as a Godly being is not to be underemphasized. But, even if it is neglected, this does not afford an excuse to do the same to one's wife. Here the husband must go beyond the formula that man and wife are as one. The honor the husband extends to his wife must rise above the constraints the husband places upon himself. Her honor is more than a function of his limited horizons.[18]

The husband who fulfills the letter and spirit of his "honor" obligations makes a significant move toward assuring that *shalom bayit* prevails in the union.[19]

To Honor One's Husband

The other side of the husband-wife *shalom bayit* equation is the honor and respect that the wife must give to her husband. It may be true that the primary *shalom bayit* responsibility rests with the husband, and that he must perforce take the lead in creating an atmosphere of respect in the home. But it is not a one-sided obligation. The husband, by being respectful, is more likely to be respected. The wife, for her part, must embark on a relationship of respectfulness by unconditionally committing herself to properly honor and respect her husband.[20]

It would be an overgeneralization to suggest that the husband's respect for his wife is respect for her as a person, whilst the wife's respect for her husband is respect not only for his person but also for his position. Yet there is an element of truth in this suggestion, for the husband does occupy a singular position of respect in the traditional Jewish family. He has priority of respect relative to the wife should this be at issue. Ladies first, as a societal norm, is not the rule in the Jewish home. Rather, it is the husband first. The traditions of the home are essentially the husband's traditions, especially if it is an either-or situation where one of the customs or practices has to give way for coherence to be maintained. There is, however, nothing wrong and much right in adopting the wife's family traditions when they make a positive impact on the home.[21]

The husband is the leader of the household, and this is reflected in the manner in which the wife should honor her husband. The husband need not, indeed should not, insist on receiving the honor due to him as the head of the household. His doing so is more likely to backfire. As leader, he must lead by example. The respect given by the wife to the husband should be the almost reflexive respect that one gives to an individual who is respectful of others and who by example elicits the respect of others. One is even likely to be in awe of a leader who assumes that role with such humility.[22]

The husband-wife dialectic, barring any special arrangements, is a maintenance-upkeep dialectic. The husband maintains the wife and provides for her needs, in return for which the wife is responsible for the upkeep of the home. It is fitting and conducive to home tranquility that the wife be amenable to carrying out the legitimate desires of her husband. The wife honors the husband in this manner. There are tasks for the wife in marriage, but again they are not to be demanded of the wife. They should be carried out by the wife's demanding this of herself.[23]

Much has been said of the supposedly slavelike tasks that the wife is obliged to perform for the husband. Firstly, in reaction to this, it should be stated that a master-slave state in marriage is unhealthy and thus undesirable. Secondly, if one were to impose a master-slave label on the union it would, as per the biblical precedent, verily make the master into a slave. For individuals in superior positions, in Jewish tradition, were burdened with superior responsibilities befitting that position. This was done to prevent superior position from developing into exaggerated self-importance with its attendant demanding, bosslike mentality. The servitude of the wife, if indeed it can be described as such, is nothing more than the dedication of one part of the body to another. It is and should always be free of any diminution of the wife's dignity.[24]

The wife should honor her husband more than enough. The "more than enough" duty serves to take the according of honor out of the realm of measurement. Instead of being bogged down in assessing what is enough honor, or how much honor is merited, the honor should come in effusive doses, spontaneously and freewillingly. The honor should be more than honor of position; it should reflect the wife's appreciation of what her husband means to her.[25]

What should evolve from the dual obligation of the husband and wife to honor and respect one another is a situation of escalating respectfulness, in which each one of the partners accords respect, elicits via that honor and respectfulness the respect of the other, and so helps to create a syndrome of escalating honor and respect. Neither should wait for the other to start lest no one begin. Let them both initiate the honor syndrome. Should they trip over each other in the rush, it will be a meeting of profound moment. There is ample confidence that they will be able to handle such eventualities more than adequately.

The escalating honor syndrome is *shalom bayit* in its most noble form.

Anger—To Be Avoided

Honor, the mode of expression that is most desirable in marriage, is underlined by the ability to communicate with genuine concern for the situation and needs of the other. Honor is humane considerateness. Anger is on the other side of the spectrum. It is communication without concern for the other. It is self-serving speech, bereft of feeling; it is talking "to" rather than "with." It is a form of letting loose rather than a form of communication.

Husband and wife, in an atmosphere of *shalom bayit*, merit that the Godly presence reside with them. God feels welcome and at home in a harmonious atmosphere. On the negative side, the consuming fire which devours the conflicting couple may in fact be the fire of anger, which in its venom provokes diatribe and insult and leaves the relationship in a state of turmoil.[26]

The propensity to anger is generally condemned as evil, and one is to keep far away from exercising anger. Anger, as verbalization that lacks control, is placed on par with idolatry, which also emanates from lack of control and is instead the expression of what one feels like doing. Anger begets angry counter-response, as well as implanting a hardness and arrogance which makes one oblivious to the truth and unconcerned about others. Anger carries with it a multitude of sins.[27]

Anger is a destructive enough force in human relations. For the married couple, who are in an enclosed environment, it can be devastating. Anger is verbal violence, and the fear engendered by anxiety over when the next tantrum will come puts the entire house on edge. Where respect builds, anger destroys. Where true respect prevails, anger is not likely to come into play, for it is not usual to explode at people whom one really respects. The presence of anger thus points to a double deficit, in that the proper respect that should obtain in the marriage is sorely lacking. It is thus extremely important never to get angry at one's mate, and not to allow for the conditions which beget anger.[28]

Whilst it is an obligation of both partners to refrain from anger and temper outbursts, the failure of one to live up to this obligation should not be seen by the other as just cause to likewise resort to anger. Hard as it may be, one should meet one's partner's anger with gentleness. That will prevent an escalation of belligerence, at the very least, and possibly calm down the boisterous party, who may even see the folly of the angry approach when the obvious and more pleasant contrast hits home.[29]

We are all prone to anger of differing intensities, and to simply speak about not becoming angry is nice, but leaves a void, the void between recommended ideal and practical reality. How to control anger is so important a matter that those in marital situations should devote some attention to it. Bottling up the emotions only works well for those who can contain an immense amount of grievances. It is worthwhile weighing at the very outset whether what is bothersome is really worth it. If it is, then the proper approach would be to sit down, in a calm setting, and discuss it with one's mate. This may head off the explosion.[30]

Before exploding, ask why. What will be gained by the tantrum? Will it bring results, or will it be merely a ventilation exercise? As a ventilation exercise, the outburst is of dubious value. The angry explosion is more likely to generate more such explosions than to get it out of the system. Awareness that anger is habit-forming should be kept in mind before expressing oneself angrily.[31]

There is probably no better technique for controlling anger than the cultivation of a balanced outlook on life which sees things in proper perspective. Advance integration of the right philosophy implants the preventive mechanism forestalling anger. Study of traditional tracts on the control of anger is helpful. This should bring with it the resolve to be extra-scrupulous about losing control. Good intentions reinforced over time usually translate into good results.[32]

Husband-Wife Communication

The question, or problem, of anger relates to the tone of the communication between husband and wife, for a communication's tone can adversely affect its actual content. What is expressed in anger is usually negative, accusative, or pejorative.

The content of husband-wife communication is a matter which on its own is worthy of elaboration. "Do not engage in excessive idle chatter with women" is seen as referring to one's own wife. Rather than being an attempt to minimize husband-wife communication, a false conclusion derived from a superficial reading of the text, the direction of this statement seems to be toward elevating the level of husband-wife conversation. A wife is not there simply for small talk, or idle chatter. If idle chatter characterizes husband-wife dialogue, it indicates a lack of true respect for the capacities and insights of the wife. Some small talk is natural; excessive idle chatter is a sad commentary on the husband's perception of his wife. The husband who disparages his wife thereby disparages himself. For it is in the normal pattern of events that a wife who is treated shabbily will react to her husband in the same way, thus doing to the husband's self-esteem what the husband did to hers. The wife may not even do this consciously; it may be a reflex response. Conversation usually develops along the lines of the assumptions which underlie the relationship between the communicators.[33]

The wife should not be compelled to live in the murky world of ignorance, not knowing what the husband does or what his concerns are. The husband should be consistently forthcoming regarding what he is doing, where he is going. He should assume that his wife cares, an assumption which is usually corroborated by the attentiveness of the wife to what her husband has to say. And this type of communication should be a two-way street, with the wife readily sharing her experiences with an equally attentive and interested husband.[34]

But husband-wife communication goes beyond mere sharing

of information. It gets to the very core of each one's inner feelings. Husband and wife will be well-served if they set aside sacred, inviolable time in which they share their true feelings with each other, feelings about how their relationship is evolving, feelings about how the home is developing, feelings about their sense of achievement and accomplishment. Whilst this type of dialogue works best when feelings are expressed openly and honestly, and not stifled or camouflaged, still neither of the partners should be used merely as a convenient receptacle for the other's ventilating of emotions. Discussion should be goal-oriented rather than catharsis-motivated. Such higher-level discussion is more conducive to really knowing the other, and to facilitating the working together toward a shared destiny.

The husband and wife who are attuned to each other in the manner described will have a greater tendency to share with each other, to consult regularly on issues of mutual interest, instead of making unilateral moves which all too often signify a lack of caring for the feelings of the other, or lack of respect for the opinions the other may have offered.[35]

Much has been made of the need to master the techniques of communication in marriage, but all the techniques are of dubious value if they are employed in the absence of *mentschlichkeit* (authentic, genuine humaneness) and are of dubious necessity among two who are exemplars of *mentschlichkeit*.[36]

The *content* of marital conversation, when it reflects positively on the opinion each of the marital partners has for the other, correspondingly links with a more sensitive *tone* of conversation. Tenderness of communication, a kindly, gentle approach, delicacy when making requests—all desired norms in the husband-wife dialectic—are more probable between a couple with true respect for each other. Tone and content are components of communication which have a way of reinforcing each other.[37]

There are times in the marriage when one of the partners will see a need to admonish the other, for whatever legitimate reason. When the normal tone and content of the marital dialogue are of the desired quality, the odd instance of admonition can be carried out in a good atmosphere, with pleasantness and without put-down. The mutual respect of the couple is too well ingrained to be jeopardized by periodic admonition. Where communication at the proper level of tone and content has not been achieved, fault-finding is likely to be more frequent, and the message is increasingly likely to be transmitted awkwardly, often leaving a bitter aftertaste.[38]

Communication at the higher level of tone and content also impacts on areas of marital life which are more functional, or at least often appear as such. The preparation of meals and the transferring of maintenance funds are usual, almost perfunctory, elements of marital sharing. In an atmosphere of admirable tone-content communication, even that sharing is of a different nature, and is accompanied by real warmth and the exuding pleasant feeling at being able to do nice things for the other.[39]

Though there are exceptions—and these exceptions, even though quite rare, often evoke the expression that life is not fair—the general rule is that goodness and kindness beget goodness and kindness, gentleness and respect generate gentleness and respect. The way one of the spouses behaves is most often a mirror reflection of how the other behaves.

If for none other than self-serving reasons, it is in the best interests of both husband and wife to be respectful, kind, considerate, gentle, and forthcoming with one another. Potentially, each has no better a friend, no more trusted a confidant, no more reliable a conduit to a life of bliss and contentedness. Potentially, too, each has no worse an enemy, no more betraying a partner, no more steady repository of misery. Whether the potentiality unfolds to either of the extremes, or to anywhere short of the extremes, depends on what each brings to the relationship. It is within the normal capacity of individuals to make proper judgments when confronted with the alternatives. And, once convinced that the alternatives are clear realities which will eventuate depending on the choice one makes, the individual is likely to make the right choice.[40]

Those in the marital situation need to confront the choice, and then take the lead. The reward most yearned for, that the other follow, is most often a natural consequence.

Good habits for self-serving reasons are better than bad habits for whatever reasons. They may not be authentic expressions at the start, but they usually integrate well into the psyche of the human being, who is better off happy and fulfilled instead of miserable and empty.

In the final analysis, however, all this is an approach which is better than the alternative, but certainly not the best alternative. The best alternative is to be gentle because that is the proper way to be, to be kind because that is the essence of true humanity, to be respectful because others, by definition, are worthy of respect. Approaching one's partner in marriage in this primary, unconditional manner is motivated not by anticipated results, but by what are perceived as primary human responsibilities. That this approach leads to a most profound manifestation of *shalom bayit* is a most welcome by-product.[41]

6

Dynamics of a Good Marriage

Some Ingredients of a Good Marriage

Shalom bayit, the marriage ideal, ensues from the effort that is put into marriage by the couple. It is the end product of the mix of positive ingredients that are put into the marriage.[1]

The basic pillars of the marriage, as reflected in the classic verse of betrothal uniting God with the community of Israel, are that it be forever, that it combine righteousness and proper behavior together with kindness and mercifulness, and that it be a union fused in faith.[2]

Forever speaks of the unconditionality of commitment to the marriage. *Righteousness and proper behavior* refers to the legal framework of the marriage, *kindness and mercifulness* to the sensitive manner with which the legal framework is permeated. *A union fused in faith* relates to a match in which the couple have faith that each is for the other, in the ultimate shared-destiny sense.

This is the structural framework of the marriage. Beyond that, or within that, are various nuances which fine-tune the relationship, giving it viability and vitality. What follows are some ingredients that make for a good mix in the marriage.

The marriage should be seen as an all-encompassing, twenty-four-hour-a-day relationship. All-embracingness has its advantages, but also its unique demands, and the partners need to be alert to the fluctuations within the totality.

No individual is the perfect being. All humans have weak-

55

nesses and frailties, along with strengths and virtues. Rather than seeing one's mate as being perfect, it is more realistic to appreciate the mate in totality, the strengths with the weaknesses, the virtues with the frailties. For individual uniqueness is in reality a unique combination of virtue and frailty; each of the partners has a measure of both.

Marriage thrives in shared intimacy. Intimacy is preserved when it is perceived as personal, private, sacred, and inviolable. This calls for fundamental discretion, and extreme care not to spill personal matters out into the public domain. It is useful to think and deliberate very carefully before talking about one's spouse to others.[3]

The marriage relationship is one of giving, bestowing to the other. It is to supply rather than to demand. When the relationship degenerates into a demand trap, it chokes off the path to true happiness.[4]

When speaking of giving, there is no more precious commodity one can give to one's spouse than time. We tend to give time to what and whom we consider important. There are some who may claim that their not having time for spouse or family is an unfortunate result of unavoidable circumstances, and such claims can, under certain conditions, have some measure of validity. Generally, however, this is not the case. On the other hand, making time for one's mate is an affirmative statement that the one with whom one shares the time is important. Therefore, establishing time that husband and wife relegate just to each other is an enhancement of the union.[5]

Most individuals have areas of life which they consider important to themselves. It could be appearance, achievement, or some other entity. Generally, these areas of importance are the selfsame areas where one puts in much time and effort. The husband and wife should seek out these areas in their mates, and go out of their way to find what is praiseworthy in the other and express the praise. It is preferable to err on the side of too much praise rather than too little.[6]

Happiness is a crucial ingredient in life. It is equally crucial to marriage. Ideally, both partners will have mastered the art of being happy and content. Failing that, if at least one of the two is a happy person, the happy one can help lift the unhappy one out of the doldrums when feeling low or in a passing mood of depression. Overcoming depression of the bearable variety is not easy, but it helps immensely to have a partner who seeks to infuse happiness. One may be able to live with feelings of depression, but it is quite difficult to thrive in such a climate. The marriage too may stagnate in an atmosphere of depression, so that helping extricate the other is quite beneficial. If both partners tend to the melancholy side, the marriage may endure, but it is less likely to prosper.[7]

Rough moments, moments of trial or tragedy, are part of life and part of married life. Pacifying, calming down, comforting, are special skills which should be in the repertoire of husband and wife for those unavoidable types of situations which demand delicate attentiveness. These situations often come suddenly, so that being prepared for the unexpected implies that one's homework be done long in advance.[8]

Most people have a definite idea of what is coming to them in honor, respect, or attention, among other things, but sometimes the one who is expected to accord these considerations may not have the same idea. The gap between what is expected and what is forthcoming often spells disappointment. For this, and other types of "wrongs," it is prudent to be forgiving, as it is best not to stand on ceremony and demand what is due. The ideal dynamic is to be meticulous in the discharge of one's own obligations, and liberal as pertains to how the other's obligations to you are discharged. All this comes under the heading of tolerance, or turning a blind eye to that which may be bothersome.[9]

These, then, are some, though by no means all, of the ingredients which, when mixed together, combine for a good marriage relationship.

Transcendence in Marriage

"If I am not for myself, who is for me? When I am for myself only, what am I? And if not now, when?" This terse statement of Hillel's is probably the most concise formulation of the dynamics of human interaction.[10]

"If I am not for myself, who is for me?" The individual cannot expect to step out into the world with a poor self-image and hope to make important contributions to human betterment. The negation of the self makes the negating person a poor choice for helping others. The beginning of all responsibility is to and for the self. The ignoramus cannot teach, the uninformed cannot enlighten, the shaky person cannot counsel. Any individual who neglects the essential components of self-growth and then asks "who is for me" must be told the blunt answer—nobody. Such a person will be for nobody, and nobody will be for that person.

Self-worth based on concern for one's development dare not become self-centeredness. The individual must always ask this question: "When I am for myself only, what am I?" In equally blunt terms, the answer is—a deficient human being. A true human being gravitates toward the other, and recognizes that existence in isolation impedes the human process, both for the self and for others.

Some individuals may recognize the primary human obligation of concern for the other quite early in life. Others may be given a rude awakening at a later stage. It will dawn on these late-bloomers that they are deficient, and they may seek to defer confrontation with responsibility. But "if not now, when?" No matter whether the awakening occurs at an early or later stage, the demands of the hour preclude procrastination. The best way to climb out of the rut of self-centeredness is not in stages of disengagement from the self. Such deferral via the installment process merely delays the inevitable and wastes precious moments of goodness. Instead, the way out of self-centeredness is now, immediately, and with finality. There is no sense in punishing oneself with guilt for past failings when present fulfillments are beckoning. Present achievements make up for the past and go a long way toward restoring the balance between responsibility for the self and concern for the other. "If not now, when?" Possibly never; therefore now.[11]

For one to be self-effacing to the point of neglect is irresponsible, and to be self-indulgent to the point of obliviousness to the other is irresponsive. The person who best relates to other people is one who has given appropriate attention to individual needs, who has a well-defined and developed sense of self and responsibility, with a realistic appreciation of the role in life to be under-taken. The honest confrontation with oneself leads to a healthy outer-directedness, to a concern with causes and for people. The classic I-thou relationship between people demands an "I" to relate to a thou, and the real "I" will intentionally gravitate to a thou not to satisfy a need but to share a self. The true relationship with another person emanates from self-transcendence rather than from self-actualization. Hillel's concise formulation argues that such a balanced approach is of immediate priority.

Marriage is the classic instance of sharing the self with an other, of extending beyond oneself to embrace another. Concerning the female relatives whom a man may not marry, Maimonides suggests that they share one common ingredient—they are constantly together with him in the home, and arranging a marriage would be a relatively easy task. At the same time Maimonides also roundly condemns the union of root and branch, and sees this as part of the reason for the prohibited consanguineous unions.[12]

These two factors, the constant togetherness and the root-branch idea, point to a vital notion in marriage. The respective spouses are obliged to marry people who are "strangers," people who can be called "other." Remaining within one's own confines is seen as abhorrent. The abhorrence stems from the reality that such a union involves not an extension of self, but a turning in of the self, a shriveling up or recoiling into a comfortable shell. It reinforces a self-centeredness that is the very antithesis of healthy human interaction.

Marriage is a union of two individuals who, if they are of mature character, should be able to live with one another. When marriage fails, the suspicion is that one or both of the partners has a deficient personality. What is referred to as marriage breakdown is often retarded personality development coming to the fore. The retarded development leads to a distorted set of values and an inability to interact with another on a truly human level. From a marital-stability standpoint, the inability or refusal to share, to extend oneself, to give of oneself, whether it stems from immaturity or from the character deficiency most easily described as self-centeredness, is a prime factor in marriage disintegration.[13]

Symbolically, the entry of a previously single individual into marriage signifies the shift from attention to oneself and toward concern for the other. But transcendence in marriage does not come automatically with the breaking of the glass. Transcendence in marriage is a reality, or has a greater chance of being a reality, if one's value-educational experience stressed this form of human expression. But if kindness, understanding, and empathy are not part of childhood experience, it can hardly be expected that the adult experience of children so raised will be characterized by kindness, understanding, and empathy. If children are taught to fend for themselves in a dog-eat-dog world, they may become self-sufficient, which is delightful for the parents but potentially harmful to the children. They may enter the adult world with caution, suspicion, and a protective, self-indulgent attitude. If they marry with that attitude, they are inviting failure.[14]

Even should a marriage of self-indulgent types endure, it would not detract from the basic thesis that transcendence is critical to marriage. Self-indulgent types may be able to persevere or to survive each other, but one could hardly label that marriage ideal, and even less the human ideal. We are less interested in marriages which survive, and more interested in marriages that thrive. And for a marriage to thrive, it needs to be predicated on the genuine capacity and desire of each of the partners to immerse the self in concern for and attentiveness to the other. Transcendence toward the other is the way to the other's heart.[15]

Showing Appreciation

There is a fundamental difference between *being* appreciative and *showing* appreciation. Each is technically independent of the other. One can be appreciative but not show it. One can show appreciation and not really mean it. The latter scenario is a less frequent occurrence than the former. Usually, when one shows appreciation, it is meant and intended, sincerely felt and effectively projected.

However, being appreciative does not automatically translate into showing appreciation. Being appreciative is a passive state; showing appreciation is an active process. Whether it be because of laziness, or because the assumption is that the other knows how you really feel, or for other reasons, people who are appreciative often do not show it. And, by not showing it, the other person, who is ostensibly unappreciated, feels slighted and hurt.

In the atmosphere of transcendence, the jump from "being" to "showing" is easily made. The transcending person strives to know what makes the other feel pleased and content, and does not hesitate to bring that feeling to the fore. And the appreciation that is conveyed is not simply the letting go of a comment or the expressing of an emotion. Appreciation is conveyed in a manner that is geared to assuring that the other is fully cognizant of the feeling and has fully absorbed its meaning.

It is admittedly not healthy for a husband or wife to stand around waiting for appreciation to be expressed. Each should go about exercising their obligations without expectation of reward. At the same time, each should see the conveying of appreciativeness to the other as quite important. The dialectic at work here and in so many other areas of marriage is that demands are made on oneself, giving is directed to the other; not vice versa.[16]

Appreciation may be conveyed in warm expression, kind comment, helpful deed, or thoughtful gift. However it may be expressed, it should not be accompanied with the thought that one has concluded or temporarily fulfilled the dictates of appreciativeness, and that the next such expression is a long way off. One should work with the thought that there is no end to the appreciation that should be conveyed to the other. This, because there is no limit to the appreciation that one actually owes to one's spouse. One who sincerely believes that limitless appreciation is owed to the other is less likely to fall short of conveying the optimal level of appreciation.[17]

It is a good practice for both husband and wife not to let one day pass in which they fail to convey gratitude to one another. The other is not perfect, neither is the one. And what is done by the one for the other may not be up to the desired standard. Yet there is always room for praise from the one as long as the other's good intentions are there, or if one benefits from the other.[18]

The recipient of the praise, though not looking for it and thereby opening the self up to disappointment, should at the same time be gracious and receptive to the praise, rather than swallow it as one does food. The bestower of gratitude needs to be sure it is accepted; the receiver of gratitude in turn should assure that the gratitude is greatly valued, not taken for granted. Exaggeration with obvious good intentions should be received in the same way.

Study Together

The husband and wife are united together in a multidimensional union. They share life in all its dimensions; they share a destiny which is reached through their common commitment to the transcending values of the Torah.

How is one to know what are the transcending values of Torah? This knowledge is gained in one's formative years, or at least should be. But even if comprehension of Jewish values is studiously digested in the earlier years of life, it remains as abstract concepts waiting to be placed into real-life practice.

Marriage affords the opportunity to carry out the most noble values of the tradition, the full gamut of person-to-person obligations that are enunciated in the Torah and further elaborated in talmudic and post-talmudic literature. Additionally, those person-God obligations which are central to the Judaic lifestyle, including the Sabbath, kashrut, *taharat hamishpaḥah,* Pesaḥ, Shavuot, Sukkot, Rosh Hashanaḥ, and Yom Kippur, among others, gain a more exalted expression in the marriage-continuity context. Also, the philosophy of purpose (*hashkafah*) with which one's life is infused has a significant impact on the direction the marriage takes.[19]

All this points to another facet of life that husband and wife share together, the navigational facet of each partner steering the other toward their transcending life purpose.

What better way to reinforce this sharing than for husband and wife to spend time together in serious study of their obligations and responsibilities, and in hammering out what should be their common *hashkafah*, or life purpose. These aspects of life are too important to be entrusted to only one of the partners, with the other totally removed from such concerns. Responsibility and life purpose are subjects of study never really completed. There are always additional insights to be gained from more study, more dialogue. Having each other as true partners in the study of responsibility and purpose is thus a tie that binds over the full length of married life.[20]

This is not to suggest that husband and wife are primarily learning partners; rather they are *also* learning partners. Most importantly are they partners in real life, where the learning is escalated from the abstract to the concrete. At the same time, the mutual respect and admiration of the husband for the wife and of the wife for the husband are also escalated. Neither is locked into a role; each shares in the other's interests.[21]

Study is also a respectful medium which can save the partners the need to admonish one another if such situations arise. When a couple study together how they should each behave or what they should each do, the text does the admonishing and the message is conveyed without put-down or ill feeling.

Study together is not a modern addition to the Jewish marriage framework. There is ample precedent for this among the sages of the past, aside from the fact that it makes eminent sense.[22]

Willingness to Adjust

Much as one may talk of the harmony that should prevail in marriage, this cannot be expected to evolve on its own. Man and woman, equal as they are, are nevertheless clearly not the same. This is over and above the general proposition that all individuals differ in appearance; they differ too in how they think, how they behave. The differences work well in intellectual exchange, where each gains from the other's perspective. In real life, the differences are more pronounced and may possibly be sources of conflict.[23]

Any talk of adjusting must be preceded with the obvious, yet the obvious must be stated with emphatic definitiveness. At no time should discussion of adjusting be an excuse for forced compliance or for making the one partner be exactly as the other partner would like. Adjusting is a give-and-take process which at all times appreciates the individuality of each of the marital partners, and is based on mutual respect and cooperation.

With the obvious having been stated, and also in the forefront of any negotiating between husband and wife, the other vital component of any mutual adjustment is the willingness of husband and wife not only to change but also to take the first step. The couple may fall over each other in the rush to be the first to move off center, and that is fine. The alternative, where each waits for the other to make the first move, is an approach and attitude laden with frustration, sure to exacerbate rather than improve the situation.[24]

If either of the partners is disappointed in the other, the disappointed partner should assume that the other is probably also disappointed, and should thus act to get at the root cause of the other's disappointment, and then correct it.

Major adjustments, changes of habit or behavior, may in some instances come quickly, but usually it takes time to undo that to which one is acclimatized or to correct a behavior flaw. The willingness to work at it should be a more than sufficient gesture, and browbeating to speed up the process is unfair. Besides, only one who is in order and of exemplary character can ask the same of the other. But precisely that type of individual is less likely to make demands.[25]

It is advisable not to have negotiating sessions regarding adjustment at inappropriate times, or when the other has not indicated a willingness to move off center. Rigidity probably has variant possible causes, but may reflect a souring of the relationship. Before any adjustment, reinvesting the union with warmth is called for, so that productive discussion becomes more plausible.[26]

Of less major import relative to adjustment are those situations when the one would like going to places the other does not enjoy, or when one must wait for the other to take care of matters before being ready. For the first situation, mature individuals can usually make balanced trade-offs. For the second, one can either think in terms of helping accelerate the other's readiness by lightening burdens, where that is possible; or failing that, can anticipate the situation and adjust to it.[27]

Marriage Counseling

Even though willingness to adjust should normally head off conflict, not everyone is willing nor is everyone able to formulate effective methods to correct situations. Ideally, husband and wife should be able to sit down and work out whatever problem affects their marriage. But sometimes the couple is not able to handle the situation, or the situation itself is quite complex.[28]

A third person, trusted by the couple and experienced in the intricacies of married life, may sometimes be able to help straighten out the situation. This is probably more useful when the outside party acts as arbitrator, or as the provider of the right advice to steer the couple through a difficult situation.[29]

In the past, the community itself had experts whose job it was to bring harmony back to a conflicted couple. Since every good marriage enhanced the community and every bad marriage had adverse affects on the community, it was undoubtedly seen to be in the best interests of the community to do whatever was possible to preserve and improve shaky marriages.[30]

The modern marriage situation is quite troubled, and marriage counselors or psychologists specializing in marital problems have no problem filling their appointment calendars with clients. Such is the gravity of the situation that it has been suggested that couples go through mandatory testing for psychological compatibility before marrying.[31]

Whether psychology, never mind psychological testing, is the answer to marital problems is in itself a serious question. There are some definite areas of value clash between psychology and Judaism. Psychologies which argue for the fullness of pleasure as the goal to be reached certainly are inconsistent with Jewish thinking. Pleasure is assuredly part of the Jewish way of life, but in the context of higher considerations. There is also a potential clash with psychologies of the self-affirmation, self-confidence orientation, which do not correlate with the Judaic appreciation of humility and sense of what is shameful. What is meant by mental health in the clinical sphere may not be in the best ultimate interests of the person as reflected in the Judaic measuring rod, the Torah tradition. It should also be kept in mind that the track record of psychology in solving problems is not nearly as successful as the psychologists would have us believe.[32]

There are those who even question the fundamental approach in the clinical setting, where the client, despite all the talk, is not really treated as an equal. Whereas Jewish tradition insists on according special care to those in unfortunate situations, or those in need of help, the client in therapy is given a limited time to talk, is sometimes not even talked to by the clinician for protracted periods, and is too often a paying customer rather than the object of real concern. It is thus not surprising that there are negative halakhic views about going to psychologists altogether.[33]

To be sure, not all psychologies are the same, nor are all psychologists the same. There are psychological systems which are truly value-oriented, there are psychologists who have great respect for their clientele, and who go out of their way to understand the "cultural baggage" of a Jewish couple in therapy. A real expert in marriage-compatibility problems is an expert because the traditions and practices of the couple are understood and respected.[34]

There is another way of approaching the crucial matter of psychological counseling. There is much within general psychology and specific psychological systems that need not be dismissed as un-Jewish. To more fully appreciate this, it is worthwhile reflecting on the talmudic discussion attempting to ascertain why it is forbidden to read the book of Ben Sira (Ecclesiasticus). One suggestion is that it may be because Ben Sira wrote, "Let not anxiety enter your heart, for it has slain many a person." The Talmud immediately rejects this suggestion by pointing to the fact that King Solomon, in Proverbs 12:25, said the same thing: "Anxiety in the heart of a person makes it stoop [yash-henna]." R. Ammi and R. Assi differ on how to interpret the word yash-henna; one view connects the word with banishing the anxiety from one's mind, the other links the word with relating the anxiety to others.[35]

Before trying to understand the views proposed by R. Ammi and R. Assi, it is worthwhile to probe into the reason why Ben Sira's statement about anxiety renders his entire treatise suspect and worthy of being banned. In the final analysis, the Talmud permits expounding upon the good things in Ben Sira, but in the process of reaching this decision entertains a wholesale prohibition for a variety of possibilities, the anxiety statement being one of them.

From a religious perspective, and, more generally, from a

human-growth perspective, anxiety is a very useful, if not necessary, ingredient. Anxiety about one's failings, anxiety about actualizing one's potential, anxiety about overstepping the letter or
spirit of the law, serves to prod the individual into more noble
human expression. Anxiety in this sense implies confrontation
with one's reality and awareness of one's responsibility. Ben Sira's
statement that we should not allow anxiety to enter our heart thus
is in sharp contrast to the basic elements of human growth and
true religious expression.

The Talmud justifiably contemplates banning the book of Ben
Sira because of this statement, but only for a fleeting moment.
Instantly it is recognized that this statement has its parallel in
Proverbs, where reference is made to the negative feature of
anxiety. For the moment at least, Ben Sira is reprieved. There is
anxiety which is inconsistent with the human endeavor, anxiety
which is stooping rather than uplifting; it is this anxiety which,
Ben Sira recommends, should not enter one's heart.

The verse in Proverbs at once discourages a type of anxiety
and recommends a "therapy" to relieve that anxiety. The therapy
is either banishing or relating, as reflected in the views of R.
Ammi and R. Assi. *Banishing* refers to erasing the anxiety from
one's mind, *relating* refers to sharing the anxiety with others, and
thus hopefully alleviating the anxiety. The ends, within this
approach, are the same, but the means are different.

At the risk of homiletic overextension, one can see in these two
approaches, banishing and relating, the antecedents of two major
trends in modern therapeutic practice, the behavioral and the
psychoanalytic. Behavioral therapies tend to separate the problem from the person. A problem is a problem the person *has*, and
the task at hand is to rid the person of the problem, a banishing
approach.

On the other hand, psychoanalytic therapies tend to see the
problem as an attribute of the person; not merely a problem the
person has, but in a definite sense a problem the person *is*. The
whole person is involved in the resolution of the difficulty, and
personal history back to the infantile stages is probed in order to
get to the root of the matter. It is a dialectical (relating) approach
to the situation.

These divergent trends have their respective strengths and weaknesses. Psychoanalytic therapies are seen as better suited for neurotic problems, and behavioral solutions more suited for short-term relief of an anxiety, a disabling symptom, or a bad habit, and possibly for psychotic depressions.

Aside from the clinical advantages and disadvantages, there is another dimension to these and other psychological systems which has caused some measure of concern—namely, the philosophy which underlies these systems.

It has been pointed out that the goals of psychotherapy have become intertwined with the emphasis on individualism, secularism, and successful adaptation characteristic of Western society. One may even conjure a case for the proposition that psychotherapy has aided and perhaps accelerated the adoption of these values. This may be even more manifest in the antiheritage orientation with which the psychotherapeutic process is identified.[36]

Does this mean that psychotherapy must be ruled out as a mode of treatment for Jews? We have seen that there are some who would espouse this position, but a legitimate response need not be a choice of extremes.

Others feel that the efficacy of therapy does not necessarily suffer if some aspects of the therapy's philosophical framework are suspended. Admittedly this is not always possible; in some instances suspending the philosophy would necessitate suspending the therapy.[37]

Another approach, one which has been gaining momentum slowly but surely, is to formulate a Jewish psychotherapeutic system.

It has been argued that in this we should not sit back and lament a bad situation, rather we should aggressively work toward an integrated therapeutic posture which is founded on Torah values and halakhic principles.[38]

The major criticism which has been leveled at the behavioral school is that it tends to see the person in a mechanistic, stimulus-response framework. Not rarely, experiments on animals were the basis for countering a human problem. The human being was conceived of in the background of the "rat model."

In 1964 the imminent demise of behaviorism was predicted. In a sense this prediction was correct, because the behaviorism of today bears little resemblance to the behaviorism of twenty years ago. Behavioral therapists now are focusing their attention on cognitive and social learning, and not merely on conditioning. A leading figure in the evolving school of cognitive behavior modification asserts that if we are going to change a behavior then we must modify the thinking which precedes the act. In this school at least, behavioral thinking has come fully within the ambience of a humanized view of the person.[39]

This development has been long overdue and is certainly welcome from a Jewish perspective. Who can deny that there are behavioral tendencies within our tradition, such as Maimonides' suggestion that the best way to establish the desirable character patterns within ourselves is through constant repetition, until the deeds come easily and the character patterns are firmly entrenched. This is a vital instance where cognition and behavior fuse in the human growth pattern.[40]

It is, of course, ridiculous to suggest that Maimonides was a behaviorist; as ridiculous as to suggest that King Solomon was psychoanalytically oriented. Nevertheless, there are elements of these schools which are operative in our own thinking. This should convince the skeptic that not all that is espoused by these schools is antithetical to Jewish thought.

At the same time, even with the strides toward cognition, there remain wide gaps between behavioral practice and Halakhah, as there remains a gulf between psychotherapy and Jewish values. On an individual, piecemeal basis, they can often be mediated by consultation with one's rabbi.

On a more general plane, a number of factors must be fully appreciated. The embracing of cognition in behavioral therapy has brought it closer to the traditional therapies. Integration of the best elements of these traditions in an eclectic, Jewishly oriented approach is not out of the question. Additionally, the pressures to rehumanize the thinking of therapists are immense. The existential slant, the humanistic therapies, the spiritually oriented system of logotherapy, are all influencing the therapeutic trend in a very positive way. What comes out of this mix will undoubtedly offer more acceptable options or combinations to the Jewish therapist and client. The eclectically oriented environment should also encourage distinctly Jewish formulations for the clinical situation.[41]

Establishing some measure of relatedness between psychology and Judaism should serve to diminish suspicions and lead to greater reflection on what may be gleaned from the respectable thinkers and practitioners of the clinic. If therapy is the essence, and its philosophy the shell, it may be instructive to collectively take the essence but discard the shell. It would be ideal to then construct our own shell, and thus give such so-called problems as anxiety and guilt a positive, future-directed thrust, transmuting "anxiety from" to "anxiety toward" and "guilt from" to "guilt toward." These and other categories could then be placed within the context of Jewish destiny as charted within halakhic parameters.[42]

All this would facilitate the setting up of counseling services for individual and marital problems which would operate along Torah guidelines. There is hardly any room for argument about the need for such services. Awareness of the need perforce must combine with the will and dedication of communal leaders to take the steps to facilitate the establishment of such services. Those who have developed proficiency in Torah-based counseling are already overbooked.

Having personnel adept in Torah-oriented counseling would bring the Jewish community back to the days of old, when such counselors were available to bring harmony back into the home. If such counselors were vital then, they are essential now.

All this is not to argue for a stampede to the clinic. Husband and wife should be friends and confidants able to help each other and able to enhance their marriage. Having counselors out there should be primarily a fallback position, a good option should the couple be unable to work matters out together.[43]

7
Love

What Is Love?

Over and above all the responsibilities, legal and extralegal, that define the husband-wife relationship, the relationship thrives and attains its most profound expression through love.

Honor and respect, caring and concern, dedication and devotion to the other, all are included in love, but love is more than the sum of all of these. Love contains all that is laudable in human relations, plus. The "plus" is a present reality, but it is also of elusive quality. One can sense its presence, but is still hard-pressed to find the proper words to describe love. In a definite sense love is ineffable, irreducible to finite terminology. This is so because it is indescribable.

Love is, and is therefore unconditional, not bound by time or circumstance.

Instructive here is the mishnaic assertion "Any love which is contingent on a thing, when the thing is nullified the love disintegrates; but a love which is independent of anything will never disintegrate. What is the prototype of a love which is contingent on a thing? This is the love of Amnon and Tamar. And what is the prototype of a love which is independent of anything? This is the love of David and Jonathan."[1]

True love, it turns out, is a relationship which is not based on the needs that are fulfilled by a partner, nor on what the partner has which is the object of desire. In such situations, it is quite natural that the thrill of receiving what one needs will eventually

71

evaporate once the needs have been fulfilled. Or, once the desire has been satisfied, the attraction for the other is not nearly as alluring.

True love is a human expression of appreciation and admiration for what the other individual is. It is a valuational relationship in which one appreciates the goodness, the warmth, the kindness, the ethical posture of the partner. In such a situation, love is linked with infinite values, and has an infinite quality of its own which will never disintegrate.

The love of Amnon and Tamar is a prototype of love which is contingent on physical attraction, on beauty which elicits a passionate desire to embrace and experience together. Once the thrill of embrace and experience has gone, the basis for the relationship is no longer solid. Whatever passions have been aroused have already gained their expression.

The love of David and Jonathan is a good example of a love independent of anything. It is a love of two individuals committed to the growth of the people of Israel, dedicated selflessly to the enhancement of the community. It is not a love which is in any way related to sensual pursuits, but is rather a love which expresses a sharing of values.[2]

The talmudic model for distorted love is between a male and female, where sensuality and its enticing power fronted as love, but was not love at all. Love may incorporate sensuality, but is independent of sensuality, as indicated by the model for true love, David and Jonathan, whose valuational union was entirely disconnected from sensuality.[3]

The aforementioned Mishnah has indicated a primary quality of love, and also what love is not, but it has not defined love. To describe what love is, how it manifests itself, what it means "to love," is to come close to the core of love, by picturing what are its essential attributes. The definition, however, remains beyond words. Thus, one can adequately answer the question "What do you like about that person?" But answering the question "Why do you love that person?" is a different matter.

The term most often assumed to describe love, *ahavah*, really is more a term for "liking." We can like many, but love does not necessarily follow from like. On the other hand, true love must emanate from like, it cannot really be love in the absence of like. To like is to know the other; one likes more, the more one knows of the other, thus leading to love.[4]

One description of love, as we have seen, is that it is a valuational union founded on the knowledge of what the other is. What passes for love in its contemporary usage, what parades as love in its infectious exhibitionism, is not love in the classical Jewish sense. Conversely, the classic love in the Jewish home may not relate to the sensually exciting picture that society associates with love, but the classical love is more meaningful. The uncompromising durability of that love is enough evidence for this.[5]

The valuational link that is love is forged out of a valuational like, a liking of the values that comprise the character and person of the beloved, and is coupled with the realization that one can fulfill and realize one's life purpose only through the valuational fusion with the beloved. The two members of the couple, while maintaining their separate individualities, fuse together into a spiritual whole, a valuationally viable unit.[6]

Where love prevails, one finds caring and empathy, immersion in the health and welfare, physical and spiritual, of the other. One finds in true love a spirit of giving where the giver experiences the sensation of receiving from the act of giving. The more one gives to the other, the more of the self is in the other, and the closeness becomes true intimacy.[7]

The love ideal, as a valuational link predicated on knowing, is a voyage of discovery which grows rather than diminishes with time. The process of knowing is a never-ending one. Marriage launches the knowing process in earnest, and the life of value-sharing that is marriage serves to develop the framework for love. Love in its ultimate sense is the holy of holies, the model of connectedness paradigmatic of the God-Israel love relationship.[8]

Marriage is a covenant of love, or more precisely, a covenant and commitment of those who like each other to like more by knowing more, and thus to facilitate love. Love is the bond that forges further mutual growth, that enables the couple to overcome whatever problems they may confront in life together. Love is what makes marriage what it is intended to be, and the human beings united in marriage what they aspire to be. In a word, love is that reality each of the partners must work to create from the mutual decision to unite in life.[9]

The First Seven Days

Love cannot be legislated, and while it is eminently fitting and proper that real love pervade the husband-wife relationship, that love cannot be ordered or mandated. However, what can be legislated is the creation of a framework in which the love has a better chance of evolving. Parts of that framework, the legal obligation, the *shalom bayit* imperative, the marriage dynamics, have already been elaborated upon. To help that framework to develop as naturally as possible, special attention and attentiveness needs to be given to the initial stages of the marriage.

The first seven days are perceived as the first crucial stage of the marriage. These are celebrative days, the days immediately following the wedding. Rather than going almost precipitously from the peak of celebration into the regular daily routine, the first seven days are days in which the bride and groom are wined and dined. More important than the wining and dining is that the groom is legally obliged to focus his attention exclusively on the bride for these seven days. It is unfortunate that the busy social calendar for these seven days, the travel obligations placed on the bride and groom to attend all the festive *sheva brakhot* (postnuptial celebrative meals), too often detracts from the attention that must be directed to each other in the first week. Even more unfortunate is that independent of these celebrative meals, the care with which one must approach the first seven days is not practiced the way it should be.[10]

During the first seven days, both bride and groom are enjoined from doing any work, even light work. A special type of work, irretrievable work, may be done by either only with the permission of the other. This legal point entrenches the notion that in the first seven days, each has a binding claim to the totality of the other's time, to be compromised only with the full agreement of the one who is about to be neglected, and then only in limited situations.

This halakhic norm is predicated on the awareness that the

first stage after the wedding is a particularly delicate period. Anxiety related to the first experience of conjugal relations almost certainly runs high, with understandable hesitancies reflecting not prudishness or fear, but a natural concern that relations go smoothly, with minimum pain and maximum understanding. The first experience is a trend-setter. Surely under normal circumstances relations will improve after the first encounter, but the warmth and caring shared in the first encounter is what paves the way for that improvement. Callousness and insensitivity in the first encounter can have deleterious effects on the course the marriage takes. Therefore, absolute attention, not only at night, but also the morning and afternoon after, indeed for the entire first week, is a must.[11]

Additionally, the first experience of conjual relations is merely an entree, a first taste of intimacy, but not an entire course. For, immediately following consummation, the bride and groom separate for a minimum of eleven days, before *tvilah* (immersion) in the *mikveh* (ritual water) and resumption of conjugal intimacy. This serves to introduce quite immediately a sense of control to the sensual dimension of the marriage. Even though the couple signify their oneness via physical union, usually immediately upon marriage, they then separate to indicate that their oneness, although also physical, is primarily a valuational and emotional oneness. To live this idea in reality aside from merely expounding it in theory, that too demands special attentiveness.[12]

The celebrative meals of the first week are communal contributions of joy and happiness for the couple. The spirit of exuberance prevailing at these gatherings maintains the ecstatic feelings of the wedding, or at least assures a residual continuity of the high emotions. This is geared to helping the couple retain an affirmative frame of mind as they embark on shaping their life together. The wedding is the beginning point, not the high point of the marriage, and for the community to suddenly and totally distance itself from the couple would not reflect this reality. Relatives and close friends do their best to create a positive postwedding environment for meaningful love to blossom.[13]

Outside encouragement and inspiration help, but essentially the couple are on their own. The legal obligations of each to the other for the first seven days are an important statement by Jewish tradition about the critical importance of the first stage of life together.[14]

The First Year

The initial experiences of closeness and withdrawal usually unfold in the first week of marriage. The absolute togetherness mandated for this period serves to ensure that personal attention and serious concern be given to this potentially upsetting time.

But there is more to marriage than can be condensed into the first week. Life together is not nearly as euphoric as the first seven days. There are pleasurable moments, but they are part of a package, a package which includes serious responsibility to financial, emotional, and valuational matters. The trend for these matters cannot be expected to unfold in the postwedding excitement of the first week. This trend unfolds over a more lengthy period, the first year, a laboratory of time and space when most of the experiences of married life, fulfillments as well as crises, have a greater likelihood of being confronted.

The absolute attentiveness of the first seven days is to ensure that the marriage does not stumble at the starting gate. The obligations of bride and groom to each other in the first year are to ensure that the foundation of the marriage is solidly entrenched; patterned with planned, mutual concern and not left to drift.

For the first year, the groom is excused from military duty so that he can be free to devote attention to his wife, his home. One can see the military exemption as a purely practical rule, in that the new groom may be so preoccupied with the new bride he left at home that he can hardly be an effective soldier.[15]

There is, however, another side to the issue. In battle, the matter at hand is the defense of the community from external threat. The objective is to neutralize those who want to destroy the community. If the objective is realized, the community can get on with their individual and collective efforts to live meaningful lives. Marrying and thus setting up the foundation for another Jewish household is one of the most important ways of investing the individual and the community with that meaning. The bride and groom, then, are also on the front lines, not fighting external threat, but rather preventing internal erosion. The soldier and the groom both defend the Jewish future. Unless it is an emergency threatening the nation, the groom is told to build within for the first year.[16]

The *mitzvah* of the first year is that the groom be free and clear of obligations that may whittle away at the time he must have available for his bride. There are those who see this commandment in uncompromising terms, that the groom must not leave the bride alone for the entire first year. Because the intent of the *mitzvah* is made clear—to make happy the wife you have taken— the husband's presence is required; he must be there to make her happy. If one is to be alert to the wishes and desires of his mate, if one is to know his partner in life, it can hardly be achieved by long distance. It makes little sense to think that the other becomes happy by the one going away. It may be true that absence increases one's yearning for the other, but first a relationship must be established for which one yearns.[17]

Generally, it is accepted that the groom may go away for the first year if it is for income purposes, but the minority view that refuses to compromise the obligation to be "clear for the home" should at least be kept in mind, so that the going is with hesitation, and the speed of coming back is accelerated. And, it is a good idea to be scrupulous regarding the obligation to be clear for the first year. Purposeless leaving is proscribed, and even the wife's agreement to this does not suffice. The stakes here are not merely the couple; at stake is the home, and ultimately the community. No one person is big enough to make a decision of such consequence.[18]

The obligation of the first year, even though directed to the groom, is basically a dual fulfillment. For the groom to carry out the *mitzvah* to make his bride happy, the bride needs to be there. The biblical command serves to program primary responsibility, and the bride's awareness of this responsibility implies that she will ensure that it be possible to fulfill, by being there in body and in spirit. The groom is not to run away; he also should not be compelled to run after. The *mitzvah* itself is intended to make sure that the bride is happy, and thus that the marriage will be patterned in a joyous mold; her being there is obviously crucial.[19]

The first year is the trend-setting year, and because of this everything in the relationship takes on added significance. To know what makes the other happy is not a prophetic gift, and will not come in a vision. It comes from concentrating fully on the other, and looking for likes and dislikes, wishes and desires, preferences and patterns of taste. No matter how naturally one may behave prior to the wedding, the real self is only revealed after the wedding, and it is the real self that the other must get to know, to like, and then to love.[20]

The first year is the energizing year, the year in which attentiveness to each other gives lasting strength to the union, through the confidence and assurance each has that the other really cares. The pattern, even the habits, have been firmly entrenched, and everything that ensues is further commentary building on the original firmament.[21]

The bride and groom are referred to as royalty, as queen and king. More than being a nice approbation, this is a title with a message. The queen and king, as royalty, are on top of matters, controlling the situation and ruling on how reality should unfold. The bride and the groom, too, are queen and king over their own personal domain; giving them the title tells them that they can make their life together what it should be.[22]

The first year is crucial, but matters do not end with the first year. Having achieved, in this vulnerable period, the firmament for love to evolve, the couple may breathe a collective sigh of relief, but that should not be accompanied by a tendency to neglect the other. For the Godly presence to pervade their union, happiness, the happiness of both, needs to be maintained. One should continually be alert to what can be done to make the other happy. Indeed, the obligation to make the other happy goes beyond the first year, and includes all the years of married life. Of special import is the obligation to honor one's wife with new clothes for every pilgrimage festival. The joy of one's mate is a Godly joy, and, on the other hand, to be happy on the festival one must be happy in life. The two, the joy of the festival and the joy of one's wife, are inextricably fused together.[23]

Love and Community

Marriage, it has been shown, is not merely a covenant of two individuals to live together in common pursuit of personal happiness. Marriage is the building block for the forging of community, and the joy of the wedding becomes, via this equation, a true reason for the community to rejoice. The couple enter married life inspired by the community, and geared, through their valuational meeting, to serving that community and enhancing its welfare.

The communal stake in every marriage goes beyond the wedding day and beyond the first seven days. It is there at all times. The requirement to praise the choice of mate may be particularly intense at the outset, but the requirement does not disappear immediately after. Instead, it prevails at all times, and one's choice of mate should continually be the object of communal praise.[24]

Whatever outsiders can do to escalate the appreciation of husband and wife for one another should be done. Guests in a home should leave tangible testimony of their appreciation for the kindness that was shown to them. And they should avoid any expression or reaction that may interfere with the harmony of the home they visit.[25]

Communal concern for the escalating love of each marital union serves a twofold purpose. It at once impacts positively on the beneficiary couple and patterns a trend of expressing appreciation that the grateful outsiders may bring to their own homes. The giving-and-receiving dynamic in marriage extends beyond the boundaries of the home, even as the impact of a good or not-so-good marriage extends beyond the home.

Communal sensitivity to the welfare of others, and collective willingness to make whatever contributions, tactful and welcome, to individual marriages, has some effects that may benefit the community and individuals within that community indirectly and directly.

Indirectly, of course, when praise is shared, appreciation shown, and the positive reinforced, a definite syndrome is set into motion. Good relations generate more good relations, and the chances of more people being happy are increased. When the community emphasizes a specific value, that value has a way of penetrating the collective communal psyche. One divorce can cause others to reinvestigate whether they are really happy, and can thus be the precipitant for more divorce. Conversely, a community that seeks ways to make others happier likewise starts a trend, a better trend at that.

There is also potential direct benefit. It is clear that one of the most important variables in how children develop is the home atmosphere in which they are raised. Deficient children are more likely to come from deficient unions; alert, proficient children are more likely to come from successful marriages. Children are not only the biological extensions of their parents; they are also the spiritual and psychological extensions. Parents who love each other will have children growing up in an atmosphere of love, children who will themselves likely be loving partners in their own married lives.[26]

What the parents intend, how they feel toward each other, reflects and is reflected in the children they have. Parents may not be able to choose the sex of their children, but they can, through their own choice of the way of life they live together, have a very potent impact on what the children will be.[27]

In the end, the child of a marriage to whose welfare an outsider has contributed may marry the child of that outsider, or a friend or relative. What was of benefit to others can, in given circumstances, come right back to the source. All this may be farfetched, but it is not farfetched to argue that any good done for others has positive side effects. This adds emphasis and meaning to the communal stake in healthy marriages and a healthful attitude to marriage.

Love, then, is a personal experience evolving from a programmed framework of attentiveness and concern; a personal experience, and a communal blessing.

8
Ethics in Marriage

The Ethics Theater

Ethics, by which we mean the proper behavior that ought to characterize human life, is directed at how the interactional dialectic between individuals is expressed. Jewish ethics springs not from a purely human invention of guidelines for a functional society. Instead, it links directly to our faith in God. God is the source of ethics, and our faith in God is indicated not only through verbally affirming that faith, but also in our being as Godly as possible in life. For to express faith in God is to attach to God, and to strive to do what is proper in God's eyes. This, in a nutshell, is what is meant by the notion of *imitatio Dei* (emulation of God).[1]

Emulation of God involves prior knowledge of the Godly ways, the ways of kindness and concern for those within reach. The dialectic travels in both directions. What is Godly elicits favor and gratitude from the beneficiaries of that ennobled, exalted human gesture. Equally is the approbation of others pleasing to God. "One in whom the spirit of humankind takes delight, the spirit of the Omnipresent takes delight. But one in whom the spirit of humankind takes no delight, the spirit of the Omnipresent takes no delight." There is a telltale sign of whether one has adequately integrated the ethical imperatives of the Torah, and that is if the individual's conduct meets with acceptance from the "spirit of humankind" (read "spiritually oriented humans").[2]

To walk humbly, to know God in everything one does, to behave in a manner that inspires others to follow and to come closer to God, who is the source for the Godly inspired conduct, all this reflects the essence of Jewish ethics.[3]

There is particular relevance to a discussion of the ethics that pertains to marriage, because the marital sphere is an ideal theater for the actual living out of all the ethical norms of Jewish tradition—honor, respect, kindness, empathy, concern, dedication, devotion, and sharing, among others. One who is exceedingly careful in relations with outsiders but cavalier with the marital partner is in breach of a basic fundamental of Jewish ethics. One can more easily get away with improper behavior at home than outside the home, where it is more likely to lead to the loss of friends. But self-serving ethics, selectively expressed rather than unconditionally kept, is merely opportunism with a friendly mask. What really counts is what one is like in the home, where the major impetus to act properly comes from within the self, not from societal pressure. Marriage is the sphere in which one's true ethical posture is put to the test. To paraphrase the Mishnah, "One in whom the spirit of one's spouse takes delight, the spirit of the Omnipresent takes delight. But one in whom the spirit of one's spouse takes no delight, the spirit of the Omnipresent takes no delight."[4]

Each of the marital partners can elicit the feeling of delight of the other through living out the basic ethical principles of Jewish tradition, even independent of the many human expressions that are unique to marriage.

Such commandments as the obligation to come to the assistance of those who are in need of help, or to do that which is upright and good, are ethical norms which easily translate into the marriage situation. To go beyond the letter of the law in order to do that which is appropriate is a desirable norm in husband-wife relations. Certainly just adhering to legalities, though better than the alternative, cuts off the spontaneous human contribution so vital to the total marital context.[5]

To push to the limit one's willingness to do nice things for one's mate, to be as scrupulous as humanly possible about causing pain to one's life partner, even as one looks the other way if such caring conduct is not reciprocated, is not only a good practice in marriage. It also accurately reflects Jewish ethics at its best.[6]

Pirkey Avot in Marriage

In the priorities to be established for mastering Jewish tradition from the source, that which pertains to everyday life must be given special importance. And among the areas of everyday life that deserve special attention is the area of marriage. *Pirkey Avot,* "Chapters of the Sages," the all-encompassing talmudic ethical treatise, is directed to life in its totality. Yet, so many of the statements of ethical import in *Pirkey Avot* relate, without resort to excessive homily, to the ethics of married life. *Pirkey Avot* itself is critical to fully understanding the ideal ethical posture to be espoused. Parts of *Pirkey Avot* are equally critical to understanding the ethical norms that are to prevail in marriage.[7]

What follows are some excerpted formulations from *Pirkey Avot,* together with a short transposition of the general comment to the specific situations of husband and wife. These follow the order in which they appear in *Pirkey Avot.*

The world stands on three things—on the Torah, on the Sacred Service, and on the practice of loving-kindness. The world of marriage should be founded on Torah values, energized through prayer and orientation around God, and predicated on the willingness of each partner to perform deeds of loving-kindness for the other.[8]

Be not like servants who serve their master for the sake of receiving a reward; rather be like servants who serve their master not for the sake of receiving a reward. Try to do nice things for your spouse without the thought that whatever you will do will be reciprocated in kind. Rather, your deed of kindness should be performed unconditionally.[9]

Do not engage in excessive idle chatter with women. This was said with regard to one's wife. Your wife should not be a repository for small talk. Since she is an equal partner in marriage, your talk with her should deal with the serious concerns you share in life, and the values and ideals you wish to emphasize in life together.[10]

Acquire a companion for yourself. There is hardly anyone who can be a better friend than one's spouse.[11]

Judge all individuals charitably. When you see something about your mate that is questionable, or you perceive that your mate is not actualizing responsibility or sensitivity, assume that there are mitigating circumstances to explain this, rather than blaming or disliking the offending mate.[12]

Love work, hate positions of lordship. Enjoy doing whatever you can, however menial, to help your mate. Hate, and keep far away from, acting as the superior and ordering your partner to perform work.[13]

Be of the disciples of Aaron, loving peace and pursuing peace. The ideal of peace should be dear to you, and the selfsame attitude to peace should be reflected in the effort you make to bring and maintain peace with your spouse.[14]

When I am for myself only, what am I? If you live a self-centered life, devoid of concern for the other, you are a poor marriage partner.[15]

Say little and do much. Do not make grand statements about what you are going to do, or how things will be better. Instead, take action, and let your actions talk.[16]

Greet all people with a cheerful countenance. Always have a smile ready for your spouse upon leaving in the morning and upon coming home in the evening.[17]

Study is not most important, rather doing. One may be proficient in what are the responsibilities to the other, but knowing is passive. More vital is that the knowledge be put into practice.[18]

The world is preserved through three things: truth, justice, and peace. The world of marriage should be a relationship built on truth, on trust. Each of the partners should be mindful of the legal obligations, the justice that accrues to the other, and both should do whatever possible to assure peace and harmony in the marriage.[19]

Which is the right path that a person should choose? That which is an honor to the one who does it and which also brings honor from humankind. Do that which is honorable for your spouse, reflecting on your own sense of respect for the other; this approach will likely be reflected in the honor that is directed to you by your appreciative partner.[20]

Be scrupulous with a light precept as with a weighty one. Do not divide marriage into matters important and matters not so important, and then neglect that which you have deemed unimportant. Instead, be careful to discharge all your responsibilities with consistent meticulousness.[21]

Concentrate on three things and you will not fall into the grip of sin: know what is above you—a seeing eye, a hearing ear, and all your deeds being recorded in a book. Do not live out marriage as a facade, putting on a good face in public but behaving less than responsibly in private. Remember that the roots of marital responsibility, like all responsibility, stem from God, and that even in the privacy of your home, you are with God, and God is with you.[22]

Do not be sure of yourself until the day of your death. At no point should you assume that you have completed your obligations in marriage. To the last breath, be attentive to the needs and desires of your marital partner, and to the best of your ability try to fulfill them.[23]

Do not judge your fellow until you have been in that person's position. At times your spouse may not approximate the standard you think is appropriate, or behavior will not be in accordance with your expectations. Instead of casting blame, assume that circumstances and conditions unique to your partner are at the root of the situation.[24]

The temperamental person cannot teach. Whatever suggestions of importance you may desire to convey to the other, for benefit to your mate and to the relationship, if it is done in anger, it will probably be counterproductive. Teach with understanding, patience, and calmness.[25]

In a place where there are no people, strive to be a person. If the conduct of your partner is less than satisfactory, do not teach the other a lesson by being worse. Instead, try to be a good example, a *mentsch*; the other may thus be inspired to change for the better.[26]

The more counsel, the more understanding. In matters that affect the marriage relationship, or the crucial matter of the home, avoid doing things without consultation. Even if you think you know more or know better, be sure to consult with your mate. Aside from strengthening the bond between you, it will also afford more understanding through the interchange, and lead to better results.[27]

Which is the good way to which a person should cleave? R. Eliezer says, "A good eye." Always try to see the good in your partner, and hold that out for praise and appreciation, and try to ignore what is less pleasing. R. Yehoshua says, "A good friend." Be a friend and trusted confidant to your mate, and establish a climate in which the other feels free to discuss problems together. R. Shimon says, "One who foresees that which will be." Try to anticipate problem situations in advance and adjust to them, heading off what could be unnecessary conflict. R. Elazar says, "A good heart." Exercise kind-heartedness toward your mate, being considerate and alert to both expressed and intimated needs.[28]

Let your friend's honor be dear to you as your own. Try to see any disrespect directed by you to your partner as in fact being disrespect shown to yourself. Be careful to maintain your partner's dignity and self-respect, which should be as important to you as the sense of dignity and respect you must have for your own self.[29]

Do not be easily provoked to anger. Undoubtedly there will be frustrating, trying moments, when matters do not flow as you think they should. Do not blame your partner, do not explode in anger. Try to better the situation, or live with it.[30]

A bad eye, bad passion, and hatred of one's fellow creatures drives a person out of the world. If you look negatively on your mate, if you see your mate only as a vehicle to exercise your passions and lust, if you thus dehumanize and effectively disdain your partner, your world of marriage is bound to collapse.[31]

Let your friend's possessions be dear to you as your own. Whatever your partner brings to the marital union should be appreciated and treated with as much care as you give to your own possessions, which, being yours, you obviously value.[32]

Let all your deeds be for the sake of Heaven. Your actions should not be for self-serving reasons. You should approach your obligations to the marital union with pure intentions, doing what must be done because that is what God asks of you.[33]

Do not consider yourself wicked. If you have a low self-image, you will feel justified in behaving less than properly because, since you are deficient, not much is expected of you. Think of yourself as good-becoming-better, and try, through the manner in which you treat your spouse, to reflect this self-perception.[34]

The day is short, the task is great, the workers are lazy, the reward is great, and the Master of the house is insistent. You may think that there is no immediate hurry to do things for the marriage, since an entire life is ahead of you. But the task of building a marriage is a great task, and the time to do all is really insufficient. Therefore, do not procrastinate, do not be lazy. The reward for your efforts, both immediately and in the future, is great, for the happiness and fulfillment from marriage and family are of real significance; therefore God insists that you do not desist from the task at hand.[35]

It is not up to you to complete the task, but you are not free to desist from it. You need not feel overwhelmed by the burdens of marriage placed upon you. Perfection is impossible to reach, but it is a good thing to strive toward.[36]

Concentrate on three things and you will not fall into the grip of sin. Know from where you came, where you are going, and before whom you will have to give account and reckoning. Humility in the household, which brings with it a compliant, cooperative spirit, helps the marriage become what it should be. Humility is best maintained by knowing and remaining aware of your humble beginnings and humble end. Your ego-bloatedness may boost your image in your own eyes or convince you that you are more respected by others, but you do not have to impress them. Ultimately you must answer to your Creator; lack of humility will interfere with your fulfilling life's purpose, and thus make your eventual meeting with God less pleasant.[37]

Two who sit together and words of Torah are exchanged between them, the Divine Presence abides with them. Husband and wife, two who often sit together, should spend time studying, exchanging ideas of Torah import, relating their lives together to their shared destiny. Orientation around the Godly brings the Divine Presence into their lives.[38]

One whose deeds exceed the person's wisdom, that person's wisdom endures. The couple, each aware of their duties to the other, are thus wise to their situation. But if that wisdom remains abstract and is not translated into action, it is not durable wisdom. Wisdom endures through its being overtaken by deeds, deeds derived from the wisdom and thus reinforcing the wisdom.[39]

One in whom the spirit of humankind takes delight, the spirit of the Omnipresent takes delight. God is delighted when partners in marriage elicit feelings of delight from each other through the love and respect they share.[40]

Receive all people with cheerfulness. All people, but primarily, have a cheerful bent toward your mate, and invest the marital home with joy and contentedness.[41]

A fence for wisdom is silence. Before rushing to complain to your spouse, think that maybe silence will be more effective, or less damaging. Weigh the worthwhileness of the words before letting them out.[42]

Everything is measured according to the multitude of deeds. One's devotion to one's mate is best reflected in the constant determination to do, and do more, for the other.[43]

If there is no Torah, there is no proper conduct; if there is no proper conduct, there is no Torah. Marriage, to be the optimal, must be predicated on the Torah conceptions for the marital relationship. Failing that, the marriage does not reach the level intended. When the marriage fails, when the marital conduct is improper, it is obvious that the Torah concepts have not been properly integrated.[44]

Who is wise? One who learns from all people. Be open and receptive to the views and ideals of your partner, and be ready to learn from them and add them to your own life concepts.[45]

Who is mighty? One who conquers one's passions. Maintain self-control, do not let passion overcome you, leading you to take advantage of your mate. Indulge your passion only in a halakhically legitimate way, and only when it meets with the full agreement of your spouse.[46]

Who is rich? One who rejoices in one's portion. Always be happy with your mate. Think, and believe, that you have the best possible partner for you, and you will be rich and enriched.[47]

Who is honored? One who honors humankind. If you bestow honor on your life partner, you will in turn be honored, not only because you are honorable, but because the honor will likely be reciprocated.[48]

Hasten to fulfill even a light precept, and flee from all sin, for one good deed generates another good deed, and one sin generates another sin.

Be ready to eagerly perform even minor deeds on behalf of your partner in life, and avoid even the most minor breaches of the honor and respect due the other. Goodness and its opposite are habit-forming and may generate trends, patterns of conduct. Goodness begets goodness, and should thus be embraced; its opposite is better avoided to the extreme.[49]

Be of an exceedingly humble spirit. Thinking positively about oneself is important, but this should bring with it an attendant humility in the face of all that remains to be achieved. For the humble, past achievement encourages future commitment instead of forestalling further action. The mood of humility in the home effectively creates this prudent syndrome.[50]

Be the initiator of greetings to all people. Do not wait for your partner to make the first move or first gesture. Instead, be the first to greet, to say nice things, to show appreciation.[51]

Do not try to assuage the anger of your friend in the height of your friend's anger. If your spouse is angry, even angry at you, react with understanding and calm, and wait for the right moment to make amends or lessen the severity of the situation.[52]

The wise person . . . does not break into another person's speech. If your mate is voicing a concern, do not rush to interrupt with your own version or views. Patiently hear out what the other has to say, and then think about your response.[53]

The wise person . . . acknowledges the truth. If you see that you have erred, or that your partner's claims or concerns are valid, be wise and acknowledge this, rather than adhere to your own previously held position from which you refuse to deviate.[54]

One who says "What is mine is yours and what is yours is yours" is a pious person. When entering marriage, think of all that you bring to the new union as being there for your mate to use and enjoy; at the same time, do not impose that attitude and make use of what belongs to your partner. For that, wait until your spouse makes a reciprocal move. Generally, if you introduce this form of piety, the appropriate response will be forthcoming.[55]

Difficult to provoke and easy to pacify—this characterizes the pious person. Another form of piety that belongs in the marriage relationship is the tight control over one's temper. Do not let trivial matters anger you, and if, human as you are, you do at one point or another unleash your anger, realize as immediately afterward as possible that such anger is unwarranted; maintain an openness to being calmed down, the anger expunged.[56]

A love which is independent of anything will never disintegrate. The love you have for your mate should be unconditional, independent of anything, and thus not vulnerable to changing conditions. The love is, and therefore is forever.[57]

Every controversy which is for the sake of Heaven will ultimately endure. It is perhaps unrealistic to think that one can go through marriage without some arguing, some controversy. Make sure the argument is about important issues, and that you do not approach it as an ego conflict which you must win. Have at heart only the pure intention of Heaven, what you think is God's will for the situation. With that attitude, the conflict will have positive results; the arguing itself will have an enduring quality.[58]

According to the exertion is the reward. What you put into the marriage, the extent to which you exert yourself, is what you will receive from the marriage. The rewardingness of the union reflects the deservingness of the couple, and the deservingness itself is a function of the effort that is placed into the marriage.

One would be hard-pressed to find a more concise, and more comprehensive, formulation of husband-wife obligations, responsibilities, and interaction than this application of selected excerpts of *Pirkey Avot* to marriage.[59]

As Yourself

There is a general obligation to like all fellow Israelites as one likes one's own self, based on the famous biblical command, "Like your neighbor as yourself" (Lev. 19:18). This *mitzvah* is seen as more than a merely attitudinal stance. One is to be careful about what belongs to the other, including the other's material possessions, the other's dignity, the other's self-respect. Behavior to others should serve to enhance the others in all possible ways. What is perceived to be contemptible, hateful, should surely not be heaped on others.[60]

Additionally, one is obliged, in the context of this commandment, to communicate praise of others, something which each individual desires. The *mitzvah* creates an interesting dialectic. For all that one would like for oneself, one should think dualistically; that is, not only to assure it for oneself, but also doing whatever possible to assure it for others.[61]

The Jew lives in the context of the Jewish community, and even in the most personal of wants and needs is urged to think in more than private, parochial terms. Desire for the community what you desire for yourself, and within the context of what is manageable, try to fill that desire for the community as you would for your own self. The harmony and interrelatedness should be as natural as that between the left hand and the right.[62]

This *mitzvah*, to like your neighbor as yourself, is seen as a great principle of the Torah. Indeed, the full gamut of loving-kindness acts which are to be extended to others is rooted in this *mitzvah*, a *mitzvah* without boundary in time or space. As a *mitzvah* without limits, it yearns for fulfillment at all times, and defies any sanctimonious statement that one has fulfilled this *mitzvah* to the full. That is simply an impossibility.[63]

To feel toward all others as you feel toward your own self, even with the active imperatives this entails, is, because of its vast scope, an attitudinal ideal one should be on the alert to translate into reality.

That alertness is specially vital and particularly directed to the one who is actually like one's own self, one's spouse. Here the *mitzvah* to like as one likes one's own self assumes very practical proportions.[64]

That one must see the other before marriage, that one must not marry one who is an unfit marriage partner, that one must not engage in self-serving pleasure which diminishes the other's dignity, that one is to be single-mindedly directed to one's mate and not to another possible mate, that one is not to be deterred by some undesirable feature of the other—all are founded on the principle of "Like the other as yourself." One could hardly call this an abstraction. These are practical manifestations in marriage.[65]

By feeling the reality that one's spouse is as one's own self, one is on the way to actualizing the full extent of the *mitzvah* to "Like the other as yourself."[66]

On the way, but not there. To get there, the feeling of oneness must be expressed in tangible, observable, other-directed deeds. Those deeds shape not only individual character; they shape the character of the marriage. Through deeds, the solidity of the marriage is firmed. Through deeds the oneness of the couple is fused.[67]

9

Potential Stumbling Blocks

Self-Centeredness

There are good marriages on the way to becoming better marriages, mediocre marriages going nowhere, and bad marriages on the way to becoming worse. So much depends on how the couple live up to their respective responsibilities, for there is much in the explication of the marriage that is in the hands of the couple. At the same time, one should not dismiss the need of the couple to have *mazal*, "luck," in large positive doses. That they start off on the right foot, that their moods bring out the best in each other, that the family is supportive but not intrusive, that financial problems do not interfere with marital harmony, that unforeseen crises do not overwhelm the couple, are among the many luck factors. One could advance the argument that even with the types of predicaments just cited, the couple can exercise control and overcome the problems. Theoretically, this may be valid. Marriage, however, is not lived in the theoretical arena; it is lived in practical reality. The practical reality is that these and other problems do interfere with relationships.

The couple, after all is said and done, need *mazal*. *Mazal* is the good fortune not to have outside circumstances derail the couple from the path of marital fulfillment. This is at the root of the blessing that is showered on the couple who marry, *Mazal Tov*, or "Good Luck." Good luck magnifies the positive attributes and attitudes of the couple, bad luck can bring out the worst in them. To say that good marriages need good luck, which effectively translates as "good marriages need the blessing of God," is not to minimize the free-will of the couple to make or break the relationship. It is rather to establish a present awareness that there are outside factors which may impact on the marriage, factors which should be seriously contemplated, not conveniently ignored.

Before elaborating on some external factors affecting the marriage, it should be pointed out that the most likely interference preventing a smoothly developing relationship is individual self-centeredness, commonly referred to as "narcissism." The spouse as consumer is not nearly as effective a partner as is the spouse as giver. The giver shares, extends, and by so doing builds bridges. The consumer takes, grabs, and by so doing builds walls.[1]

Self-centeredness often holds a partner back from admitting to being wrong, as if such an admission were a blow to one's self-image. Marriage is not, or at least should not be, an ego game. Ideal marriages reinforce egos, but are not entered into for ego purposes. The ego fulfillment comes from mutual giving rather than from individual demanding.

Self-centeredness blocks the human capacity to care, to be attentive to the other, even to be respectful of the other. The self-centered person thinks in terms of the self; marriage means thinking primarily in terms of the other.[2]

The self-centered person looks more at the self than at the other, and is thus more likely to be oblivious to obvious failings in the marriage. Instead of growing together, the marital partners may be drifting apart, slowly but surely, with one or the other or both not noticing. They may do less and less together, and even when together are together in body only.[3]

Luck may sometimes be a hidden factor. One of the marital partners may take the bold step, necessary but sometimes difficult, of deliberately exposing the self to the other; trying to gain the other's attention and understanding by giving up of the self, divulging feelings and sharing emotions. The other may not really appreciate the magnitude of the gesture, and may totally ignore it. The initiator is thus left exposed and hurt, rejected and defeated. This can cause a downward spiral, with the hurt and rejection feeding on itself; everything which ensues from that fateful moment may be viewed in a negative light. A missed opportunity, the bad luck of not understanding or reading the mind and heart of the other, is sometimes all that it takes to set the marriage off course.

It is not asking too much to suggest that each of the couple be alert to the hidden agenda in the requests or initiatives of the other. It always helps when each feels free to verbalize what exactly is at issue in what they are putting forward. But early on in the marriage, or at other critical junctures, it is unrealistic to expect that everything can or will be put into words. Holding back in that manner is itself a defense against outright rejection and the immediate conflict likely to follow.

But there is usually a critical moment, or a buildup of smaller moments, leading to one or the other or both of the couple making the leap, taking the fateful step of placing oneself into the other's trust. This is the step that ideally destroys any of the walls that exist between two different individuals who unite in marriage. When the walls crumble, the way is paved for true oneness to evolve, in which the physical, spiritual, emotional self of each is fully shared with the other. After that, the marriage is likely to build on itself, to grow naturally and flow smoothly. Failing that, each of the partners remains on guard, not totally forthcoming, perhaps even withdrawn. If the attempt or attempts at breaking the walls are unsuccessful, or meet with rebuff, the divide between the couple widens, and they may grow apart.[4]

The observation that most marriages are failures, even those which do not eventuate in divorce, is a telling comment on the inability of couples to make the jump from partnership to union, from being together to actually feeling and acting together. And this, more often than not, relates to either one or both of the couple being too wrapped up in the self to be able to extend to the other, or to be meaningfully attuned to the other.[5]

Financial Problems

Long before sophisticated survey techniques uncovered this, it was emphatically stated in the Talmud that the primary source of conflict in marriage related to not having adequate sustenance. Generations have come and gone, but this seems to have remained a constant. It is understandable that in a house lacking food, there will be screams of frustration, perhaps also screams of recrimination. Everyone wants to live, and most prefer to live in comfort, in varying degrees. Much depends on the standards to which one is accustomed, and to general societal norms. When the basic comforts are missing, the road to conflict is opened. Financial problems, however, are not always related to poverty. Quite often, they relate to lack of harmony and trust.[6]

There are different possibilities for how a couple gain financial resources. The husband may work, and support his wife, who is either caring for the children or attending school, or both. The wife may work, to support her husband who is engrossed in his studies. Or they may both share the burden of marital income. By mutual agreement between the parties they can decide on whichever setup suits their own particular situation. In the absence of any specific agreement, the primary onus for sustenance belongs to the husband. He makes the money, the wife spends it. This fact in itself can trigger much ill will among the marital partners. The husband may resent that all his hard-earned money is seemingly squandered; the wife may in turn resent the charge that she is squandering money when really she is making an immense effort to fight off the ravages of inflation and the decreasing buying power of the money her husband earns. Or, she is trying to manage the home on a less than adequate salary. These types of conflict are instances of financial problems which are less related to poverty, and more associated with lack of harmony or trust.[7]

Marriage is a relationship of trust, in which each ideally has full confidence that the other will do whatever is best for both. That trust relates quite significantly to the realm of finances. In marrying, each in fact entrusts the other with the totality of one's being, and money is only a part of that totality. Emotional, spiritual, purely physical sharing are also very much involved. If those elements of sharing are problematic, financial conflict may also rise to the surface. If true sharing and love prevail, the chances that money will come between the couple are appreciably reduced.[8]

Money can reflect on the essential nature of the relationship. It can also be used as the vehicle for firming the relationship. If both husband and wife agree to forget about a "mine-yours" arrangement, and instead shift to a genuine "we" arrangement, they will go a long way toward avoiding money clashes. That "we"-type trust in matters financial will likely spill over into the more intimate dimensions of the marriage.

Rather than argue over who should control the finances, the couple is probably best off managing matters jointly. Working jointly for each other's benefit, the husband should not entertain questioning his wife's management or harbor doubts about her exercising restraint, and the wife, for her part, should be uninhibited in freely sharing with her husband how the money was spent. It is self-evident that being entrusted automatically implies that the one entrusted be worthy of that trust. This places a crucial responsibility on the wife to be prudent in her spending habits.[9]

Marriage is a balanced relationship in which neither of the couple feels they are giving more to the marriage. Instead, each is an equal and full member of the marital union. Either husband or wife may generate all the income, but the other should not just sit back and collect. Nor should the provider seek to translate the power of the purse into a position of supremacy in the relationship. That works all too well to distort the marriage balance, and the marriage itself.

No matter how the income is generated, the obligations of prudence rest with both of the partners, to spend within their means, to borrow only with a payment schedule they can adequately handle, to buy with respect for the effort which went into earning the money in the first place.[10]

Carefulness with money can itself lead to an equally undesirable extreme, where one of the partners, usually the husband, is less than forthcoming in giving his wife what she needs in order to manage, and the wife, wary of the husband, feels so constrained as to shiver before spending any money. Autonomy rather than control is the desired financial climate for the home. The husband who clamps down financially on his wife will soon find the entire relationship strained. It is in the husband's own best interests to create a climate of autonomy, to allow his wife to feel trusted and respected, and for him to acknowledge and appreciate her management, and even the occasional dress or coat she may buy for herself. The dialectic with finances, as with other components of the marriage, is that both partners set high standards of personal responsibleness for themselves and assume the best of each other's intentions and actions.[11]

Either or both marital partners may embark on an excessively demanding work schedule in order to gain wealth or status, or both. It is evident that the marriage will suffer, even as the hard worker rationalizes that it is for the eventual betterment of the marriage, and whatever components of the marriage have been neglected will be more than compensated for later. Deferred payments may work with bank obligations, but they rarely work for marital obligations. By the time success has been achieved, either the achiever is too entrenched in the workaholic pattern and enslaved by it, or the supposed beneficiary of all this plenty has had enough of neglect. The two may have grown too far apart, with too much animosity separating them, for such an anticipated reunion to actually work. Less wealth in favor of more togetherness is a worthwhile investment. The couple will have fewer funds, but at least what they have they will enjoy, instead of spending the money on lawyers.

Richness in marriage, as in life, resides not in the material but in the spiritual. A couple devoted to each other, supportive of each other in times of crisis, willing to adjust in whatever manner to make the relationship work, and uncompromisingly caring for one another no matter what the circumstances or financial conditions, are blessed beyond monetary value. Prudence dictates that the couple marry only when it is realistically within their means to support their basic requirements. Loyalty dictates that if, in spite of all the carefully worked out assessments, financial difficulties still arise, then each will support the other, encourage the other, and do the best to extricate from the difficulties. The agony of poverty, the stress from being in need, is too intense to downplay, but spiritual wealth, the richness of having one another, at least helps to make a bad situation more manageable, with the couple more likely to cope, and eventually to overcome.[12]

In-Laws

Though financial matters pose an almost steady threat to marital stability, the right attitude and approach serves to anticipate and thus minimize the dangers posed by financial matters. This also applies to another area of potential conflict in marriage, which is particularly acute primarily in the early stages of marriage, the problem of in-laws.[13]

Parents-in-law are a potential source of conflict, as indeed are parents, essentially if and because the marrying couple, who desire to responsibly set up their marital home, feel that their parents are interfering, imposing, denying them the opportunity to work matters out between themselves. In-law problems are more peculiar to marriage, since each of the partners comes into the marriage with the relation to their respective parents already established. If the relationship is sound, then barring some major problem, such as the parents' rejection of the child's choice, the relationship will probably continue to be sound during the marriage. If the relationship is unsound and shaky, marriage is not likely to improve the parent-child relationship.

Possessive parents who are reluctant to let go of their children may see the marital partner of their child as the cause of the child leaving, and will have a mental block against developing a positive relationship with the child-in-law. Another potential sore point is that one of the partners, usually the wife, keeps in close contact with her mother, but the other, usually the husband, keeps more distant contact with his mother. The husband's mother may feel neglected, jealous of the daughter-in-law, and angry at her son. The husband then becomes locked into a tug-of-war between his mother and his wife. Of course, the tendency of parents to think that no one is good enough for their son or daughter is the biggest obstacle to protective parents ever really appreciating the new son-in-law or daughter-in-law. If the new addition is not appreciated, the parent-in-law–child relationship will be strained from the very outset. Parents-in-law who act in accordance with such distorted thinking will evoke negative reactions from the not-so-accepted child-in-law, which will in turn convince the parents-in-law that they were right all along. This is a bad trap, one which must be avoided and discouraged.[14]

Parents who really love their child should think carefully about their actions before acting. They, like the rest of the community, and more so because they are so close to the scene, must do all in their power to increase the love of husband and wife. They do this best by interfering as little as possible, by truly accepting their child's choice and extending a complete welcome, and by saying nice things about the child-in-law to their own child. Optimally, the new addition should be treated as a full equal with the other children. If husband and wife are one, with all the attendant obligations and fulfillments deriving therefrom, this surely imposes upon the parents the duty to treat the spouse of their child as one, as one of their own.[15]

So much for parent-in-law responsibility. Child-in-law responsibility is of a different nature entirely. It is a legally binding, unconditional duty to respect the parents of the spouse, even as one must respect one's own parents. Parents, and parents-in-law, are asked to accept and support, but respect in the classic parent-child sense must flow primarily from the child generation to the parent generation.

The famous biblical story of Ruth is a vivid illustration of what is true honor and respect for in-laws; in Ruth's case her mother-in-law. Her refusal to let herself be separated from the mother-in-law, Naomi, her insistence that she return and provide for her, projects the exquisite ideal of child–parent-in-law relations. Boaz was obviously overwhelmed by Ruth's kindness, and this may be seen as a reflection of the times—that is, Ruth's respect and honor for her mother-in-law was probably atypical of her times. And, truth be told, atypical of modern times, perhaps even more atypical. King David and King Solomon were direct descendants of Boaz and Ruth, who united in marriage primarily because Boaz was so impressed with Ruth's treatment of her mother-in-law.[16]

The marital couple, since they are now one, have four parents rather than two. And they are thus obliged to honor and respect all four equally. Each of the couple, happy with the partner, should naturally be effusively grateful to the two people who were most instrumental in making the spouse such an ideal mate, somewhat akin to the respect owed to parents for bringing one into the world. This dynamic applies equally to husband and wife. And, as in parent-child relations, the respect and honor accorded, though rooted in the concept of gratitude, is not subject to the whim of the child-in-law. The ungrateful child-in-law, like the ungrateful child, is not thereby excused from respecting and honoring. The Halakhah insists on that respect and honor being given, as if to say to those who are ungrateful that they should feel grateful, even if they may find excuses to justify their ingratitude.[17]

Under normal circumstances, each of the partners according respect and honor to the other's parents is greatly appreciated by the other, and binds the marriage in a tighter transgenerational link. If either of the partners evokes invective against the other's parents, it is grounds for the offended partner to apply for divorce.[18]

Husband and wife, alert in advance to the possible problems posed by their respective parents, are well served if they indicate to one another how important each views the need to have good relations with the parents and the parents-in-law. At the same time, they should make it clear that each will keep personal matters totally private, to be shared between husband and wife only, and each will stand by the other and persevere if relations with the parents-in-law do not work out smoothly. Here again, if both the children and the parents actualize what is asked of them, the children to respect, the parents to accept, many of the potential problems will probably not materialize.[19]

Taking the Marriage for Granted

Marriage, even though it may start out smoothly and develop rather positively, can sometimes run into an unexpected snag somewhere in the relationship. There may be no arguments, no apparent discord, but the relationship is not what it used to be, or what the couple want it to be. What precipitates this uneasy feeling? Mostly, it stems from the familiarity that develops between husband and wife, to the point that each is so confident of the other that there is little excitement, and less of an inclination to do special things for the other; for example, to put on specially attractive attire for the other. The lifetime marriage contract seems just about guaranteed, and this allows laxity to set in.

Husband-wife responsibilities never lapse, even as the obligations to eat only that which is kosher and to observe the Sabbath are constants. Commandments do not function along the lines of building up credits, whereby after one full year of steady observance, one gets a day or week's vacation from the *mitzvah*. The *mitzvah* is an inextricable part of life, sacred and therefore always inviolable. That sense of inviolability should prevail for the marital partners. Honor, respect, appreciation, attentiveness, caring, and the other fundamentals of marriage remain essential even after years of meticulous adherence to the letter and spirit of the laws pertaining to them.

But people are human, and the Jewish legal tradition for marriage, realistic as it is, should not be oblivious to the possibility, perhaps even the likelihood, that there will be lapses even among the best-intentioned. Jewish legal tradition should not be oblivious, and it is not. Once again, the tradition does not disappoint. Instead, it shows a most perceptive grasp of life's realities.[20]

The manna which sustained the Israelite community for the forty years following the exodus from Egypt came down from Heaven together with spices, spices for use by the Israelite women to maintain their attractiveness. What does this mean? It means that God, concerned with the well-being of Israel, provided what was essential to their well-being. That food was one of the essentials is understandable. That an instrumentality to keep the husband-wife relationship fresh and vibrant was another essential is at once astounding and instructive. It firmly establishes a Godly imperative to keep marriage on an affirmative footing. It also shows a singular awareness that measures are needed to prevent marriages from losing their luster and falling into a rut.[21]

Later on, the great scribe Ezra arranged for perfumers to go from place to place to ensure proper provision of enticing scents. Ezra, dedicated to reshaping the splintered community, went right to the root of family stability. No one would suggest that perfume saves marriages. The suggestion is that if each of the couple makes the extra effort to maintain their attractiveness to the other, normally good marriages will not go the way of almost natural attrition with the passing years. The tradition from the very outset was aware of this pitfall, and took measures to prevent it from occurring.[22]

In the present era, some comment is forthcoming concerning a pattern within marriage that, though almost universally practiced, deviates from the norm that should obtain for marriage to retain its excitement. The reference is to the trend that both husband and wife incline to dress more attractively when going out to work or to a social event, but are attired in less than ideal fashion when in the home. If this reflects what and who is considered important, it is a distortion of priorities, for the obligation of each is to be attractive to the other, not to the outside world. This is not to say that one should not dress in a respectable manner when appearing in public. But it is to say that special attractiveness should be reserved for the special person in one's life.[23]

This is nothing new under the sun. Adornments were long ago perceived to be essentially for the home, and special care not to engage in any home activity that would repulse the other was more than merely acceptable. Dress and adornment may be superficial decoration, and it would be folly to think that the marital union should be obsessed with superficialities. Dress is, however, a signal; a signal to the other that the relationship is greatly valued, that the affections of the other are continually desired, that the love of the other will not be taken for granted.[24]

In practical terms, husbands who shave when they come home from work instead of when they go out to work, or wives who administer facial makeup for when their husbands are home instead of when they go out in the daytime, make powerful statements about what is important to them. As a standard practice in the home, it can serve as a reminder to each of the partners of their obligations to the other, the need to continually win over the other, the duty to ensure that the relationship continues to grow and the love continues to intensify.[25]

10

Conjugality: The Concept

The Holiness of Conjugal Relations

In the background of the essential legal obligations binding on husband and wife, in the framework for love created by adherence to the marital imperatives in letter and spirit, it is possible to discuss that component of marriage which is best described as the unique language of husband and wife, the sexual, which I prefer to call "conjugal relations." This phrase is preferred not in order to hide behind a euphemism; rather it is to signify that the intimate expression of marital relations is not simply a biological act. It is a profound expression of love in its purest human form, and in the conjugal setting. Hence, the use of the term "conjugal relations."

Conjugal relations are a powerful factor in the marital union, yet this alone, even when satisfactory, is no guarantee that the marriage is what it should be. Nor is a less than satisfactory conjugality necessarily indicative that the marriage is a failure. A good marriage and satisfying conjugality, however, do reinforce each other, and the appropriate marriage dynamics, including respect, care, and concern for the other, when brought to the conjugal sphere, go a long way toward ensuring that the partners will be uplifted and drawn even closer via the physical intimacy.[1]

Conjugal relations effect the ultimate closeness, the physical union of the marriage partners, which in itself is a tangible manifestation of the spiritual union of husband and wife. Conjugal relations are a potent instrumentality in the forging of *shalom bayit* in its ideal form.[2]

Jewish tradition, far from trivializing or denigrating conjugality, in actuality accords conjugality great importance and considers it holy. When conjugal relations are experienced in the purest form, there is nothing more holy. The Godly presence is seen to abide among the couple who experience this most blissful intimacy. The ecstasy of intimacy is linked to the profound contentedness of the Sabbath, bringing together the holy act with the holy day, the Sabbath, since the Sabbath is perceived as the ideal time for conjugal relations.[3]

Rejected is the notion that conjugality is shameful. Personal, private, and sacred, yes; but shameful or sinful, absolutely no. And this derives from faith in God, and refusal to believe that God would create so vital a component of human life simply to be avoided. The very experience which is basic to the existence of the world cannot possibly be deemed shameful, for then all of human life, emanating from a shameful act, would itself be shameful. But human life is potentially service to God and living the Godly ideal—far from being shameful.[4]

There is shame in life, as there is shame in conjugal relations. The shame inheres in the abuse of life, in the insensitivity to what and who matters. In conjugal relations, the shame is in the use of the other for one's own purposes; in feeding one's sensuality rather than sharing peak pleasure with one's spouse. Precisely because husband-wife relations as they ought to be are the holy of holies, precisely for this reason is the abuse of conjugality a most shameful, disgraceful human conduct. Human choice, the choice to be human in the Godly sense, or the choice to deny that humaneness, to reject the spiritual and thereby reduce human behavior to the animal level, is the factor which colors all of life, and equally the life of conjugal intimacy. Human conjugality in its pristine form is sacred. Human abuse reduces it to an ugly, repulsive act.[5]

The human generative organ, on which is imprinted the covenantal bond at the earliest stage of viable life, apparently underwent a change at the time that Adam and Eve failed to observe the specific command of God when in the Garden of

Eden. Prior to the breach, the generative organ was like any other of the body organs, and the conjugality experienced via that organ was as natural an experience as eating or putting on *tefilin*. Adam's rude awakening after the breach came together with an awareness that this organ was now different from the others, an organ which could be beyond control. The generative organ is unique in its potentialities for fulfillment or destruction, unique in the power it can exercise over the entire person. But it exercises power over the person primarily if the person allows; by not exercising control, by not subordinating libidinal resources to the more encompassing and meaningful spiritual union of husband and wife. It is in the exercise of control, in achieving *mitzvah* fulfillment via the generative organ, not in unbridled sensuality, that one is likely to find paradise.[6]

Inspired by the inner and outer beauty of one's mate, the conjugality which derives therefrom is an exalted spiritual union of souls which in turn generates more souls. That the proper exercise of conjugality is of critical importance for the Jewish community is seen in the choice of biblical reading for Yom Kippur afternoon. On this solemn day of self-investigation and resolve to mend one's ways, none other than the text outlining the parameters for the sacred expression of conjugality is the choice for the afternoon reading.[7]

Preparatory expressions which are the norm prior to the performance of deeds with religious significance are suggested in anticipation of conjugal relations, even including the possible recitation of a blessing. The sanctity of the conjugal experience is likewise reflected in the obligation to know thoroughly the halakhic parameters for the proper conjugal expression. Equally is it advisable to be conversant with the classic works in this area, which place conjugality into proper Judaic perspective, *The Holy Letter* attributed to Naḥmanides and *Baalay HaNefesh*, by Rabad. These works, aside from projecting the letter and the spirit of the Judaic approach to conjugality, will also, if followed, serve the marital partners much more effectively than what today parades as scientific literature or sound advice.[8]

In the light of this short introduction, clearly illustrating the affirmative attitude to conjugality in Jewish tradition, the tone is set for further exploring the many nuances associated with conjugality, always bearing in mind that halakhic parameters or restrictions are intended not to program denial; instead, they are intended to promote fulfillment.[9]

Yetzer Energy and Its Use

The human propensity for good or evil, that which unfolds relative to human choice, is broadly subsumed under the categories of *yetzer tov* and *yetzer hara*. Every person has both a *yetzer tov* and a *yetzer hara*. What exactly are *yetzer tov* and *yetzer hara* is open to interpretation. If we assume *yetzer* to refer to creative energy, then *yetzer tov* is the human capacity to generate energy for actualizing the good, and *yetzer hara* is the human capacity to generate energy for actualizing the bad. For human beings to have true choice, or free-will, they must be capable of both forms of behavior. If only angelic behavior is possible, it cannot be attributed to the human being for praise, any more than a person who has only the capacity for evil can be blamed for bestial behavior. The world was judged by God to be "very good" after it was created. "Very good" is interpreted as referring to the *yetzer hara*. Only with *yetzer hara* is the world complete, free-choice a reality, and human praiseworthiness a possibility.[10]

Further, the human being is asked to serve God with the two *yetzer* tendencies. This imperative calls for a more studied analysis of the terms *yetzer tov* and *yetzer hara*, for it can hardly be expected that one may actually serve God with the energy for evil. Possibly, then, *yetzer tov* signifies creative spiritual energy, the type of energy that is likely to generate good deeds. And *yetzer hara* refers to creative instinctual energy, energy which, if left to its own devices, more often than not tends to evil. To serve God with the two energies, one must fuse the instinctual and the spiritual, raising instinctual gratification to the spiritual dimension. This is far removed from espousing denial. Instead, it is directed toward sanctifying and uplifting indulgence into a meaningful experience.[11]

The human appetite for food is a response to the pangs of hunger which begin to tell the person that the body needs nourishment. Eating is a distinct form of instinctual gratification, ennobled in Jewish tradition through blessings before and after the eating, as well as through its being a primary way of celebrating the Sabbath, the festivals, and other joyous occasions. We effectively thank God for giving us the need to eat, the instinct for food, so that we will naturally desire to regularly enjoy the good things God has placed on the earth. We eat in order to live, we live in order to achieve and appreciate. The mix of spiritual intention with instinctual need raises eating above the mundane, beyond being an exercise in self-gratification, an exercise in which the practitioner is likely to be spiritually gross and to become physically obese.[12]

Human sensual desire, itself another form of appetite, also derives from an instinctual need. That need too, if catered to indiscriminately, results in sensuality expressed for its own sake and pursued for its own purposes. Like food, it is not appreciated; it is devoured. Worse, unlike food, which though it must be respected cannot be dehumanized, sensual desire pursued for its own sake abuses the partner in the act, leaving wounds which often never heal.

Sensual desire too is ennobled when it is fused together with creative spirituality. This comes through quite clearly in the Judaic view that when properly expressed, conjugality is the holy of holies. Attendant to this, it is worthwhile to analyze some aspects of one of the more serious breaches of Jewish law, the wasteful emission of seed (*hotza'at zera l'vatalah*). Primarily, wasteful emission refers to masturbation.[13]

Wasteful emission is itself not directly related to procreation. There is no obligation that one engage in conjugal relations only when such relations can lead to procreation. The woman, in fact, is the only female of any species that can mate with a male when pregnant, a mating which is removed from procreative considerations. Additionally, having conjugal relations with a wife who is incapable of bearing children is not in contravention of the prohibition against destroying seed. Technically, any conjugal relation which cannot generate a conception is as biologically unproductive as spilling the seed on wood or stones. But it is not wasteful, because the seed is emitted in the course of sharing pleasure with one's partner. The spiritual creativity of shared intimacy transmutes what could be perceived as a biological waste into a humanly fulfilling act. Seed that is spilled is essentially sensuality without spirituality, and is categorically condemned. Special efforts are made to avoid the spillage of seed wastefully, the most specific example being the permissibility of conjugal relations at a time when one is overcome with desire, even when the prevailing custom is not to engage in such relations at these times.[14]

The human being, then, possesses sensual desires, but as a human being is obliged to ensure that these desires do not take over. To achieve this, the path should not be toward killing the desire. That would bring with it physical and spiritual starvation. If God had wanted the human not to have, God would not have blessed the world with such Godly bounty. Denial is at once denial of the opportunity to enjoy God's goodness, a removal from God's world. Such abstinence in the face of opportunity to appreciate God is considered sinful. The sin is compounded if, in consequence of an ascetic lifestyle, one's marital partner is denied the normally forthcoming pleasures of conjugal visitation.[15]

The way to proper balance is achieved through gaining control over the sensual. The strong one is the one who "conquers," not the one who kills instinctual energy. The word "conquers" is instructive, for in conquest the one who is conquered is slave and subordinate to a more powerful master. The human being as spiritual being should reign supreme, with the instincts subordinated to the spiritual. Those with greater sensual drives have a tougher battle, but if they overcome these drives, they reach a higher level of achievement.[16]

The suggested dialectic in encountering the sensual is that the left hand should push away and the right hand draw near. The right hand, the more powerful hand, should grasp the sensual and direct it to its proper human expression. The left hand, the weaker hand, should push away, ensuring that sensuality is not embraced in totality, but that there is some distancing from it, enough distancing to maintain some capacity to be independent of sensual expression, some measure of control. This dialectical balance helps to avoid some of the more serious problems in marriage deriving from uncontrolled passion, from making one partner feel used and manipulated just to satisfy the other partner's greedy sensuality.[17]

Taharat HaMishpahah

It is nice to talk of control, of the need to be the master over one's drives. But actually achieving control is much more complicated than simply acknowledging that control is needed. The program for control is too much of a challenge to be left totally to the couple to devise. The couple may have the best intentions, but they will be hard-pressed to prevent personal preference, be it toward overindulgence or overdenial, from interfering with a fair and balanced approach. An approach which in its general framework is the same for all, but which at the same time allows for individual differences and preferences, is the norm that is projected for the Jewish community.

The rules which govern the conjugal relationship are generally thought of as the *taharat hamishpahah* legislation. *Taharat hamishpahah* translates literally as "the purity of the family." *Taharat hamishpahah* is more the description of a theme than merely a description of the laws involved. The laws, in brief, proscribe conjugal relations for a period of not less than five days from the onset of menstruation, and, following the cessation of the menstrual flow, for another seven consecutive days when no menstrual presence is detected. Following that, the wife immerses in a specially constructed and filled pool of water called a *mikveh*, after which conjugal relations between husband and wife are resumed.

These rules are primarily rules for the wife. They are more *taharat ha'ishah*, "purity of the woman," than purity of family. The thematic description of these rules as being *taharat hamishpahah* laws contains a message that should not be lost on the husband, the couple, or the community. Though it is the woman on whom the major onus of the laws is placed, the entire *taharat hamishpahah* process enhances and uplifts the whole family; that is, the husband and wife, and the spiritual-biological extensions of their union, their children. The husband dare not remove himself from being as involved as possible in the obligations of the wife. Emotional support and encouragement, understanding and appreciation of her dedication, are just some of the ways the husband can show his wife that she is not completely alone. By so doing, the husband confirms his fully comprehending that the rules are rules for the family, and that the benefits from adherence to the rules are family benefits.

An explanation of the term *taharah*, or "purity," is in order. The woman who is in a menstrual state is not unclean, or impure; she is *ta'may*. There is no English word to adequately convey what *ta'may* means. When one is *ta'may*, one is in a state of limbo, not yet ready to assume or resume certain interactional involvements. The state of limbo is a contemplative state, when one focuses on the inner causes and implications of the *ta'may* condition. Invariably, the state of being *ta'may* arises from the inner experience of loss of life potential, as in the case of menstruation, or from having direct contact with or being in immediate proximity to that which itself is now lifeless.[18]

The act of immersion in the *mikveh* at the culmination of the *ta'may* state signifies one's reentry into interactional life energized by the contemplation in the period of separateness. The *mikveh* itself is filled with water that never was drawn in a receptacle, or, in other words, water that never took the shape of the limitations of human use. *Mikveh* water is God's water taking its shape and initiating its usefulness in the *mikveh* itself. The person—in our case, the wife—who immerses in the *mikveh* is symbolically surrounded by life, by water, in its pristine and spiritual sense. She emerges from the *mikveh* ready and eager to resume spiritually creative intimacy with her husband, to shape life together. That ready eagerness is what we call *taharah*. It is immediately obvious that the translation of *taharah* as "purity" is quite inaccurate and misleading, and at best incomplete.[19]

The purpose for the biblically mandated separation during the menstrual period and for the week following is clearly enunciated in the Talmud. It is to recreate the excitement and thrill of the wedding day for the husband and wife. The law actually effects a renewal, an emotional reunion on a monthly basis. This, even more than the previously cited provisions for spices and perfumes, serves to prevent the relationship from becoming routinized. The separation during the menstrual period, as per the Talmud, is patently directed to the affirmation of the marital bond, not to its denial. It is enforced separateness for the purpose of effecting a tighter togetherness. The thrust and purpose of the menstrual laws is to make possible a more intense intimacy.[20]

Several other benefits accrue from this sensitive complex of rules. The husband, the one generally more likely to be overcome by sensual pressure, is programmed to adjust not to his need schedule but to his wife's availability schedule. The wife need not impose this discipline, and thereby possibly incur the husband's wrath. The Torah does it for her, and the husband, equally dedicated to the union, is obliged to respect his wife's timetable. More than making him respect his wife's schedule, the law serves to inculcate respect for the wife, for her dignity as a person, for her being entrusted with control of the rhythm of family life.

Another benefit concerns the possibility of the couple arguing because the one is not responsive enough to the sensual needs of the other. This possibility is significantly minimized, since responsiveness during certain times is impossible, and at other times is obligatory. The obligation of responsiveness is clearly delineated. Additionally, potential conflict arising from uncoordinated desires, in which one or the other is in the mood but the partner is not, is likewise minimized. Almost two weeks apart is an effective way to establish correlated moods. This is not to suggest that the *taharat hamishpahah* rules guarantee the couple will be blissfully happy. There is still plenty of room to create problems, since the Halakhah only establishes a framework but refrains from legislating all the nuances within the framework. This would ruin the excitement and openness the Halakhah itself endeavors to create. Under normal circumstances, however, the couple who live by the *letter* and *intent* of the *taharat hamishpahah* regulations cannot help but be better off for it. The community, too, is much better off with happy couples, so much so that, in the scale of priorities, the building of a *mikveh*, the effector of closeness, takes precedence over the building of a shul or the writing of a Torah scroll. The foundation, happy and committed families, comes first. The rest follows.[21]

There are also some long-range benefits from these regulations. The couple who are accustomed over the years to periods of physical separateness will be better able to adjust to the realities of the later years of life, when sensuality, although still present, is usually not as intense. The husband and wife have learned that high-quality conjugality springing from heightened anticipation during the period of being apart is an exciting feature of marriage. This they can more easily extrapolate to their situation in later years.[22]

Taharat hamishpahah has embedded itself in the collective Jewish psyche. The Jew, through the practice of *taharat hamishpahah*, has learned to endure momentary frustration for the sake of fulfillment sometime in the future. The Jew does not demand instant gratification, and can live with a bad situation as long as there is hope in the future. *Taharat hamishpahah* discipline has thus helped the Jew endure some excruciatingly painful times, times of trauma and tragedy. The Jew endured the present pain because the messianic hope that salvation from the misery will eventually come never left the Jewish consciousness. Trained to wait, they were able to persevere.[23]

Taharat hamishpahah is not free of difficulty. Aside from the natural difficulty of being together with but apart from the one you love, the separation itself comes at a time when the wife needs her husband's support. The couple should realize that although the time for separating is ideally situated in the menstrual period, when conjugal relations are less desirable, this should in no way be an excuse for total withdrawal. If physical intimacy is not possible, emotional intimacy is more than possible; it is highly desirable. With conjugality out of the question, the couple can and should forge ahead in their developing a caring relationship. This is an ideal time to comprehend what each is going through, how they really feel, what aspects of the relationship can be improved.[24]

The couple who effectively use the separation period to prepare for a greater, more meaningful togetherness will be more likely to view the night of immersion as more than a mere reunion. For them, it is a festival of its own, an event to be celebrated.[25]

The Onah Obligation

The precise biblical term for conjugal visitation is *onah* (Exod. 21:10). The word *onah* is itself associated with the notion of time, so that *onah* can be interpreted as referring to "her time," the time in the marriage which belongs exclusively to the wife. *Onah*, or conjugal visitation, is the biblically prescribed obligation of the husband to share his very being with his wife via conjugal relations. In the language of the Torah, the husband is prohibited from diminishing the time that belongs to her, which translates as a prohibition against denying one's wife the conjugal visitations that are her right by the dictates of Halakhah. The Torah legislates minimums, but establishes no upper limit. Beyond the minimum, the couple can and should have a good mutual understanding of what is appropriate for their relationship. In the view of some, the original biblical obligation includes not only the visitation; it includes also the duty to provide true intimacy, as well as the comforts basic to a pleasant conjugal experience.[26]

The language of the Torah clearly indicates that the *onah* obligation rests with the husband. The Torah concern is that the wife's rights in marriage should not be subject to the husband's whim. The Torah chooses to introduce the *onah* legislation when discussing the claims of the Israelite maidservant on her master, rather than when discussing the usual husband-wife relationship. Precisely in this most obvious circumstance of woman's vulnerability is where the Torah intervenes to protect the woman, a protection which logically extends to all marital situations. That *onah* is the husband's obligation is consistent with the general pattern for marriage, which places the primary responsibilities on the husband, and cooperative responsibilities on the wife subsequent to her agreeing to marry. This dynamic helps prevent the wife from being forced into uncomfortable situations or being denied what is her due.

Onah, to be sure, is not only the husband's duty. It also is a marital benefit that he derives as well as bestows. Thus, the failure of the husband to live up to his *onah* duty, and also the failure of the wife to cooperate in the exercise of the husband's *onah* fulfillment, is grounds for the deprived party to divorce. *Onah* underpins the relationship, is fundamental to it, so that it should never be used by either of the partners as a weapon. *Onah* is designed to forge togetherness. When it is manipulated, the relationship tears apart.[27]

Onah is perceived as the husband's marital debt. It belongs to his wife, the husband owes it to his wife. Thus the husband who for whatever reason is unable to pay his marital debt is akin to a monetary debtor, and should repay the debt when he can. It is only logical that *onah* which is unfulfilled, for whatever understandable reason, should be recompensed when the conditions allow for it. Marriage admittedly is not a balance sheet of credits and debits; husband and wife who conduct their relationship by the scoresheet are bereft of the spontaneity which characterizes marriage as it should be. Projecting *onah* as a debt is not intended to rob the relationship of that spontaneity. The intention, instead, is to impress upon the husband the full extent of his responsibility, that he is indebted to his wife, and that he should genuinely appreciate this as he discharges his obligations.[28]

For the husband to deny his wife her *onah*, especially when the intent of the denial is to cause her pain, is considered sinful. Even his desire to subjugate his sensual drive through self-control is no excuse for denying the wife her due. Godliness is a reason for being closer with one's marital partner; it is not an excuse for distancing from one's partner. The husband and wife, however, can by mutual agreement establish an altered and more moderate *onah* schedule. And, subsequent to the fulfillment of procreation requirements, the wife can waive her *onah* claims if she so desires and her husband agrees. Unlike the husband, the wife who waives her *onah* claim has the right to renew that claim if life without the *onah* proves to be painful to her. Pain, her pain, is too serious an issue to stand on ceremony. The husband is advised to be careful not to induce her to waive her *onah*. She may not really mean it when she agrees, and is compliant rather than eager. The husband should be sensitive to what his wife really feels, and should then act with prudence.[29]

The biblically mandated *onah* obligation expresses itself in more than merely fulfilling the prohibition admonishing the husband not to diminish the conjugal visitation accruing to his wife. There is an active, positive component to the *onah* regulations, contained in the husband's obligation to gladden, to make his wife happy. That *mitzvah* includes the duty to confer pleasure to his wife via conjugal visitation. This *mitzvah* is of inestimable significance for the conjugal experience, for it drastically expands the meaning of *onah*. *Onah* becomes more than merely the consummation of the marital act, although it surely includes that aspect. The actual consummation, when approached properly, is a moment of intense, even indescribable pleasure. And it is precisely the feeling of being pleased, happy, and loved that must accompany the conjugal experience. The Torah is not applying "performance" pressure, but it is definitely applying pressure for an affectionate approach to conjugality.[30]

The *mitzvah* then, independent of but certainly related to consummation, is that the husband shower his affections on his wife, ensuring that she feels truly loved, and then, with that feeling permeating the conjugal chambers, uniting together in that ultimate form of togetherness, as one. The key element of *onah* is the shared intimacy, the felt love. With that, the rest is a commentary which writes of itself. Even when distance separates husband and wife, the capacity to share affection verbally is a source of profound satisfaction. Affection is not merely a prelude to the conjugal act; it is the most vital mood creator affecting all aspects of the marriage.[31]

Onah in its true sense now reads as the husband's obligation to share himself in totality with his wife, leading up to the affectionate expression of love in the conjugal act which leaves the wife happy and pleased.

There are specific times when the culminating *onah* duty is obligatory. Foremost among these times is the night the wife immerses in the *mikveh* at the conclusion of separation, whether separation because of menstruation or because of childbirth.

Additionally, the husband is obliged to provide conjugal visitation immediately prior to his embarking on a journey. The common legal denominator is that these are times when one can logically assume the wife's desire for affectionate embrace and more. These times are at the conclusion of a prolonged separation or just prior to the onset of a separation of distance.[32]

The common denominator itself points to an almost inescapable conclusion, the realization that the essential obligation of *onah* is when the wife desires it, over and above the legal minimum. To the *onah* obligation just enunciated, one must add the responsibility of the husband to be sensitive and alert to the desires of his wife, and to respond accordingly when he senses his wife's desire for conjugal relations. The husband is in violation of his *onah* duty when he ignores his wife's intimated wishes.[33]

Onah itself is part of the marriage compact. Upon entry into marriage, the frequency of *onah*, the minimum legal obligation, is subject to the same considerations as the provision of maintenance; subject to the same considerations, but not spelled out, for obvious reasons. Conjugality is a legal construct, but it is also highly personal and private.

The husband's *onah* capacity is a function of his strength and his availability. If he is employed in a profession which saps his strength, or which places considerable travel demands on him, the *onah* responsibilities are correspondingly lowered. As with maintenance, the husband is not expected to provide what is beyond his means, be it material or physical. The husband who is relatively comfortable, or who has a satisfying job within the city, is obviously able to provide more frequent conjugal visitation.[34]

The wife's right to conjugal visitation is directly related to the type of person she marries, and the nature of her husband's occupation. Whether it be once a week as the visitation norm, twice a week for a regular in-city worker, or every day, as for a healthy, vigorous, vocationally satisfied person, the obligation, though unspoken, is clear. The husband cannot, after marriage, change to a job which will be more enervating and thus compromises his capacity to provide the *onah* that was implicitly agreed to upon marriage.[35]

These legalities once more impress upon the husband how

important *onah* is to his wife, and that he therefore dare not treat this obligation cavalierly. The Halakhah makes maximalist arguments on the wife's behalf, to which the husband must submit. However, an understanding wife will surely refrain from demanding the frequency of visitation belonging to her by right when she sees that her husband cannot oblige. Surely a husband who moves to a more demanding, less satisfying job because of the unemployment squeeze can expect his wife's empathy for his plight, for their predicament. Also, it is in no one's interests to insist on excessive conjugality. Overindulgence beyond capacity can be frustrating and self-defeating, and may adversely affect both conjugal quality and marital harmony.[36]

The classic *onah*-frequency formula is that of talmudic scholars, who engage in conjugal relations "from Sabbath eve to Sabbath eve." This at once reflects the perceived strength, the physical prowess, of the talmudic scholar and the special attractiveness of Friday night, Sabbath eve. The actual conjugal act is simultaneously exhilarating and exhausting; the energizing extra spirit of the Sabbath is thus conducive to a more fulfilling conjugal experience. Additionally, the Sabbath, as a truly spiritual moment, is the most appropriate time for the spiritual experience of conjugal fusion. The host of Sabbath regulations effectively eliminates most of the diversions that may compromise full concentration on the conjugal experience.[37]

Even this classical formulation for talmudic scholars, from Sabbath eve to Sabbath eve, is subject to modification upwards consistent with modern exigencies.[38]

In sum, the *onah* reality reflects the full profundity of the Halakhah regarding the conjugal experience. *Onah* is a delicate combination of legal requirement and affection imperative. The legalities are the minimum, the affection imperative a *mitzvah* without limit. Full appreciation and understanding of *onah* by both husband and wife, he as primarily responsible, she as cooperatively responsible, is essential for the marriage becoming a spiritually blissful union.[39]

11
Conjugality: The Practice

The Ambience for Conjugality

The appropriate atmosphere for conjugality is created long before the actual conjugal experience. Without authentic love, physical intimacy loses its true meaning. Functionally, such relations may succeed once or twice, but over a longer duration, conjugality cannot effectively materialize from a sudden burst of affection. Conjugality is an expression of love; love itself is an ever-evolving reality, not a machine to be turned on or off when it so suits the desirous partner. Biologically, arousal is possible without love, but true human intimacy is more than a biological act. It is a spiritually infused emotion, an emotion which yearns for an unconditional loving and caring relationship.[1]

It is absurd to focus on what is commonly and unfortunately called "foreplay" and not give proper attention to the prime elements of the marriage. Foreplay conjures the notion of a game plan, a technique by which to turn the other on, setting up the other to be ready for the one's sensual ventilation. But conjugal relations is not a combination of foreplay, play, and afterplay; it is not play or a game. Conjugal relations is a periodic contextual peak, evolving from a growing love and itself intensifying that love.[2]

The most important "foreplay" for conjugal relations is the daily infusion and effusion of love between husband and wife. All the niceties that are then expressed immediately prior to a desired conjugal experience are appreciated as a genuine, sincere reflec-

119

tion of how the partner really feels, and will less likely be seen as manipulative words designed to get what one wants. There are times when one or another of the partners is genuinely tired, though the other is in the mood, but too often the tiredness is a convenient shield hiding a disappointment at the way one is being treated. More than a night's worth of niceties and entreaties need be forthcoming for this, a problem which itself developed over time rather than suddenly.[3]

Though it is clear that adequate preparation for conjugal relations is a long-range matter, there are nevertheless areas of relevance to conjugality which require more immediate preparation. In anticipation of conjugal union, one should neither overeat nor undereat. One should have a moderate, balanced meal and allow for the food to digest. The ideal approach to conjugality is in an atmosphere of moderation, free of desperation or uncontrolled passion. Drunkenness, too, is not a state of being which conduces to good conjugality. The drunk is unaware, and likely to abuse. The same is true of the desperate or the overly passionate.[4]

It is self-understood that immediate preparation includes making oneself appear attractive and enticing to the other, avoiding any habits that may appear repulsive to the other. Spiritual preparedness is another vital area of preconjugal activity. Introspection prior to the conjugal experience, where both partners ask themselves what their real desire is, and resolve to enter the conjugal chamber in a receptive, giving spirit rather than in a demanding frame of mind, is very advisable. All these preparations help create the right ambience for conjugality.[5]

Insofar as choice of time most conducive to conjugality, the middle of the night is highly recommended. Early in the evening, or early in the morning, one is more likely to be disturbed by either outside noises, noises in the home, or the telephone. The middle of the night is more likely to be free of disturbance, allowing the couple maximal concentration on each other, the opportunity to be in their own world and to express their love for each other.[6]

The crescendo-like buildup to the ultimate conjugal fusion starts from a pre-existent love, and in the moments immediately prior, includes verbal expression and physical embrace which help the husband and wife to become physically and emotionally aroused. How much more or less expression and embrace is needed is a matter that depends on the couple involved, and on what their precise state of mind and heart are as they embark on the conjugal experience. It may differ from time to time, but a caring couple will be alert enough to the realities of the moment to sense what is proper. There is no textbook or technique that helps more than having a genuine concern for the situation of one's mate. The build up of an arousal-evoking mood is of utmost importance for both. Neither partner should assume the readiness of the spouse simply because he or she feels ready. Focusing on the other's readiness helps correlate the moods and effects a mutually satisfying conjugal experience.[7]

The aftermath of consummation, the period following the climactic moment, is also important. Ultimate togetherness followed by sudden separation can turn a blissful experience into a traumatic one. The shared intimacy is an idyllic experience which should be cherished, and extended naturally into a blissful, relaxing sleep of husband and wife beloved by one another.[8]

The human being is a rational being, not a machine. The human being yearns for happiness and fulfillment, yet the yearning is not for any type of happiness. The human desire is for happiness with reasons, not happiness that is caused. Techniques may cause temporary happiness; real happiness, lasting contentedness, emanates from reasons. For the couple, peak conjugal bliss is connected with reasons, none more important than the unconditional love each has for the other.[9]

Dignity in Conjugality

The way the couple engage in conjugal relations often mirrors how the couple relate to each other in the other dimensions of marriage, and at the same time may dictate how they will relate in the other spheres of marriage. Conjugality in the absence of love is repellent, and is both physically and emotionally painful.[10]

Biologically, the concept of coercion in conjugality implies the husband as agressor and the wife as victim. The husband cannot engage in conjugal relations unless properly aroused, the wife can be coerced by a physically stronger and aroused husband even though she is not desirous of conjugality. The wife has a definite responsibility to encourage the husband's desire and capacity, but the primary responsibility to avoid abuse and ensure readiness resides with the husband. This derives from the fact that he is the one more likely to abuse, the one more likely to accelerate his own readiness and thus not synchronize with his wife.[11]

Conjugal relations without the wife's willingness is tantamount to illicit relations. The previously cited obligations to create the proper ambience for conjugality are designed to prevent such illicit sensual expression. It is assumed that the husband wants, or else the union cannot be consummated. What remains to be clarified is the wife's desire. The husband who wants is obliged to ensure the reality of a wife who truly desires, not simply a wife who goes along.[12]

The actual prohibition is directed to conjugal relations against the will of the wife. The desired union is that which is forged with the wife's *eagerness*. Any statement about the license given the husband for conjugal expression works with the assumption of the wife's agreement. Failing that, the husband has license for nothing. This even includes the normal *onah* visitations, for while the wife may be obliged to cooperate, still the husband cannot use coercion. The excuse that *onah* fulfillment drives him is dismissed, since coercive conjugal relations do not gladden, and are not a fulfillment of the *onah* obligation, which must achieve the happiness of the wife.[13]

Assumption of the wife's agreement is not sufficient even in situations where the assumption has a reasonable foundation. The husband who, after consummation, desires an encore, cannot assume his wife's willingness, even if she was eager for the first conjugal experience. It is the husband's obligation to make sure that his wife's intentions and desires correlate with his.[14]

Conjugal relations in its ideal expression takes place between two individuals with mutual respect and love for each other, respect and love that prevails in thought, in word, and in deed. Mutuality in the relationship and mutuality in conjugal relations usually go together. The law of coercion deals with a base-level relationship; mutuality approaches to the most exalted level of the relationship.

Mutuality alone, the correlation of desires, however vital, is only part of the conjugality package. Husband and wife, in the mutual desire to confer pleasure on each other and to derive pleasure from each other, are to maintain their dignity and self-respect in the process. This falls under the general heading of walking modestly with God (Mic. 6:8). Walking modestly or humbly is an all-encompassing prescription, applying to dress, to speech, to behavior.

It applies also to the conjugal experience. Modesty and humility in conjugality do not diminish the pleasure experienced. They actually enhance the pleasure, in that each approaches the conjugal experience with a measure of self-control and respect for the other, rather than being under the influence of unbridled sensuality. In control and respect, combined of course with love, each moves caringly with the other toward the blissful peak.[15]

Modesty as a requirement applies equally to men and women. In the conjugal context, there are a few regulations to help create a climate of modesty. One is that the husband is forbidden to stare at the wife's most private area, the place of conjugal consummation. One must appreciate this in the context of the affirmative attitude to conjugality in Jewish tradition. The intent is to prevent the wife's being reduced to a sensual repository. Her dignity needs to remain intact, and that is best preserved through not allowing her to be compartmentalized and scrutinized. The husband and wife engage in conjugality with the total being of the other, not just with a vital part. Staring at a vital part may engender obliviousness to the whole, and is thus proscribed. Husband and wife are asked to embrace what the other is, not what the other has.[16]

A second modesty requirement is that conjugality not take place in daylight or where lights are on. This is based on the *mitzvah* to love one's neighbor (wife) as oneself. In the light, the husband may see an unseemly thing in her, and be repulsed. Here too the ultimate rationale is that the wife not be reduced to an arousal instrument at the price of her sense of self. With one another there is no need to feel ashamed, yet there is a need for each to respect and love the other's person, rather than the other's body. Conjugality is a spiritual union, and that spirituality enhances the physical expression in conjugal relations. Daylight eats away at the mystique, and erodes the spiritual nature of the experience.[17]

Another element of restraint, of modesty, is particularly the woman's province. In dealing with the question of initiating the conjugal encounter, the Talmud comments that the male asks with his mouth, whilst the woman asks with her heart, and this is a superior characteristic of woman. Before rushing to the conclusion that the woman is a passive partner in the relationship, it should be stated that there is enough evidence from tradition to totally contradict this allegation. The selfsame Talmudic passage which speaks of the difference between man and woman in initiating also lauds the woman who entices her husband to the conjugal encounter, hardly an espousal of passivity.[18]

Additionally, the Israelite women, during the enslavement of the Israelites in Egypt, were fiercely determined to foil Pharaoh's designs. Pharaoh placed the Israelite husbands far away from their homes. The work load was so heavy that they could not return home, a tidy way of making husband-wife conjugality impossible, and the birth of more Israelites likewise impossible. The Israelite wives refused to buckle under, and instead went to their husbands' work locations, and actively inspired their physically and mentally enervated husbands to conjugality. This defiant action is accorded high praise in the tradition, again hardly an endorsement of passivity.[19]

Further, talmudically reported advice for how women can activate their husbands' desire indicates that they were more than passive partners in the conjugal chambers. What, then, is the significance of the wife asking with her heart? It is perhaps that the woman has enough sense and self-respect not to demand. Or perhaps that the woman recognizes that the man cannot adequately respond to a demand situation, and that he responds most effectively in a natural setting where his wife's attractiveness in turn triggers his own attraction to and desire for her. Frankly, there would be nothing wrong if the husband were to adopt the same modest approach as the wife; that is, rather than ask directly, he should show his own eagerness through appropriate and well-appreciated gestures. The wife, too, is far from at her best when responding to a demand situation.[20]

Ideally, in a true loving relationship, the couple are so well attuned to each other that all this evolves naturally and spontaneously, with the mutuality coloring the conjugal experience from the very outset.[21]

The Conjugal Act

Much has been said about the importance of conjugal compatibility between husband and wife for marriage to work. The feeling is, however, that where there is compatibility, respect, and love in the waking hours, there will be compatibility, respect, and love in the resting hours. Jewish law creates the legal framework for love to evolve. This assumes, and the assumption is well founded, that love is not instantaneous, that it evolves over the years as the couple come to know each other, the faults and the virtues, the idiosyncrasies and the good habits, and adjust to each other as they gradually increase their love for one another. It stands to reason that the warmth and intimacy of the conjugal union, and with it the pleasure sensation, likewise evolves over the years. In a marriage where the love grows, the experience of conjugality grows and becomes more fulfilling. Where love attenuates, the conjugal experience usually follows the same pattern. The question of which came first is itself conjectural, and varies with each couple.[22]

As with love, conjugality also needs knowing. Each member of the couple needs to know the internal chemistry of the other—how they respond, to what they respond, the time it takes them to respond. There are no textbook rules for this. Conjugality is a process of mutual discovery, of getting to know one another. No individual works by a textbook pattern. Each is unique, and it is for the other to discover that uniqueness. Additionally, discovery is not a once-and-for-all matter. Husband and wife respond differently in different moods, in different settings, at different stages in life. This means that being attuned to one another should not cause the couple to routinize their approach, with the assumption that what worked once will automatically work again. Every new experience demands new attentiveness.

Conjugal dynamics, like marriage dynamics, is ideally the dynamics of self-transcendence rather than self-gratification. Marriage is the opportunity to live out the caring, sharing, loving values that are central to Jewish life. Marriage is an ethics theater par excellence, in which transcending toward the other forges an ideal union, with both together mutually orienting toward the Godly values that they share and actualize together.

Conjugality, too, both from an ethical and a functional perspective, becomes more fulfilling and meaningful if it emanates from the transcending approach of the husband and wife. From a Judaic standpoint, there is no greater transcendingness than when both share themselves with each other in order that they may be able to share themselves with others. This is philosophical hyperbole for the simple statement that the conjugal experience is most laudable when its aim is to procreate. This is a union of ultimate sharing.[23]

But conjugality, though enhanced by the prospect of procreation, is itself independent of procreation. It is the language of expression for husband and wife even when the wife's childbearing years have passed. The most noble conjugality in this context is when each approaches the experience with the primary thought and intention of conferring pleasure on the other, and brings that intention to fruition. It has already been shown that it is precisely in this manner that the husband fulfills his *onah* obligation.[24]

Jewish tradition frowns on conjugality which is intended only for self-serving pleasure. This is considered a humanly deficient act. The husband is urged by tradition to intend, via the conjugal act, to bring his wife to the peak of pleasure. What about the husband? Does the conjugal act constitute a theoretical instance of self-denial? Must the husband forget entirely about himself? The answer here is definitely in the negative. The husband enters the conjugal chambers with the pleasure of his wife as his main focus, but he is likewise open to and warmly welcomes the pleasure that he will receive. He receives pleasure spiritually from feeling the ecstasy of his wife. He receives his own sensual pleasure in the very process of giving pleasure to his wife. In the ideal conjugal experience, each receives much more from the giving process than from intending to receive and neglecting to give. The conjugal experience, the pleasant, even ecstatic results which come from sharing and caring for the other, is thus a paradigm for the totality of marriage.[25]

There are some general guidelines which are advisable for conjugality. The essentiality of these guidelines may vary from time to time, from couple to couple. But they are worth keeping in mind as both husband and wife attempt to give maximum pleasure to each other.

Talking, saying nice things to one's mate, words that are genuinely felt and meant, expressions of love, affection, tenderness, can be a very important means for each to feel truly appreciated as a person, and thus eager to share. Conjugality is much more than a functional act, and the verbal expression launching the togetherness serves to imprint that point. However, as the couple approach the climactic moment, talking is ill-advised, as it diverts concentration from the pure, blissful, "beyond-words pleasure" of that moment.[26]

A second important point, and this applies mostly, though not exclusively, to the husband, is that one should not be in a hurry to become aroused. The husband can quickly become overly passionate, but the wife may lag behind. True love means being able to wait for each other. And, to be fair, it also means not keeping the other waiting unnecessarily. Even after the actual physical fusion, when the husband and wife are linked through his being inside his wife, speed, overexertion, rapid and penetrating thrusts may cater to the husband's desires, but may not correlate with the wife's preferences. It is vital to be alert to the buildup of the other's excitement, and to control and coordinate accordingly. The husband who reaches his peak moment too soon is then less able to further stimulate his wife. This can leave them both frustrated, and she moreso than he.[27]

Finally, even with the best of intentions, the conjugal union does not always live up to expectations. Unanticipated distractions may interrupt the couple at a critical moment, recovery from which can be difficult. One or the other may be too physically worn out to sustain vigorous activity and may thus not be able to extend pleasure to the other. Or, one or the other may be overcome with passionate zeal and reach the climactic moment before the other, leaving the other short of the expected high. For whatever reason, the conjugal experience may not click. But even when one may not be able to generate a functionally successful union, it should always be possible to transmit feelings of love, of warmth, of affection, of caring; in words, in embrace. That, in and of itself, is as vital as, if not more vital than, conjugal success. And that, in and of itself, is more likely to generate conjugal success.

The cyclic pattern of conjugality, with time off every month during the wife's menstrual period, is on its own a lesson in control; specifically, the ability to hold back one's desires in anticipation of a rewarding reunion. That selfsame discipline is worth extending to the actual conjugal experience, in that each patiently and caringly assures the readiness of the other for the moment of ultimate bliss.

The matter of the relative positions of husband and wife for the peak moment, the moment when the wife achieves her climactic pleasure and the approximate time the husband's seed is emitted, is given more than passing attention in Jewish tradition. The main concern appears to be that in the moment of ultimate fusion husband and wife should face each other directly. In the context of all that has been enunciated on the Judaic approach to conjugality, this concern follows a consistent pattern. Jewish law is ever concerned that neither of the partners, with the wife being most vulnerable, be abused in the conjugal union. Face-to-back positions remove the personal-encounter component from the conjugal peak. Instead, the wife is reduced to a mere body which serves to enable the husband to experience sensual pleasure.[28]

In the face-to-face union, the accepted norm is for the husband to be on his wife, perhaps projecting the essential responsibility, in conjugality, for the husband to give, to confer pleasure on his wife, and for the wife to receive that pleasure, and in the process also effect the husband's pleasure.[29]

Generally, assuming the wife's full consent, and that is an exceedingly crucial factor, the husband can freely express himself in the conjugal chamber. And if face-to-face conjugality with the wife on top enhances her pleasure, that can be part of the couple's conjugal vocabulary. Additionally, if the fulfillment of *onah* is at stake, and the only possible positioning for conjugal relations is standing up, allowances are made to permit such conjugal expression.[30]

The license for variety is not intended to destroy what is perceived as the norm, but such license does serve to reduce the inhibitions of the couple as they focus on extending pleasure to one another. Control and discipline are at all times helpful in maintaining the dignity and enhancing the pleasure of the conjugal act, but husband and wife should feel free to unabashedly express the love and affection they have for one another.[31]

Avoiding Problems

The husband or wife, or both, may have problems related to biological function which may affect the ability to achieve consummation, problems which may call for responsible medical intervention. However, given the general good health of the couple, the majority of problems in conjugal relations derive from exaggerated expectations or fear of inadequacy, the fear of failure.

Consistent with the understandable pattern that one who has a little bit of a good thing wants even more of the good thing, the husband or wife who has experienced exhilarating conjugality may approach the next encounter with slightly higher expectations, that it will get even better. The expectations may be realized once, twice, or even more times, but there is an obvious limit to how much "peakier" the peak can be. When the expectations are frustrated, when there is excessive focus of attention on the self and on aggrandizing pleasure instead of approaching the conjugal experience naturally, impotence or frigidity may develop.[32]

A good way to counter this situation is to switch the focus away from self-realization, from gaining pleasure, toward the partner and how pleasure can be given to the partner. Selfless conjugality is, over extended time, much more fulfilling and productive than selfish conjugality. It may seem surprising that attitudes, healthy or otherwise, can affect what seems to be a biological problem, but that is indeed the case. When conjugality is a demand situation, whether it be implicit demands placed on the other to fulfill expectations or demands of the self toward the self, it is usually the harbinger of problems.[33]

The problem of premature ejaculation, which may be linked to deep-seated problems, is also amenable to an outer-directed, transcending approach. The husband with such a problem is well served to slow down, to perhaps, if possible, forget about himself, and channel his energies toward his wife and what pleases her. He should follow her tempo, letting her dictate the flow, with him concentrating fully and completely on her. This can go a long way toward letting nature take its course, with his pleasure pattern unfolding as it normally should.

The fear of failure, of not being able to deliver the anticipated delight to one's partner, may result from having a demanding mate who imposes excessively; it may derive from one's own sense of general inadequacy or from exaggerated demands placed on the self toward pleasing the other, among other possibilities. Understanding is here absolutely critical. Without adequate understanding, the fear of failure, which blocks off the natural capacity to stimulate and to be stimulated, is likely to be a self-fulfilling prophecy. From fear of failure comes failure itself.

The partner who fears failure needs to be understanding of the realities of life. Failure always looms as a possibility. People are human, and cannot be expected to reach ultimate standards at all times. This is unrealistic. Life has its peaks, it also has its valleys and its plateaus. That a person has failed does not mean that the person *is* a failure. It simply means that one should do one's best to improve the next time.

The other partner, aware of what is disturbing the spouse, must likewise provide understanding. The partner can indicate that being loved is the most important factor in the relationship, that the marriage can function quite well without the conjugal act. In fact, for two who really love each other, this is the truth. Witness that in true love, the fact that one or the other is ill for a prolonged period and cannot be a conjugal partner does not destroy the marriage. Instead, the devotion shown in that period of nonconjugality actually increases the love between the couple.

Additionally, the sensitive partner can provide understanding by stating that failure in conjugality can come from either side, and probably will; but the love that exists between the couple will not be compromised no matter who is the cause of a failed conjugal experience. There is nothing to fear from failure, because failure is assumed to be likely in the best of marriages, and only serves to make the successes which follow even more meaningful.

Finally, in a situation of an actual failure of the conjugal act itself, the one who was unable to play an adequate role should be more tightly embraced and shown more affection than under more pleasuring circumstances. This, better than any soothing comments or reassuring arguments, will be proof positive that a failed conjugal encounter does not indicate an abating of love.

One actually hesitates to use the word "failure" to describe a conjugal experience in which the ultimate pleasure did not materialize. It is precisely this mentality that causes so many marital partners to be fixated on success and in dread of a poor "performance," as if they were on trial, as if the ability to perform successfully were what makes a marriage last. Love, affection, caring, and respect should be catapulted into the forefront as the primary components of a solid marriage, and the nonclimactic conjugal experience should interfere with the relationship no more than if some water spills. It can even be transmuted into an ideal opportunity to show that the love between the partners is indeed unconditional; it can, borrowing the unfortunate contemporary terminology, become the success of failure.

There is a fascinating story in the Talmud about a student who stealthily made his way to his rebbe's bedroom and hid under the bed. In the evening, he listened to how his rebbe engaged in the conjugal act with his wife, and muttered to himself about the passion with which the rebbe approached his wife. The rebbe heard, and in understandable amazement, but astoundingly without anger, asked the student what he was doing under the bed. The student's answer must rank as a classic response: "It is Torah, and I need to learn!"[34]

Indeed, how to engage in conjugal relations is Torah. And conjugal relations at its best is Torah at its best. There is much literature available offering advice for this most delicate aspect of marriage, unfortunately literature which all too often is colored by a hedonistic philosophy and which caters to the entire smorgasbord of sensual expression, implicitly giving credibility to these forms of expression by discussing them with the same scientific seriousness. The student of the talmudic story had a good teacher, but what about the student of today?[35]

It may seem surprising, but the Jewish parent of yesteryear was able, in a matter-of-fact, serious, and enlightened manner, to discuss all this with the child prior to marriage. Too few are able to do so today. The soon-to-be-married bride or groom would be helped significantly through being able to discuss, candidly and completely, the full scope of healthy conjugality with a capable, knowledgeable person, prior to marriage.[36]

It is lamentable that not enough attention is given to the *onah* obligations and fulfillment prior to marriage. Lamentable because *onah* obligations, properly carried out in letter and in spirit, are an ideal paradigm for marriage as a whole, and can engender an upward spiral of respect and love which invests the marital home with *shalom bayit,* domestic bliss, in the full implications of the term. In the present climate of dissatisfaction with marriage, an overdose of *shalom bayit* is necessary medicine, and *onah* is one of the most pleasant ways to administer it.

12

Death and Divorce

Reacting to Death

Marriage, like life itself, is not forever. The marital union can terminate either through external forces, the forces of death, which take away one of the partners, or due to internal conditions, the dissatisfaction of either or both partners with the marriage and the subsequent decision to divorce. Both types of dissolution are tragic in their own way, leaving a lasting impact on the surviving partner or the ex-partners. Both of these contingencies merit discussion; death because it is an unavoidable part of life, divorce because it is becoming much more prevalent in contemporary society.

When marriage approaches the ideal, when it is suffused with love, caring and respect, when the two actually live as one, the death of one of the partners is a severe, crushing blow to the surviving member of the marriage. When the marriage is short of the ideal, when the partners survive but do not thrive, when the marriage is characterized by missed opportunities to share, to help, to love, then the death of one of the partners may elicit the guilt-laden grief of the other. The death of one of the partners, then, no matter what the quality of the marriage, usually brings with that passing its own particular devastation.

When a husband or a wife dies, the death is keenly felt by the surviving spouse. It is as if part of the surviving partner has died. Whether the surviving partner recovers, how that recovery evolves, how long the recovery takes, are all matters which relate

133

to the circumstances of the marriage and the personality of the surviving partner. That the world blackens for one who loses a marital partner is natural; how long it takes for the blackness to lift depends on the attitude with which the tragedy is confronted.[1]

There are, among the many talmudic observations concerning the death of one's mate, two instructive comments, one anticipating the inevitable, the other reacting to the inevitable.

The Talmud considers one's wife among those with whom the dialectic should be: the left hand pushing away, and the right hand drawing near. On the surface, this statement is little short of surprising, considering all that has been said about the husband and wife being as one corpus, united in a spiritual, physical, emotional bond. This would seem to point to a total embrace, with both hands, left and right. Why, then, the pushing away with the left?[2]

It may be that the Talmud is hereby incorporating realism into the marital relationship. For, if the conceptual projection for marriage is realized, in that the husband and wife actually become as one, then the death of the one presages, or perhaps almost implies, the death of the other, at least the partial death. Conjugal closeness is blissful in life, but that very bliss creates overwhelming adjustment problems at death; theoretically at least, perhaps insurmountable problems.

To lessen the severity of the blow that is felt upon the death of one's spouse, the Talmud suggests pushing away with the left, and drawing near with the right. The primary, right-hand action should be a pull toward; the secondary, left-hand action should be a push away. The closeness of the couple is real and genuine, but also balanced. Pushing away with the left is designed to prevent either of the partners from becoming so immersed in the other as to become dependent, over-reliant, unable to function alone. The marriage is a union of mutual interdependence which does not foreclose the possibilities of either exercising independence.

The language of the Talmud suggests that the husband initiate the left-right dialectic, but the effect is felt by both husband and wife. The husband, by pushing—the pushing is obviously a mental, attitudinal process, not a physical shove—maintains just enough of a distance from total dependence to protect himself in the eventuality that he survives his wife. The wife, herself held back, is thereby encouraged not to place all her eggs in the husband's basket, but to maintain enough distance so that her autonomy can be reasserted should she survive her husband.

One of the husband's obligations, as spelled out in the *ketuvah* document, is that he assume responsibility for the dignified burial of his wife. Beyond concern for the physical corpus of the other, the left-right approach serves to ensure the dignity and capacity of husband or wife to survive following the death of the other.

In the background of this interjected balance in the marital closeness, another statement of the Talmud may be seen as extending the concern for life after the death of one's spouse one step further. This is the statement that a person who has married in his earlier years should marry in his later years. This statement is understandably directed to the male, since, as has been pointed out, the woman is not obligated to marry. The husband alone is obliged, and that obligation challenges him to find someone so enamored with him that she is willing to share her life with him.[3]

Another implication of this talmudic statement relates to its "if-then" structure. If the person married in his earlier years, *then* he should marry in his later years. One can dismiss this inferential syntax with the explanation that since the overwhelming majority do marry, the "if" part merely reflects reality, and the statement indicates that the husband is not simply to get married, he is to *be* married. If he was married in his earlier years, but that marriage terminated, the male should not feel that he has discharged his obligation. He did get married, true, but he is not now married. The concern that the husband marry is less a concern with an act, and more a concern with a state of being. That state of being is desirable even in later years.

There is perhaps a hidden meaning in the "if-then" structure of the talmudic statement. If the person married early in life, then he should marry in his later years. But if the person did not marry in his earlier years, then there is no imperative to marry in the later years. There may be extenuating circumstances to explain why the person did not marry early in life, including that he could not find the right mate. Generally, however, the one who does not marry makes a telling statement about his priorities, maybe about negative attitudes to women and children, maybe about assuming responsibility. Such a person goes through the major portion of life without sharing himself with another. The capacity to love, to care, to embrace is not exercised as it should, and tends to atrophy. To insist that such a person marry later on in life is unfair to the partner in such a marriage who, ostensibly accustomed to being loved, cared for, and embraced, may find the change too drastic and the lack of true feeling intolerable. One hesitates to read any halakhic directive or any waiving of obligation into the talmudic statement, yet it is worthwhile not to overlook the innuendo.[4]

However the talmudic statement is interpreted, one conclusion is clear: that after the termination of the marriage, and presumably, since divorce was relatively rare, this means after the death of one's first wife, the husband should remarry. This is not to suggest that the second marriage will be as fulfilling as the first. The intimate union of the first marriage may be a once-in-a-lifetime experience, not likely to be duplicated. Remarriage, however, is better than remaining single. It reaffirms the primacy placed on a caring, sharing lifestyle, even if the intimacy of caring and sharing is on a reduced level. The husband or wife who remarries following the death of the spouse is hardly being disloyal to the deceased partner. Remarriage confirms that the first marriage was an affirmative, meaningful union, that marriage itself is a desirable way to live, that the values of life so sacred in Judaism yearn for expression up to the last moment.[5]

The husband or wife whose first marriage was as one, but within the left-right dialectic, is theoretically better able to cope with loss, and to thus be more open to potential further gain.

After Divorce, and Before

Divorce, like death, is a tragedy. Unlike death, divorce is often an avoidable tragedy. The fact of contemporary life is that many have chosen not to avoid the trauma of divorce, and have opted to extricate themselves from unpleasant or unfulfilling unions. It is feared that soon one of every two marriages will end in divorce, and that fear-cum-prediction has been extended even to Jewish marriages.[6]

Very few are able to exit from marriage without adverse effects and negative feelings. Even the initiator of a divorce must wrestle with the lonely, exposed feeling that divorce can cause. Divorce is testimony to a failed marriage. To some it is nothing more than a failed experiment, to others it may be interpreted as a personal failure, or indicative of personal failings.

There are today so many postdivorce singles that communal leaders are hesitant to talk in public about the virtues of marriage or the negative impact of divorce, for fear that they may hurt the feelings of divorced individuals. A cycle of acceptability is thus generated, changing divorce from a personal and communal tragedy to a fact of life.[7]

To be sure, divorce is a fact of life; unfortunate, but a fact of life nevertheless. Jewish law long ago accepted the possibility of divorce in theory, as is evident from the biblical source and the development of relatively equal claims for divorce for either husband or wife who is short-changed in marriage. The modern institution of no-fault divorce was long ago incorporated as a legally justified contingency in Jewish law. Yet divorce was rare, and rabbis went out of their way to preserve marriages with which many of today's marriage counselors would not waste their time. A radical shift in attitude has unfolded over the past few decades, away from saving marriages and toward saving the individuals inside the marriage. This attitude, itself a manifestation of the self-realization, me-first, narcissistic ethic spreading over the free world, has spilled over into the Jewish community.[8]

There is an eloquent talmudic statement projecting the traditional attitude to divorce. The statement is that when one divorces one's first mate, even the altar in the Holy Temple sheds tears. Why the altar? Why the tears?[9]

The altar was that place in the Temple where Israelites expressed their closeness to God. One who deviated brought an offering which was to effect atonement and bridge the distance to God, distance caused by or indicated in the deviation. An appreciative person brought an offering expressing gratitude and

appreciation to God for God's kindness. The penitent has the
courage to admit being in error, and to take definite steps to
correct the error. The appreciative one has the kindness of
character to acknowledge a benefit bestowed, and to make a
tangible gesture showing that appreciation.[10]

These two fundamental emotions, penitence and appreciation, are evoked at the altar. They are also two critical ingredients
in marriage. Being penitent speaks of the ability to see that one
has erred, that one has not lived up to one's responsibilities, and
that one has the courage and the desire to correct the situation.
Being appreciative is an essential part of the outer-directedness
dynamic of marriage. Expressing appreciation to one's spouse
binds the relationship with the glue of caring and attentiveness.
Marriages that fail invariably lack the outer-directedness and
"willingness to adjust" ingredients. The altar, which also thrives
on these ingredients, cries when a couple divorce, when the
ingredients it thrives on are lacking in marriage.

But why tears? Why not rage? Why not anger? Why not
screams? Because divorce is unfortunate, a situation to lament,
but not a reason to condemn. One cries *for* others, but one
screams *at* others. The altar commiserates, but it refuses to point
an accusing finger. Character flaws may be at the root of the
marital disintegration, but who can claim to be perfect? Moreover, the fact that other marriages survive intact is no proof that
the partners in such marriages are characterologically superior.
They may just be more lucky.[11]

Using this paradigm, then, one can at once laud the marriage
ideal and lament divorce, yet refrain from pointing an accusing
finger, or condemning anyone who has suffered the pain of
divorce.

In the talmudic sequence, the tractate on divorce (*Gittin*) is
placed before the tractate on marriage (*Kiddushin*). Obviously, it is
impossible to divorce before marrying. But it is possible, even
recommended, to learn about divorce before marrying. One who
learns about divorce, the pain and trauma that it brings not only
to the couple, but also to their parents, their children, their family
and friends, will probably hesitate before marrying, and that is

good. It is not good if the hesitation is an excuse for procrastination. It is good if the hesitation is translated into seriously studying what makes for a good marriage, what makes for a good partner in marriage, what are the parameters for compatibility.[12]

In today's rush-to-divorce climate, one is tempted to reverse the aforementioned recommendation, and to suggest that couples learn about marriage before divorcing. Unless it was a total mistake from the outset, the couple, at least in the initial stages, were reasonably convinced that theirs could be a good marriage. Marital life did not go according to plan, and probably both have contributed to the derailment. Before divorce, a couple with honesty, courage, and will can get back on track; learning about marriage, what makes good marriages work, may forestall divorce.[13]

The hope remains that the rush to divorce is a passing phase, that the vast numbers who have run away from marriage because it was not the answer will collectively realize that divorce, too, as a general trend, is not the answer, and indeed may be an even greater problem. This is only said in reaction to divorce that is pursued because some segments of society have declared open season on marriage. It is hardly desirable that people remain in less than happy marriages because divorce is worse. But the realization that divorce is not the answer may possibly prod many would be divorcers to seek the answer in making their marriages better, by willing and working toward that goal.[14]

The procedure for divorce is much more complicated than the procedure for marriage, perhaps consistent with the notion that husband and wife uniting is natural, husband and wife separating is unnatural, and therefore complicated. The granting of a divorce is a painstaking process, itself affirming the sanctity of marriage even at its dissolution. This is akin to the pattern on Sabbaths and festivals, which are ushered in with a sanctification (*Kiddush*) and are concluded with a *Havdalah* ceremony, *Havdalah* signifying the separateness and distinctiveness of the Sabbath or the festival from the regular weekday period. What is sacred at the start is sacred at the conclusion. That which demands a sanctification procedure to be properly launched demands an equivalent procedure to be properly terminated. The point is that sanctity does not evaporate on a personal whim, even as it is not launched by a personal whim.[15]

Similarly, there is a halakhic ethic for divorce just as there is a halakhic ethic for marriage. Thus, conjugal relations with one's spouse after having decided, within one's own mind, to pursue divorce, is prohibited. The normal household duties that one may normally expect to be carried out in marriage can no longer be expected once the intent to divorce has been firmly entrenched in the mind. Admittedly these are rules that are beyond enforceability, since what is in one's mind is not open to public scrutiny; but the rules are there, and they serve as basic rudiments of a halakhic divorce ethic, an ethic which begins with the insistence, as reflected in these laws, that neither partner be exploited by the other.[16]

In marriage the impact of the obligation to love one's mate as oneself, since both are as one, calls for each to respect the other as a full and dignified partner in their life of shared values and shared destiny. In divorce, the impact of the obligation to love one's neighbor as oneself calls for each to respect the other as a person, as a fellow Israelite. Realistically, it may be too much to ask that respect, which did not prevail during the marriage, be present after divorce. Halakhah, however, is less concerned with surrendering to human callousness, and insists on standards of decency even in situations where conflict and enmity are the rule rather than the exception.[17]

Considering the rarity of divorce in talmudic times, there is still ample evidence, from the conduct of the talmudic sages, for the sensitive treatment that must be extended to one's former mate. For the present situation, one can derive much from the famous edict of Rabbenu Gershom, which, through removing from the husband the right to divorce his wife against her will, effected a more equal and equitable situation between husband and wife. If husband and wife are now more or less equal in the grounds for divorce, it stands to reason that they should be equal and equitable concerning the ground they are on after divorce. Husband and wife should try, without recrimination and vindictiveness, to agree on the terms of the divorce. Instead of remote-control wrangling which benefits only the lawyers, they should resolve to behave as befits responsible adults; not merely for the sake of the children, but for their own sakes, for the sake of each one's dignity and self-respect as a person.[18]

The husband may not be legally bound to sustain his wife after divorce, but there still remains an extralegal, "within the boundary of the law" fulfillment that deserves his consideration. Leaving the wife with no means of support runs contrary to the admonition warning against being oblivious to one's own flesh. This applies likewise to the matter of adequate living quarters.[19]

Child support and child visitation should also not be items for barter. The animosity that erupts over these issues usually lasts for years after the divorce, and has a damaging effect on the children over whose welfare the parents are allegedly fighting.[20]

The husband and wife who set out to get each other, who use the divorce as occasion to let loose all the anger and animosity they have for each other, would see, if they only opened their eyes, that all the hatred directed at the other boomerangs back. The low road has few victors and many victims. The hatred one directs at another is not a hatred that leaves, it is a hatred that stays, and that eats at the dispenser of the hate. From a purely practical view, even before ethical considerations, hatred yields very few positive results and an abundance of negative results, for the hater and for the hated. The hater is very much a loser, much less capable of enjoying whatever is left of life.

The host of condemnations of hate in Jewish tradition applies most forcefully to the divorce situation. Hate should be eliminated from the dialectic of former mates. This is a halakhic statement more than amply reinforced by experience in the theater of human relations. After divorce, the couple should maintain good relations, helping and cooperating with one another if for none other than self-serving motives. Through the self-serving motives, they will eventually see the wisdom of Halakhah, its insistence on decency and dignity even in the most difficult of circumstances.[21]

Conclusion

If one has done a little wrong to another, it should appear to the doer as much wrong. If one has done much good for the other, it should appear to the doer as minimal. If another has done much harm, the victim should perceive it as trivial. If another has done a little good, it should appear to the beneficiary as of major significance. This is the advice from Jewish tradition about the attitude people should bring to their interactions with others.[1]

This advice runs contrary to the typical pattern, in which people are more consumers than bestowers, aggrandizing rather than sharing. Whatever good is gained is not enough; whatever is dispensed, however trivial, seems overly significant. Being of fragile ego, even a minor slight punctures the ego balloon. On the other hand, concern with one's own self often blinds the person to the harm that one is doing to others.

The advice from tradition, then, proposes that people be givers more than receivers, forthcoming rather than stingy with appreciation, secure enough to be more concerned with others than obsessed with themselves. This advice is offered for human relations in general, and is to be integrated into one's personality as a natural expression.

Much of what has been spelled out in this volume on husband-wife relations from a halakhic perspective flows in this direction. In all of the essential components of marriage—honor, respect, caring, attentiveness, appreciativeness, affection—all the key ingredients allowing for love to evolve, each of the partners is obliged to be a giver, to live up to their own responsibility. Once the marital union falls into a demand pattern, the relationship becomes filled with unrequited expectations, feelings of frustration and neglect, all creating distance between the partners instead of the closeness that is effected through giving. It seems clear that when each lives up to the letter and spirit of their marital obligations, the marriage cannot help but be a blissful union.

All this is not technique, it is human essence. It is obvious that the Halakhah programs the rudiments of *mentschlichkeit* (being a true human being in the ultimate sense) for all people on all occasions, whether young or old, whether married or divorced. Human beings constantly wrestle with their own base instincts, but as human beings have the power to overcome. Adopting good habits, even at a point when one does not feel like it, may not quite fit in with the self-expression ethic, but that matters little. We are less concerned with people expressing and reflecting what they actually are, and more concerned that they become what they are capable of being.

To reach beyond, to strive toward, demands an external focus, a goal orientation that is real, yet not finite and limited. One senses that in many of the failed marriages of today there is not merely a frustration with one's partner; there is also a frustration with life itself. Happiness is pursued, but it does not ensue. Material delights bring only momentary satisfaction, satisfaction which rapidly turns to disappointment when it becomes obvious that this too is not the answer. The work-leisure pattern seems like an unending cycle going nowhere. What is missing? In a word, life is missing a sense of meaning and purpose.

That Jewish marriage worked so well in the past, and was the envy of many, was in large measure due to the fact that meaning and purpose were salient features of family life. Husband and wife, and then the children, were all involved with Jewish life and Jewish destiny. This was all natural, not catalogued. The well-intentioned attempts to recapture the legacy of the past and reinvigorate Jewish marriage all too often become technique without spirit. But technique does not create spirit; rather, spirit energizes the technique. Technique itself without spirit is self-limiting, working well for a time, for some longer than for others. Technique can generate mutually reinforcing good habits, but all the play-action yearns for a goal to make the effort meaningful and purposeful.[2]

In a word, then, the halakhic ethic for marriage herein projected, the Torah for marriage, probably works well for a time purely as a technique. Ultimately, however, it cannot really work without Torah itself, without genuine orientation around the Torah as the focus of one's value expressions. When that happens, there is less worry about what to do, about how to inspire the children. The authentic, Torah-inspired, loving marriage usually generates its own perpetuating energy.[3]

The sages of the past composed various prayers related to marriage. Prayer itself serves a twofold purpose. Prayer orients the praying individual beyond the self, and toward God as the source of blessing. At the same time, prayer expresses one's own particular set of priorities, since one prays for what one considers to be important. Prayer does not thereby leave matters in God's hands. Prayer as request is genuine prayer when it is combined with personal commitment. The individual who prays thereby asserts readiness to do all that is possible to bring the prayed-for request to realization, yet is ever-cognizant that human beings are finite beings, and can only go so far. The rest is up to God. One can pray for good health, and work hard to take care of oneself, even do all that is possible; yet there is still a missing ingredient, God's blessing, that which people sometimes erroneously refer to as luck. On the other hand, one who neglects the self, and abuses the body, cannot legitimately ask for God's help. Such supplication is more of a challenge than a request. True prayer is orientation and cooperation.[4]

Prayer with this attitude is a welcome ingredient in the home. The couple, at the very start of the marriage, would be well advised to compose a collective prayer expressing their hopes and aspirations within marriage, how each would like to bestow on the other, what each would like to glean from the other, that they should grow together through love and devotion, and promulgate a meaningful life, a meaningful posterity. Or, each may compose their own prayer, reflecting their own requests, and have that prayed for by the other. Such prayer entrenches transcending orientation and mutual cooperativeness, which are the body and spirit of the marriage ideal.

To those skeptics who question whether marriage has a chance, we can then say unequivocally that marriage has a prayer.

The Dynamics of Halakhah

It is the purpose of this volume to suggest parameters, halakhic parameters, for the Jewish family, and a dynamic of marital interaction which works within those parameters. Consistent with this purpose, it would seem appropriate to spell out the conception of Halakhah that is the basic premise upon which this volume is built.

Law in History

One of the unique features of classical Judaism as it has been transmitted over the ages is the element of *mitzvah*, "commandment." Unlike other religions with which it has been indiscriminately compared, Judaism is not a faith system per se. Rather, it is a commitment to life that is rooted in and springs forward from faith. Some Jewish thinkers even refused to include faith in God as one of the 613 commandments, since faith is the base upon which Judaism is built, that which makes Judaism possible, the source which gives birth to commands, but itself not a command-ment.[1]

The 613 commandments, the *mitzvot*, their development in talmudic literature and subsequent codification into Halakhah, are the warp and woof of Judaism. No full appreciation of Judaism is possible without an understanding of the individual laws as well as the role of law in faith.

Generally speaking, it is possible to view law (Halakhah) as the vehicle through which man actualizes himself, exercising responsiveness to his Creator and fulfilling his purpose in life. Law is thus conceived as affirmation of the individual, who becomes, by his actions, the agent of his own salvation.

In the course of Jewish history, there has been an almost perpetual tension within the ranks regarding the law. It begins almost immediately after the Sinai experience, with the ups and downs of the forty years wandering in the desert, and continues through the period of the Judges and Kings, with their sometimes hostile attitude to Jewish law. The Pharisees and Sadducees fan the flames in their own conflicts, the Karaites offer their own version of Bible interpretation, Sabbateanism negates the validity of observance amongst other things, the Frankists turn moral law upside down, Reform attacks the ritual laws, even Hasidism challenges the Orthodox approach to observance. These conflicts, bitter as they sometimes were, are almost insignificant when compared with the great cleavage in Jewish ranks resulting from the rise of Christianity. Here the matter of law occupies center stage, as Christianity proposes vicarious atonement and salvation, with an accompanying abrogation of the law in its theology. Christianity, a less demanding religion, eventually attracts great masses, whilst Judaism remains a minority group expression. Judaism and Christianity clash constantly, often not on an intellectual level.[2]

We propose a view of Jewish law which is not so much novel as it is either unknown, neglected, or obscured in the controversy over legalism.

Mistaken Notions

Immanuel Kant saw Judaism as a national-political entity, which fails as a religion to inculcate the inner-appropriateness of morals, instead demanding external obedience to statutes and laws. Closer to home, Martin Buber asserted: "I do not believe that *revelation* is ever a formulation of law. It is only through man in his self-contradiction that revelation becomes legislation. This is the fact of man. I cannot admit the law transformed by man into the realm of my will, if I am to hold myself ready as well for the unmediated word of God directed to a specific hour of life."[3]

Accordingly, in these views, the law, rather than affirming the individual, represses personal development and precludes spontaneous reaction to the Divine call, reducing man to a halakhically programmed computer. At the risk of oversimplification, one senses in Kant and Buber a view of Jewish law as an end in itself, as the purpose and expression of life. Whilst this is in some measure corroborated by the religious behavior of some individuals, it nevertheless assumes a view not totally consistent with the design or intent of the law.

In coming to grips with the role of the individual in Jewish law, it should be noted that the very all-embracingness of the law presents problems. Jewish law contains not only a full measure of *bayn adam LaMakom* laws, ordinances revolving around man and his Creator, it also projects *bayn adam lahavero* regulations, a full corpus of laws covering the legal, ethical, and moral aspects of social interaction. Whilst such comprehensiveness is likely to evoke an expression of chauvinistic pride, it nonetheless points to an acute problem which, in the present atmosphere of existentialistic pressures, cannot be avoided.[4]

According to a leading contemporary Jewish thinker: "For Judaism sheer compliance with the Law as such was never regarded as the ultimate value, it rather represented a means to the fulfillment of the Divine Will." In support of this view, one need only think of the multitude of open-ended categories in applying Jewish law. For our purposes, it will be helpful to treat separately the realms of *bayn adam LaMakom,* ritual law, which, for obvious reasons, I prefer to call transcending laws, and *bayn adam lahavero,* social legislation.[5]

Within the Border

In the domain of social legislation one frequently encounters the notion of *lifnim meshurat hadin,* which is often erroneously translated as "beyond the requirements of the law." *Lifnim* actually means "inside, within," suggesting a profoundly symbolic category of *within the boundary of the law.* What is proposed as social legislation in Judaism is not the *summum bonum,* the ultimate. It is the lower, irreducible limit, the boundary line. Within the pale of the law, man oscillates between straddling the border and approaching the core, the heart and soul of the law. Straddling the border has its own dangers, including the likelihood that in straddling one may overstep, as well as the danger that the law can become a veneer, used by man as a camouflage for his own interests. *Lifnim* is thus recommended for legal as well as humanistic reasons.[6]

The notion of *lifnim* has its counterpart in open society. There, human life, humane life, has self-evident boundaries beyond which resides the dimension of the animalistic. Self-evident boundaries, such as the illegitimacy of theft, rape, murder, etc., are the outer periphery, beyond which is something less than the human dimension. These boundaries leave wide-open areas for human expression within the perimeter. Humanness, in this setting, is not limited by boundaries, rather it is made possible by boundaries. An analogy from Viktor Frankl's concept of freedom is useful. "Certainly man is free, but he is not floating freely in airless space. He is always surrounded by a host of restrictions. These restrictions, however, are the jumping-off points for his freedom. Freedom presupposes restrictions, is contingent upon restrictions."[7]

In a parallel sense, the thrust of Judaic social legislation is toward circumscribing a frontier within which man has ample room for being himself and expressing himself. Thus, the Talmud interprets the scriptural passage concerning the obligation to make known to the people the deeds *that they are to do* (Exod. 18:20) as a reference to *lifnim meshurat hadin*, within the line of the law into the human dimension. What *they are to do*, what is an authentic expression of man's higher development, is *within* the borders of the legal framework.[8]

Lifnim as Essential

Lifnim meshurat hadin is more than just a higher form of expression of Judaic law. It has already been pointed out that all of the eleven principles of virtue to which King David condensed the 613 *mitzvot* are, without exception, expressions of the notion of *lifnim meshurat hadin*.[9]

For example, the virtue of *nor does he evil to his fellow* (Ps. 15:3) is interpreted beyond the passive state of not harming a neighbor.

It is taken as referring to the meticulous detail man should give in order to refrain from even indirect harm. *Speaks truth in his heart* (Ps. 15:2) is applied to the behavior of men like Rav Safra, who in his scrupulous adherence to truth refused a higher offer simply because in his mind alone he had accepted the original offer. *Nor does he take a bribe against the innocent* (Ps. 15:5), hardly an excelling virtue, is applied to such as R. Ishmael b. R. Jose, who avoided even the slightest possibility of conflict of interest in deference to the purity of judicial inquiry.[10]

At least in the realm of social legislation, where the concept of *lifnim meshurat hadin* is applicable, Judaism seems to posit a strong dosage of human contribution. The ultimate importance attached to this concept is seen in the talmudic assertion that one of the reasons why Jerusalem *had* to be destroyed was "because they based their judgments [strictly] upon biblical law, and did not go *lifnim meshurat hadin*." One must appreciate this as a declaration that law perfunctorily observed, albeit even scrupulously, is not authentic Judaism. Judaism demands man.[11]

Lifnim meshurat hadin does not exhaust the categories in social legislation where virtue depends on man. There are such other notions as *midot hasidut*, the way of the pious; *lazet yeday shamayim*, fulfilling the desires of Heaven; *v'aseeta hayashar v'hatov*, doing that which is upright and good; and *l'maan telekh b'derekh tovim*, to walk in the way of good people. These categories do not lend themselves merely to a legal framework. Instead they function within the legal framework in accordance with the ethical growth of man. For the Jew, sensitivity and conscience development, tightly bounded by the full gamut of social legislation, are nevertheless, through this boundedness, given the room, more than ample room, to mature. God's word can go only so far. After that it is up to man to take up the baton, to give to the body of laws meaningfulness and life with his heart and soul. Here enforceable Judaism ends, and responsive and responsible man enters.[12]

Transcending Law

Having dealt with social legislation, although somewhat superficially, the next step is to comprehend the thrust of transcending legislation, the *bayn adam LaMakom* ("between man and God") laws. In the social realm the construct is, to a large extent, one-dimensional, in that the law serves to thrust man into the core, away from the outer border, but in the transcending ordinances, the *mitzvot* function in terms of man's dialogue with God, propelling man into the dimension of transcendence.[13]

Again, reference to a Franklian analogy is useful. "The ground upon which man walks is always being transcended in the process of walking, and serves as ground only to the extent that it is transcended, that it provides a springboard." In the domain of transcending legislation, attention will be focused on how the law serves as a springboard to literally propel man into a transcending dimension.[14]

Here too, illustration is the best method of elucidating the point.

The commandments regarding the Sabbath are perhaps the most minute and exacting in the vast expanse of Jewish law, yet the great preponderance of these regulations are geared mainly toward interpreting the prohibitive aspect of the Sabbath, the *shamor* component (Deut. 5:12). As for the *zakhor* component (Exod. 20:8), the positive human contribution to the day, each individual, in his unique situation, decides how to best parlay the Sabbath into a meaningful experience. The law here is extremely restrictive, it divorces man almost totally from materially creative concerns, but in cutting off all these options the law forces man into a higher dimension, where his concerns are purely intellectual and spiritual. The Sabbath still remains, paradoxically, the subject of more laws than most other precepts, and, at the same time, a symbol of *human* freedom.[15]

As an aside, one senses in the challenging questions constantly hurled at rabbis, "Why can't I drive?", "Why can't I switch on a light?", "Why can't I watch television?", an attitude which obviously negates the primary thrust of Sabbath law. If the Sabbath laws are springboards, these questions testify that some people are still grounded. There is a dimensional difference between the one experiencing the true Sabbath and the one questioning the Sabbath. This difference is rarely overcome by intellectual intrigue, and is most often effectively countered with a suggestion to "try it."

Even more radical than the Sabbath in its restrictiveness is

Yom Kippur, the Day of Atonement. Superimposed upon all the restrictions which pertain to a regular Sabbath are more ordinances dictating abstinence from eating, drinking, washing, etc. But these regulations are not intended as an exercise in abstinence, as is evident from the procedure followed in public fasting. The elder would address the fasting community in the following manner: "Our brethren, neither sackcloth nor fastings are effective but only penitence and good deeds, for we find that of the men of Nineveh Scripture does not say, 'And God saw their sackcloth and fasting,' but, *'God saw their works that they turned from their evil way.'* " This, of course, echoes the message of the prophet which is read as the Haftorah on Yom Kippur morning.[16]

Fasting is not the ultimate value on Yom Kippur. Through fasting, however, man is divorced not only from material creativity but also from any immediate material concerns. He is then forced into a purely spiritual dimension, where the concerns are self-investigation, confrontation with responsibility, acknowledgment of previous failings, and, in the spirit of *teshuvah* (repentance), resolution for the future. To be sprung into the spiritual realm, the law, in its exacting stringency, ordains a negation of the material. Man's response to this situation, as in the case of the Sabbath, is facilitated by law, but not programmed by law. Each person's *teshuvah* is a reflection of the peculiar position and nature of the *baal teshuvah*, the one engaged in the process of return.[17]

In the realm of experience, Jewish law manifests its concern not only in advocating the experience; it also creates, through the mechanism of prohibitive commandments, the setting in which such experience is not only possible, but also evoked.[18]

Individual Responsibility

The role of the individual does not end here. In the exercise of prayer, where the matter of prescribed textual entreaties is a controversial topic, the Talmud asserts: "If a man makes his prayers a fixed task, it is not a [genuine] supplication." By fixed task the Talmud means, according to one view, the prayer which is looked upon as a burden. It would be appropriate to introduce here the concept of attitude to commandments. The attitude one has in approaching a commandment is of singular importance. Prayer pronounced as a task, a burden, is not prayer in the intended attitude. Lacking the proper motivation, it becomes a rote exercise, something less than sincere prayer.[19]

Attitude plays a major role in other situations. Regarding the honor due to parents, the Talmud says the following: "One may give his father pheasants as food, yet [this] drives him from the world; whereas another may make him grind in a mill, and [this] brings him to the world-to-come." The differentiation made here is between one who performs his duty, but grudgingly, and another, who cannot do what he would really like, but does whatever he can with love. In the talmudic view, "Charity is rewarded only according to the kindness accompanying it." The Talmud recognized that whilst machines can coin money, only humans can transmit concern. Within the legal framework, concern cannot be pinpointed, but the ultimate value of the deed is again dependent on the individual human contribution. The deed is the structure which effects human response.[20]

In fact, as much as deed-structure is considered of ultimate necessity, there is recognition that where the value of the deed has been elicited without actualization of the deed, the purpose has been realized. Thus, "Even if one [merely] thinks of performing a precept but is forcibly prevented, the Writ ascribes it to him as though he has performed it." In the view of transcending law as springboard, even the sincere desire to fulfill a *mitzvah* propels man into the transcending dimension.[21]

In the area of attitudes there is an almost inexhaustible number of categories which are distinctly human contributions. As examples, the following may be cited: *v'anvayhu*, adorning the precepts; *hidur mitzvah*, beautifying the commandment; *hivuv mitzvah*, love of the commandment; *lishmah*, the intent for fulfilling the precept; *kavanah*, single-mindedness in fulfilling the command; *zerizut*, eagerness to fulfill the ordinance. Some combination of various of these categories is imperative to make *mitzvah* a meaningful endeavor. The proper attitude in fulfilling law is expressed with these means of approach, which are normally linked to the transcending laws, though many can be equally applied to social laws.[22]

The Human Component

As a further indication that transcending laws are deficient and miss the point when performed mechanistically, the prophet castigates the people because their fear of God "is a commandment of men learned by rote" (Isa. 29:13). Instructive here is the commentary of RaDak, who explains, "*learned by rote*, because one who does only what he is commanded and does not add of his own, does not do because he really wants or wills to."

In simple words, the law is the jumping-off point, and the real spirit of the law is captured in adding the human ingredient to it. The prophet condemns the programmed Jew, who is perfunctorily exact but who has thus reduced himself to a lifeless person, not responding to situations in the freedom and spontaneity of human conscience within the guidelines of Judaism.

In the classic talmudic definition, a *hasid shoteh*, or foolish pietist, is termed a destructive force and described as one who sees a woman drowning in the river and yet proclaims, "It is improper for me to look upon her and rescue her." This again reveals an awareness of the distortions that arise from man's interpreting law as the ultimate reality, in the process projecting stringency upon stringency to the point of denying life. Perhaps this is what the Hasidic sage had in mind when he cautioned his followers that man can make idolatry even out of commandment.[23]

Finally, it would be appropriate to mention the concept of *averah lishmah*, a transgression performed with good intentions. As the law is generally directed toward an affirmation of life, it is recognized that at times man may transgress for a greater value. To be sure, carte blanche in this instance is not forthcoming, but the mere existence of the notion is itself meaningful. Also, it is paralleled by the famous charge "live thereby," on which is based the right, even the responsibility of man to transgress in order to preserve life. If the law, properly understood, is for man and for life, a clash with life militates strongly in favor of disregarding a precept in order to preserve life. Put succinctly, the law is a means. If it is made an end, or if man would face his end because of it, the law, with few exceptions, humbly withdraws itself temporarily.[24]

Having cursorily examined the various types of law, and the categories linked to its fulfillment, it would seem ridiculous to even suggest that Judaism is legalistic. In allowing the Torah and Talmud to speak for themselves, it appears perfectly obvious that it is not in the law, but rather (in social legislation) *within* and (in transcending legislation) *through* the law that authentic Judaism is expressed. The law is the framework carefully constructed to elicit the highest level of man's social and spiritual essence. And it is this concept of Jewish law, Halakhah, which must be applied in the home if the Jewish family is to reemerge as the strong foundation of a vibrant Jewish community. For it is clear that piety, adherence to the law, is all too often superficial, and is not supported "by personal behavior behind closed doors."[25]

Appendix 2

The Marriage Crisis

The family today, aside from being one of the prime topics in social science literature, is a primary concern of all who are committed to Jewish continuity. Within the literature, there are those who insist that the family is here to stay, others who wave a happy and final goodbye to the traditional family, and many in between. For Jews, the family is much more than a subject of conversation or a museum piece to be admired. For Jews, the family is the guts of Jewish survival and growth. For ultimately, in the fate of the family inheres the fate of the Jewish community. Judaism's genesis was in the family. Judaism emerged from a union between a father, his four wives, and their twelve children; and the ensuing extended family, which moved as a group to a new location, expanded and proliferated, was redeemed, and received the Torah as a collective family.

With other religions it was the reverse. A prophet or a redeemer, claiming to have received a directive from God, shared this message with disciples who would gather up more followers voluntarily or by force. The revelation came first; the family of followers second. In Judaism the family came first; the revelation was directed to an existent family.

This societal-theological evolution of Judaism is linked to the conception of Judaism as a way of life emanating from monotheistic faith, rather than being a mere affirmation of faith. As a way of life, it flourishes when lived out in a harmonious environment.

156

For a long time the extended family, extending into a community, or later a *shtetl*, was most conducive to and appropriate for actualizing one's Jewishness.

Though there are a number of *shtetl*-like Jewish communities in North America, *shtetl* life is more history than prospect. The realities of the American lifestyle are with us, and solutions to whatever problems confront the Jewish family must be found within the context of the existing structure. Whilst one may make a very strong argument for the reintroduction of the *shtetl*, this is not likely to unfold with immediacy, nor is it likely to encompass a majority, or even a large segment, of the Jewish population. We may learn from the *shtetl*, and perhaps try to infuse the Jewish home of today with some of the values of the *shtetl*, but we must begin with the notion that we do not have the *shtetl* per se, only the memory of it.

Theological Programming

Already in the Torah there is an explicit formulation which is geared toward evolving a family structure within the Israelite community. The legislation referred to is the "sheep for each household." At the time that the Israelites were breaking loose from the yoke imposed upon them by Egypt, the commandment that was to bind them together in common observance was that each family gather to celebrate freedom by eating from a sheep. Since it was obligatory that nothing of the sheep be left over, people had to gather together in groups of significant size. The *bet avot*, or patriarchal household, as these groups were termed, comprised more than just merely a father, mother, and children. It was undoubtedly an extended family which incorporated brothers and sisters, aunts and uncles, nieces and nephews. This was a most effective countermeasure to the strategy of the Pharaohs, who, in order to destroy the fabric of the Israelite community, separated husband from wife by placing husbands far away from their homes and in extremely demanding work conditions, so that any cohabitation between husband and wife was almost impossible. I say almost impossible, because midrashic tradition indicates that the dedicated wives of yesteryear found a way around the edict, and the Israelite community was saved from extinction.[1]

However, to invigorate the community on a family basis, the notion of celebrating as a family was introduced, by the Torah, to counter the aforementioned strategy of splitting families at the very core. The extended family was a response to the undermining of the family through enforced separation of husband from wife.

Marital Stability

From the strategy it seems clear, and experience bears out this observation, that family stability and coherence begin with a solid relationship between husband and wife. Since they are the ones who generate the family that emanates from them, they also dictate the nature and conditions of family life. A healthy marriage is the prime requisite for a healthy family. An unstable marriage gives birth to a family which is built on shaky foundations.

There are many factors which have imposed themselves on the American family of today, yet the most important factor impacting on the family is the rate of divorce, or, in more general terms, the pervasiveness of marital unhappiness. Demographic projections indicate that half of the first marriages now taking place will end in divorce, and that, on the whole, over 40 percent of all individuals who are now of marriageable age will at some time or another in their lives experience a divorce. This must have a devastating effect on the entire notion of family.[2]

Of course, many side matters become affected by the increasing rate of divorce. Alternative types of arrangements, such as cohabitating without marriage, seem to flourish in this type of environment. Childbearing, with the risks that are involved for the child from a ruptured marriage, is also affected.

As in so many of these situations, the chicken-egg problem prevails. There are those who claim that it is precisely the desire to have fewer children that has led to a higher rate of marital instability, rather than marital instability leading to having fewer children. Whatever the case, the prospect for American society is not a very optimistic one, and beckons for a massive effort to examine what is at the root of the problem, and how to stem this dangerous tide.[3]

The Jewish Scene

The situation in America generally has impacted on the American Jewish community. Admittedly, reliable statistics on divorce are not so forthcoming, and we are left essentially with conjectures based on observation, and based on reports of the feverish activity that goes on in most Jewish courts to finalize divorces. Given that the allegation that the divorce rate amongst American Jews is about the same as the general American divorce rate is slightly exaggerated, nevertheless even the fact that some talk in these terms indicates how the situation has deteriorated. A recent study indicated that in 1977 there were approximately 1,000 divorces amongst Canada's Jews, and the number of divorces in the years since then have been at least that number. Extrapolated to the United States, this would mean that there have been close to 18,000 divorces yearly. This is based on the assumed Canadian Jewish population of 300,000 and the assumed American Jewish population of approximately 5.5 million. The fact that a recent study showed that 31,700 Jewish families in the New York metropolitan area are single-parent families would seem to be indication enough that the estimate of 18,000 divorces per year in the last few years is not that off base. Added to this is the natural tendency of Canada to be more conservative than the United States. Give or take a few thousand, the 18,000 statistic is not only astounding but also quite alarming. It indicates the depths of the crisis and the necessity for immediate and effective action to counter this encroachment upon the basic fabric of the Jewish family, and hence, upon the foundation of the Jewish community.[4]

Why the Increase in Divorce?

Whilst every divorce is a personal situation, and it is difficult to deal with personal, private situations in grandiose, generalized terms, nevertheless analysts of American society have tried to pinpoint the reasons for the spate of divorces. According to Robert Weiss, a leading sociologist, the ethic of self-realization is a prime factor in the increasing rate of divorce. Weiss contends that in all the divorces he has studied the ethic of self-realization has been an important factor in the split, if not the primary factor. This is narcissism at its very worst. A recent analysis of the growing divorce rate in Orthodox Jewish life attributes part of the blame to the lack of ability to give of oneself and to show even a small degree of selflessness within marriage. This observation indicates that what has impacted on American life in general has crept into Jewish family dynamics.[5]

Among other reasons suggested for the increasing rate of divorce amongst Jews are that (1) people can afford to get divorced today and manage economically afterwards; (2) there is less emphasis on "we" and more on "I" in the family context; (3) there is an increasing boredom with day-to-day family life; (4) there is less commitment to working out problems; (5) there is no more backdrop of Jewish religious family values to serve as an inspiration; (6) Jewish males have forgotten what it means to be a father and husband and instead see themselves as wage-earner, golfer, and organization man; and (7) Jewish women, in their rush to emancipation, desire to play too many roles at the same time—something has to give, and often it is the family.[6]

Another view of the situation suggests that the American family is being undermined by divisive societal forces making harmony, cooperation, and affection a rarity both in and out of families. The trend toward self-aggrandizement, exploitativeness, and titillation instead of commitment, involvement, and tenderness is a major factor in the problem. Individualism has become egocentrism. Anything done for someone else must bring personal gain, so that young children are often seen as a pleasureless burden. The family itself becomes the main arena for the exercises of self-fulfillment, and young people therefore see their families as prisons. The possibilities of family, which previously excited parents, now scare them. Additionally, caring seems to be equated with losing and mutual protectiveness is missing.[7]

This apparent consumerism of emotions has reduced human

life to its base functionality and stripped it of its spontaneity and warmth. The result is not only a higher divorce rate and increasing level of marital unhappiness, but also family disintegration, with a concomitant increase in such problems as drug and alcohol abuse, crime, delinquency, and suicide. The spiral effect that this can engender is further cause for alarm. People see the failure of marriage, and thus are likely to be very careful about getting married. This is reflected in the statistics concerning the Jewish community, amongst which the study of the Boston Jewish population is most revealing. There, 73 percent of the adult Jewish population were married in 1965, but by 1975 only 56 percent were married. In the same period, those within the twenty-one to twenty-nine age group had a rate of 42 percent married in 1975, as compared to 58 percent in 1965. Additionally, within the same ten-year span, the percentage of the Jewish population which was single rose from 14 percent to 32 percent.[8]

No part of the Jewish community seems to be immune from the trend to divorce. According to the estimates of the guidance counselor in a large girls' high school in Boro Park, Brooklyn, 8 percent of the approximately 1,000 girls came from homes where the parents were divorced. This indicates the inroads that divorce is making even in circles which heretofore were thought to be immune to American social trends. Even a more *shtetl*-like community such as Boro Park cannot claim to be that separate an entity from American society as a whole. This has led to the very sobering prediction of one noted student of the American Jewish scene that one out of every two Jews who marry in the 1980s will be divorced by 1990. That prediction, in fact, correlates with the exact same prediction that is made by demographers for American society as a whole.[9]

Success as Failure

We should not leave the problem area of divorce without pointing to an observation made more than a decade ago concerning the possibility that some marriages fail not because they are bad but because they are good. Richard Farson suggested that good marriages fail more often than bad ones and that they fail precisely because they are good. Akin to the finding that revolutions break out not when conditions are at their worst, but when they have just begun to get better, marriages, too, fall prey to the syndrome of rising expectations.[10]

It is not rare, in this period when so many marriages are disintegrating, that we are on occasion taken aback by the collapse of what overtly seemed to be a most admirable union. The natural reaction, of course, is to retroactively analyze the situation and shoot holes into the relationship so that one can rationalize away the separation with the argument that the marriage was not so good after all. However, many rabbis and counselors who are on the inside of such situations and are privy to the real condition of the marriage will remain perplexed about the need for divorce even after they know most of the facts.

There are situations where the marriage not only looks good, it actually is good, and yet separation ensues. The couple may still like each other, may enjoy each other's company, have their present and future well taken care of, have common leisure-time pursuits, respect each other, and even be in love. This does not seem to penetrate the logical brain of the typical Western Hemisphere individual. If things are so good, why are they so bad? The types of comments which usually flow from the separation of a good union are (1) We have simply grown apart; (2) I feel trapped in the relationship; (3) We are not communicating; or (4) There must be more to life than what we are getting from this marriage.

Farson suggests that it is highly probable there is nothing wrong with this type of marriage, nothing that makes it worse than others. There is no brutality, mental anguish, adultery, or any of the common justifications for divorce. Instead, the separation emanates from the perception of what the marriage is and the higher order of possibilities that are presently just a dream and which do not seem realizable in the context of marriage. As in the case of revolutions, such infatuation with possibility stems from having a taste of the good life, from having a relatively successful marriage which has whetted the appetite for more peaks. Illogical as it may sound, good marriages may fail because they are good and generate the hope for better things. Farson lists eight sources for the discontent that may be present in a good marriage.

1. *Discontent arises because the basic needs of the marriage have been satisfied.* Human beings often seem to be dissatisfied with what they have, especially when they are aware that there is more to have. The satisfaction of a certain level of needs may often give birth to higher-level needs. This is a type of demand situation which can exert great pressure on good marriages. Farson suggests that marriage was never intended to be as good as it is. It evolved from a survival mechanism to a security mechanism to a convenience mechanism. Now, however, marriage is expected to include intellectual companionship, moments of intimacy, value-sharing, romantic love, etc. There is pressure on marriage to be everybody's panacea. The fact that it is an almost impossible task leads to more frustration and discontent.[11]

2. *Discontent arises because mass education and mass media have taught people to expect too much from marriage.* So many today are exposed to the marriage ideal in song, in book, in television, in film; the American ideal of a smoothly functioning nuclear family. Aside from the fact that the nuclear family is falling by the wayside, what with the high divorce rate and the increasing number of single-parent families, the fact is that the nuclear family is not as ideal a setup as the Hollywood moguls would have the public believe. People have unrealistic expectations based on false media projections. Just seeing the idyllic bliss of a plastic marriage either on television or in the movies, with all of its peak pleasures, may subtly work on a couple and convince them that theirs does not measure up to the Hollywood ideal. Hollywood, of course, is a disaster area of its own, but its grand and unrealistic visions have certainly not helped those outside its perimeter. When it becomes obvious that their marriage does not conform to the ideal, a couple may decide to call it quits, erroneously and unfortunately.[12]

3. *Discontent arises because couples succeed in fulfilling their masculine and feminine roles.* Contrary to the view that the tender, gentle, understanding, feminine woman is a perfect companion for the firm, strong, aggressive, dominant male, it seems as if such apparently perfect matches are too limiting and demanding. Both men and women are seeking liberation from these stereotypes. Marriage reinforces the stereotypes and often allows for no escape within the marriage context from these imposed rules.

When either spouse demands this role of the other it creates pressures which are so intense they lead to separation.[13]

4. *Discontent arises because marriage now embraces a new concept of sexual fulfillment.* There is a new and wider range of sexual performance which is expected within marriage. "How to" books proliferate, and the successful peak experience only gives rise to the expectations of an even peakier experience next time. Ups and downs are not allowed, only highs.[14]

5. *Discontent arises because marriage counseling, psychotherapy, and other efforts to improve marriage actually make it more difficult.* Counselors often urge couples to live at their best, which increases rather than decreases the pressure on and the complexity of the relationship. Added to this, if decent communication is achieved in the therapeutic hour, the partners of an apparently failing marriage must wonder why this cannot carry over into the home. They reach the conclusion that it is the other partner who is at fault. Farson suggests that counseling gives the person the feeling of being in charge of life when in fact individuals are often locked into situations over which they have no control. Initiatives are frustratingly lacking when it is a nonchangeable situation that is at the root of the difficulty. Counseling does very little to change marriages. The fact that psychotherapists and marriage counselors have a high incidence of separation and divorce is an example of damage rendered by constant attention to marriage.[15]

6. *Discontent arises because marriages suffer from the gains made in the consciousness revolution.* Over 6 million Americans have participated in encounter groups of one form or another, experiences which have their moments of intimate beauty, giving birth to the rising-expectation syndrome. The premium placed on complete truthfulness in these groups is something which cannot carry over into marriage. Also, the encounter experience is divorced from reality. The level of intimacy when one is divorced from reality is obviously higher than what should be expected amidst the daily demands placed on a couple.[16]

7. *Discontent arises because of fantasies about what other marriages are like.* We sometimes fall prey to the images of the marriages of friends who feel they must camouflage their difficulties by posturing a most blissful union. Too many people fall for this ruse and think that therefore their union is not as healthy.[17]

8. *Discontent arises from comparing the marriage relationship with itself in its better moments.* Couples often have good moments together which are followed by valleys. This is to be expected, but often may lead to the frustrating question, "Why can't today be like yesterday?" The birth of children and the focusing away of the wife from the husband toward the child is an acute crisis.[18]

Inflated expectations, exaggerated notions of pleasurable fulfillment, an awkward, imbalanced focus on the self, all symptomatic of the narcissistic personality, are at work in the scenario that is spelled out by Farson.

Farson's insights indicate how far-reaching the problem is. Divorce has become an expected "luxury," almost a function of a distinct North American philosophy, but it is a luxury that society can ill afford if it is to remain stable, and if its products, namely the children, are to develop as wholesome individuals.

Agenda for the Future

Perhaps the realization that present trends are heading toward massive, overwhelming problems has led to a serious soul-searching. The American couple of today is preoccupied with questions of immediate moment dealing with the marital relationship. Questions of how men and women should relate to each other, what is fair and just, where should compromise operate, what are the rightful provinces of the male and the female, whose needs will prevail in steering their relationship, how should the breakdown of responsibilities for earning a livelihood and taking care of the house and the children unfold, and primarily, over and above everything else, "is there any formula which can make marriage work," occupy the attention of the American couple. "There are many couples in America today who would accept any division of household chores, of emotional skills, of dominance, if they could just protect, preserve, or restore their relationship."[19]

The problem, however, is that there are so many different problem areas that can impact upon the marriage, and also so many different variables, that choosing the right options is an almost impossible task. "Perhaps the older arrangement, in retrospect, was not so glorious, but it was structured and orderly. There were few choices and it was not considered appropriate to complain. Now there are so many decisions that one is liable to make serious errors in judgement. Everything is in flux and the priorities are not clear."[20]

What about the Jewish couple? Is the Jewish couple in the same bind as the American couple? Is the Jewish couple faced with the same multitude of choices and thus burdened with weighty decisions? The answer is yes and no. The Jewish couple has as many choices, or almost as many choices, as its non-Jewish counterpart. However, as in the past, there is a corpus of legislation, known as the Halakhah, which has always guided Jewish life, and which beckons to be reintegrated, on a profound level, into the contemporary Jewish family. The Halakhah is a framework which creates a context, as well as a dynamic and an ethic which establish the basis for interaction. The Halakhah does not take away individual choice, not does it choke off individual contributions, but it does establish a basic contextual framework within which it is easier for the couple, committed to the concept and the intent of the Halakhah, to bring out the best in each other, and to thus forge a family unit which can serve as the solid foundation for the Jewish community of today and tomorrow.

Notes

1. The reference is to Philip Blumstein and Pepper Schwartz, *American Couples*. Here four groups are treated together—married couples, cohabitors (men and women living together but not legally married), gay couples, and lesbian couples—and conclusions are drawn comparing the four.

2. Regarding loneliness being a pervasive condition, see Robert Weiss, *Loneliness*. Here it is claimed that at any time, about 25 percent of the population are likely to say they are lonely (p. 1). For some, the loneliness may be a passing phase, so that the 25 percent does not involve the same people at all times.

3. On intermarriage rates, see Fred Massarik, *Intermarriage*. The intermarriage rate derived from this early (1970) study was 37 percent (i.e., more than one out of three marriages involving Jews were intermarriages.) Also, 43 percent of the population surveyed saw nothing wrong with intermarrige, and among the then twenty to twenty-nine age group, about three-quarters saw nothing wrong with intermarriage. The statistics of actual intermarriage are actually much better than the statistics for potential intermarriage, and suggest that things may get much worse before they get better.

4. See *Kiddushin* 68b and further in *Even HaEzer* 44:8 and *Hilkhot Ishut* 4:15. Rambam states that they are as married after the ceremony as before.

5. On the unmarried person being incomplete, see *Yevamot* 63a. The *Zohar* to Leviticus (1:2) asserts that anyone who does not marry is deficient and that a male without a female is not a total person. The talmudic idea that a man without a wife, a he without a she, and therefore not part of a "them," is not a person (*adam*) derives from the language of the Torah, which says that God called "them" Adam (Gen. 5:2).

6. Pertaining to original creation, see *Eruvin* 18a. See Rashi to Gen. 2:22, that the word *tzela* refers to a side; thus original Adam had two equal sides, a male and a female side, and Eve came into autonomous being through something akin to a Siamese section.

Relevant to the oneness of the male and female, see *Akedat Yitzhak* to Gen. 2:21 (*Shaar* 8, *Perek HaHibur*—entire section), who suggests that woman was made from Adam so that they would be more similar and their love stronger.

On marriage being the natural condition of man and woman, see Rabad's

167

introduction to his classic work *Baaley HaNefesh*, where he stresses this point. On the mystical side, the *Reshit Ḥakhmah* of Eliyahu de Vidas remarks that when souls are created, male and female souls are created together, and they reunite at the wedding (*Shaar Kedushah* 16).

7. On marrying even in the twilight years, see *Yevamot* 61b and 62b. See further *Even HaEzer* 1:8 and *Hilkhot Ishut* 15:16.

8. On the notion of emulating God, see *Sotah* 14a, where clothing the needy, visiting the sick, and comforting the mourners are included in the imperative to emulate God. See further *Hilkhot De'ot* 1:5 and 1:6. There the Rambam argues that the balanced approach fulfills the primary obligation to emulate God.

For more on achieving completeness by focusing outward, see R. Shlomoh Wolbe, *Aley Shur*, p. 255. R. Eliyahu Dessler (*Mikhtav M'Eliyahu, Kuntrus Ha-Ḥesed*, chap. 6) states that ideal love comes through each completing the other, since a person who is alone is deficient and cannot fulfill the purpose of life; therefore when each engenders the other's completeness, the love for one another is enhanced.

9. Related to the longer life expectancy associated with marriage, Frances Kobrin and Gerry Hendershot, in a 1976 presentation to the American Sociological Association, reported that lonely men have a mortality rate 94 percent higher than married men. This report is further reviewed in *Family and Marriage Newsletter* 1, no. 1 (1977).

A more thorough treatment of the connection between marriage and longevity is found in James Lynch, *The Broken Heart*, pp. 38–55. Lynch musters a wealth of data to support his claim that for both sexes of all races and at all ages in the United States, the death rate for nonmarrieds is always higher than for marrieds, and sometimes five times higher.

Relative to the link between marriage and depression, see *Family and Marriage Newsletter* 5, no. 1 (1980), for elaboration on the study of George Warkeit and Charles Holzer, which monitored 7,000 adult subjects over ten years. They concluded that people without husbands or wives are most susceptible to depression.

10. On the expounding of the laws of the festival thirty days before the festival, see for example *Pesaḥim* 6a.

The point about more than thirty days being needed to prepare for marriage is found in the approbation of R. Shlomoh Wolbe to *Binyan Aday Aḥd*. The name of the author of this publication is not given. In the handwritten approbation of R. Wolbe, the name of the author is whited out. From the appellation preceding the white-out, it appears to have been written by a rabbi of distinction, and aside from certain inaccuracies is a very useful work.

On the responsibility of parents and teachers to the next generation, see R. Shlomoh Wolbe, *Kuntrus Hadrakhah LeKalot*, where the author claims that the present generation, unlike the pre–World War II generation, has much difficulty in handling problems, and is likely to run to psychologists or to swallow tranquilizers. The author of *Binyan Aday Ahd* suggests that yeshivot should be alert to the need for personality development (p. 15). For a fuller treatment of this issue, see my "Divorce: The Problem and the Challenge."

11. Regarding locus of search, it is worth noting that matchmakers, or the modern counterpart, the computer, are being used by some segments of society. For more on the *shadkhan*, see below, n. 28.

On the essentiality of meaningful personal encounter before deciding to marry, see *Yevamot* 52a and *Kiddushin* 12b, *Even HaEzer* 26:4, and Rambam, *Hilkhot Ishut* 3:22 and *Hilkhot Isuray Biah* 21:14. The prohibition forbidding marriage without *shidukh* (deliberate efforts at matchmaking) is designed to prevent haphazard unions that are entered into without proper care and consideration.

12. Relative to dating, textbooks such as *Marriage,* by Bob and Margaret Blood, reflecting the societal pattern, see the dating period as an end in itself, a form of recreation (p. 18).

On the matter of dating as an opportunity for a good time, it is obvious that this can lead to exploitation. Lester Kirkendall, *Premarital Intercourse and Interpersonal Relations,* has some vivid illustrations of this (pp. 84–114). See also Suzanne Gordon, *Lonely in America,* pp. 65–84, 213–246. Generally men resort more to sexual exploitation and women to economic exploitation. Hardly recreation.

On the quality of the time spent together, R. Eliyahu Dessler, in *Mikhtav M'Eliyahu* (pt. 1, p. 74) makes the telling point that today, with more knowing before the wedding, one would assume that marriage would work better than when the parents chose, but in fact the opposite is true, and marriage today is in crisis.

There may be more than a casual link between long premarital getting-to-know and marriage failure, although some are likely to claim that the spate of divorces presently being encountered reflects liberalization of the attitude to divorce more than anything else, and that many in previous generations would have divorced if it had been as acceptable. That is a conjecture difficult to prove or disprove. What can be stated is that long periods of getting-to-know may at times reflect a distancing and analytic approach, instead of throwing oneself into the relationship. Constant scrutiny will eventually yield reasons for terminating the union. Acceptance of the other, once the main compatibility concerns have been ironed out, is more likely to lead to unconditional partnership.

13. On the matter of telling lies, see Exod. 23:7 and Lev. 19:11. See further on this the discussion of *shalom bayit* in Chapter 5.

14. See *Ketuvot* 17a, where the ultimate compliment given to a bride is that though she has no makeup or flamboyant hair-style, she is still full of grace. The natural self is more real, and thus more worthy of praise. The one who is well made up *looks* beautiful, the one who naturally effuses gracefulness *is* beautiful.

15. R. Shlomoh Wolbe, in *Maamaray Hadrakhah LeHatanim,* p. 1, warns that this is a real danger. This volume and Wolbe's aforementioned *Kuntrus Ha-*

drakhah LeKalot are relatively recent and quite insightful pamphlets, the former for grooms, the latter for brides.

16. Concerning winning over one's mate on a continual basis, R. Tsvi Travis, in *Pirkey Hanhagat HaBayit*, pt. 1, emphasizes this point. He asserts that one knows how to win over a woman prior to marriage (p. 46) and this should serve as a model for after marriage (p. 49).

17. Concerning economic crisis and the addition of children, modern texts on marriage view finances and children as major crises that can affect the marriage. See, for example, the relatively popular university text by Bob and Margaret Blood, *Marriage*, the first edition of which appeared in 1962 and the third in 1978.

18. Compare Exod. 19:16 and 20:15 with Exod. 34:29 and the lack of any fanfare in the transmission of the second set of commandments. See also Rashi to Exod. 34:3.

19. On the matter of euphoria at having found one who can do no wrong, see Louis Birner, "Unconscious Resistance to Pre-marital Counseling." He sees undeflatable elation as a potentially negative sign (p. 25).

Relative to the issue of falling in love, Ernest Havemann once observed that orientals get married first and then fall in love, but in the west the order is reversed.

The idea of marriage as a significant plateau on the way up is a model suggested by Isaac, who took Rebekah as his wife and then liked her (Gen. 24:67). Rebekah fit the parameters for a marital partner, Isaac embarked on his life journey in marriage with her, and the love came as the relationship evolved.

Relative to ultimate significance, infatuation obscures the long-range perspective. The long-range perspective allows one to maintain control. Thus, Jacob, who saw in Rachel the ideal partner for his life, worked seven years to gain her hand, and those seven years were like a few days (Gen. 29:20). In real love, renunciation is possible, and a long time is like a short time; not the reverse, as with infatuation.

20. See *Sotah* 2a, where the Talmud associates the ease of matchmaking—the heavenly voice–type, with one's first marriage, and the complicated matchmaking—the splitting-of-the-sea type, with second marriage. Meiri ad loc. sees any marriage entered into after twenty years of age as a second marriage, i.e., in the more-difficult-to-arrange category.

21. Concerning deservedness, Rambam, in the eighth chapter of *Shmonah Prakim*, asserts that with all the Heavenly intervention, the choice of one's mate is a free-willed human choice, and depends on individual deservedness.

On the evolving nature of marriage, see *Akedat Yitzhak* to Genesis (*Shaar* 8, end of first section), who claims that "second marriage" (see above, n. 20) refers to a person's choice, and that effectively most marriages fit into that category. *Binyan Aday Ahd* (p. 82) cites a view that the day after the wedding the marriage becomes a second marriage. To this is applied the talmudic statement that a person is matched with the mate that is deserved (*Sotah* 2a). How marriage unfolds, then, is effectively a matter of deservedness, and one is ill-advised to rely on luck. The luck part ends on the day after the wedding; or, in the view of the *Akedah*, never really started.

22. On the importance of physical attractiveness, see Rambam, *Hilkhot Ishut* 3:19 and *Hilkhot Isuray Biah* 21:3, where, following *Kiddushin* 41a, he asserts that it is proper to actually look carefully *(lehistakel)* at one's prospective mate before marrying. See Rabad's rejection of Rambam's position, and the defense of Rambam by the *Maggid Mishnah*. See also *Even HaEzer* 35:1.

Binyan Aday Ahd, acknowledging that undesirable features may discourage a prospective mate, and that this occurred even among the luminaries of Jewish tradition, suggests that if the blemish continues to be irksome one should call off the relationship, but if it bothers the concerned party less and less, then the relationship is worth furthering.

Concerning misrepresentation, *Sefer Ḥasidim* (sec. 507) insists that there be no coverup of blemishes or faults that may possibly cause the other party to call off the marriage.

Relative to height, see *Bekhorot* 45b, where it is stated that a tall man should not marry a tall woman, lest their children be excessively tall, and a short man should not marry a short woman, lest their children be exceedingly short.

On the matter of age, see *Yevamot* 101b. The community intervened to prevent marriages between an old person and a young mate. See also *Sanhedrin* 76b.

23. Pertinent to beauty and marrying one who is characterologically fit, R. Eliezer Papo, in *Pele Yo'etz*, under the word *yofee*, encourages the match which combines virtue and beauty. However, marriage with an unfit type is severely condemned (*Kiddushin* 70a). See further Tosefta, *Sotah* 5:6. The Hebrew for "face," *panim*, relates to the Hebrew for "inside," *pnim*. The external, *panim*, beauty derives from the inner, *pnim*, beauty of character.

24. On the importance of one's mate being of noble character, R. Shlomoh Aviner, in *Pirkey Ahavah Bayn Ish L'Ishto*, p. 20, asserts that having a mate who is of good character even though not the daughter of a sage is more important and better than having a mate who emanates from sages but is of poor character.

Having sensitivity, a sense of responsibility, and acting kindly—this is a reference to the three classic identification traits of the Israelite people— *rahamanim* (sensitive), *byshanim* (lit., having a sense of shame, which translates as guilt for not living up to responsibility; thus *byshanim* equals having a sense of responsibility), and *gomlay ḥasadim* (inclined to act kindly) (*Yevamot* 79a). See *Hilkhot Isuray Biah* 19:17.

Relative to brazenness, see *Hilkhot Isuray Biah* 19:17, where Rambam states that arrogance actually raises questions of pedigree.

Maharal, in *Netivot Olam*, claims that the arrogant person refuses to be influenced for the better and cannot give to others (*Netiv HaBushah*, chap. 2). Such behavior hardly conduces to marriage.

Concerning the statement that those of deficient character should be avoided as marriage partners, Blood and Blood (*Marriage*, p. 115) remark that it is foolhardy to think that change will come automatically after marriage. Marriage does not change personality.

The matter of communal education toward proper behavior is a major crisis facing the Jewish community. For further reading on this issue, see *Reuven P. Bulka*, ed., *Dimensions of Orthodox Judaism*, especially the introduction and the article by Irving Levitz, "Crisis in Orthodoxy: The Ethical Paradox."

25. On the importance of one's family background, see *Pesaḥim* 49; also *Even HaEzer* 6:2, *Hilkhot Isuray Biah* 21:32.

On the overriding importance of the stature of the potential partner, R. Joseph Epstein, in *Sefer Mitzvot HaBayit*, vol. 2, in "Kuntrus HaB'ḥirah V'haGzerah," cites the *Ollelot Efrayim* that the entire issue of pedigree is presently in doubt, that *yiḥus* (pedigree) is more linked with wealth and honor than with real essentials, so that attention should be focused on the plant itself, not on the roots (p. 128).

That a child may surpass the parents is self-evident. It is interesting to note that *Toray Zahav* to *Even HaEzer* 2, n. 3, states that a woman who understands the meaning of Torah for life is not in the category of "daughter of a boor" even if in fact her father is one. *Binyan Aday Ahd* cites the Ḥazon Ish as having stated that a girl who attends a *haredi* school is in fact a "daughter of a sage," a daughter who is herself as a sage (p. 26).

26. On the primacy of virtuous behavior, see *Pesaḥim* 49b. A girl from a family of sages is considered most preferable. If such is not available, a *gadol hador* (people of action and righteousness) family is next on the preference list, followed by heads of congregations (rabbis), and then by the *gabba'ay zedakah* (dispensers of charity), who, as Rashi comments, are invariably good and trustworthy people. The accent, it is clear, is on families with traditions of virtuous behavior.

That scholarship which does not translate into deeds is not true scholarship is reflected in the statement that "Study is not the essential, deed is the essential" (*Avot* 1:17). The very term for "scholar," *talmid ḥakham* (lit. "wise student"), is instructive. Wise yes, but yet a student, aware there is much to learn, much to improve. The true sage is humble and eager, and as such is accorded the priority of family preference.

The division between intellectual capacity and personality comes through in the remark by Wolbe, in *Maamaray Hadrakhah LeHatanim*, cautioning against looking for a learning partner when choosing a mate (p. 14).

27. The matter of choosing a mate with whom one is at ease reflects the statement of *Birkay Yosef* to *Even HaEzer* 2:3, who suggests that if one is more comfortable with a mate who is of simple pedigree but noble character than with a possible choice from an imposing family which makes one feel less than comfortable, then the more comfortable choice is the better one. The comment (*Yalkut Shimoni* to Proverbs 5) that happy is the one whose mate is from the same

city points to this notion. One is more likely to be familiar and at ease with a hometown person.

The importance of parental input into the choice of marital partner is evident in the findings of Ernest Burgess and Paul Wallin, in *Engagement and Marriage*, that when both parents objected, the chances of the relationship breaking up were significantly greater than when both approved (pp. 560–562). This may also point to the power of parents to influence children, but at the same time reflects the insight parents have into what are their children's needs.

Too much association with parents can be harmful, as per the observation of Stewart Ostrov, in "Problems Confronting the Orthodox Jewish Family in America," who points out that there is a problem with marriages in which the child chooses a mate to fit the parents' image (p. 23).

On the right of a child to reject parental choice, see the gloss of R. Moshe Isserles to *Yoreh Deah* 140:25, who states that a son is not obliged to heed his father's objections of marital choice. See also *Ziz Eliezer* (vol. 13, sec. 78), who states that the rule applies equally for a daughter relative to parental objections.

Examples of exceptions to the general circumstance where parents desire what is best for their children are when parents look at status or wealth for their children, and in the process, however well intentioned, impose a choice that may be uncomfortable and undesired.

28. Concerning the matchmaker, the observations of Eleanor Stoker Boll in "Should Parents or Cupid Arrange Marriages?" are quite interesting. Keeping in mind that the piece was written in 1959, the merits of what she says have not lapsed with time. The review of her piece which follows originally appeared in the *Family and Marriage Newsletter* 3, no. 1 (1978).

"Boll begins her article by referring to a remark of Dr. Marie Finger Bale, who after five years in India observed that there might be fewer divorces in the United States if Americans took a cue from the Indians. She observed that in India divorce is almost unknown because 'parents select their children's spouses and control their children's lives even after marriage.' It is obviously difficult to transport a foreign custom into an alien culture and expect it to work miracles, yet Boll points out that something must be done because the United States is becoming conspicious for marital failure, with a divorce rate of about one for every four marriages. It is, therefore, useful to at least see if some parts of the Indian system of arranged marriages could be adopted, says Boll.

"The Hindu joint family system is geared towards achieving continuity of the family line—its reputation, status, and property. Families negotiate mating of children with those of similar religion and status, and who are of good health and character. The children themselves are considered too immature to make this terribly important decision; parents often will engage their children at an early age to a member of another family. The parents maintain control even after marriage, because the young couple live permanently with the parents of the bridegroom, who control, through strict supervision, the personal, social, and family life of the couple. The bridegroom's mother also controls the finances. Anything earned by the children goes into a family purse, which is disbursed by the mother at her discretion. The system perpetuates itself through the oldest son and his wife taking over control when the parents die.

"This type of arrangement and control is not indigenous to India, and is practiced in such countries as China, Japan, and in the Arab world. Free choice does exist, but the old tradition does not wither away so quickly, especially since it worked quite well in maintaining the stability of the family, protecting it and ensuring its survival.

"Boll points out that the argument for 'arranged marriages in the United States' and if not arranged marriages, at least more parental input and control, is based on the fact that the average marriage takes place at an early age. One out of every three girls who marries for the first time is 18 or under and the most frequent ages for first marriages are 21 and 22 for boys and 18 and 19 for girls. The judgment of those who marry at such a young age seems questionable. Dr. Judson Landis of the University of California found that divorce rates where both spouses were under 21 at the time of marriage were six times higher than in marriages where both spouses were 31 or over at the time of marriage. According to a selected sampling in the United Nations Demographic Year Book of 1958, 22.5% of divorced women were 24 or under and 24% of those who had been divorced were married for less than two years.

"Another argument for parental input is the fact that young people are inexperienced. They are in high school until the age of 18, in college until the age of 22, and then they go into education for career specialization. During this time, many want to marry, but they are ill-prepared for marriage and parenthood. Intellectual compatibility is often mistaken for an abiding love. (One senses a trend away from the rush to marry amongst college students today. The liberal trends have opened up other options for many, but the problems Boll speaks about have not disappeared.)

"Boll further points out that one out of every five Americans changes residence every year, so that many children are likely to have moved to different neighborhoods and schools five times before completing high school. This makes it increasingly difficult for American youngsters to learn more about the qualities of their friends, and is all the more reason why parental guidance and assistance is most desirable. Children today live in a melting pot with other individuals of different religious, racial, social, and economic backgrounds. The child who rebels against family traditions is likely, at least for a fleeting period, to be enticed by what appears to be different, but Boll points out that many studies indicate that inter-racial and inter-religious marriages lead to more broken homes than when the backgrounds are similar. Moreover, if marriage ends in disaster, it is often left for the family to help heal the wounds of the disappointed lover. This might involve children of a young lady who is often too immature to handle the kids, who now become children of their grandparents.

"Since so much of the burden of failed marriages falls onto the shoulders of the parents, it is not unreasonable to allow them some input into the marriage itself. This point is accentuated by the observation of Dr. Carle C. Zimmerman of Harvard, who found in a study of the family throughout history that the strength of a nation follows in close parallel to the solidarity of its family system. Thus, those young lovers who feel that what they are doing is 'their own thing' may, in fact, be contributing to the undermining of society.

"This is the one side of the coin. On the other hand, Boll points out, arranged marriages are not particularly suited to the free-flowing society in which we live. Arranged marriages are often insensitive and reflect only parental whim, without taking into account the child's feelings. Often the female of the species is hit the hardest because she is in a most vulnerable position. Male chauvinism and arranged marriages are a particularly bad mix. It is not unheard of in some situations that an older man would be married to a very young girl to bear him children. He will then die and she will be left a widow from the age of 20 or so. Even if this is an unlikely scenario in our part of the world, nevertheless the danger of insensitivity to children's desires still exists. Old world parents might want to restrict their children to their own mold; they might be status-seekers who would sacrifice their children on the altar of social prominence; they may place such a great emphasis on marriage that they push their children into early disaster; or, for self-serving reasons, they might want to prevent an early marriage. Added to this, it may be argued that if the children themselves only know their mates superficially, the parents could not really know the mates any better.

"The higher education the younger generation receives today also may make it difficult for the parents to really know what their children need. The trump card of arranged marriages, which is, of course, the financial and emotional support system, is perhaps not so prominent where children are able to support themselves.

"Boll points out that another fly in the ointment is the thinness of family emotional relationships. This is precisely what drives many children into early marriage, and it is entirely dubious whether parents who have fared poorly in their own marriages can do much better for their children. Culturally, there is also a vast gap in conceptions of love between 'arranged marriage societies' and America. Love is a minor factor in arranged marriages, especially when the couple to be wed have not even seen each other before the wedding and where romance before marriage is looked upon suspiciously. Americans have placed a primacy on love and romantic affection as a basis for marriage. This may be a questionable choice, but when it is combined with a sharing of common values, it provides for a good family and a healthy atmosphere for children. This generates and perpetuates a content and happy atmosphere for future generations.

"These are the two sides of the coin. What is the mediating point between the two alternatives? Boll, after having conducted many studies on American marriage at the William T. Carter Foundation, reaches the conclusion that there should be more control over marriages exerted by the law, by the parents, by the public, and by educators. She questions the wisdom of laws which allow boys in certain states to marry without parental consent at the age of 18 and girls at 16. Laws cannot solve problems, but should also not encourage problems. She recommends that parents take a more active role in conditioning children towards good marriage in their earlier years. Children should feel that marriage is a responsibility to the family and parents should give the children a sense of pride in the traditions and values of their family, race, religion, and/or social class. This would hopefully avoid the conflicts of cross-cultural marriages. The parents should control the selection of their children's friends from an early age, so that the children learn to prefer certain types. Of course, this places an obligation upon the parents to choose an environment where the desired choices are available. Furthermore, parents should be open enough with their children to discuss the ups and downs of their own marriage, so that the children have a realistic view of the good and bad points as they enter into the age of marital eligibility.

"Boll further points out that public opinion must be mobilized to back up the parental role. If what she writes was true in 1959, it is even more true today that the parental role in marriage is looked upon with skepticism at least, and most often disdain. The American ideal of equality militates in favor of cross-cultural marriages, flying in the face of evidence that where values are not shared, the union is likely to fail. The emphasis in marriage on personal compatibility, to the exclusion of traditional continuity, does not bode well for parental input. Experts in the field of marital counseling are likely to take anti-parent approaches when counseling a soon-to-be-married couple.

"In the final analysis, it is up to the parents to instill a confidence in their children through openness and true concern, which reflects back when the time comes. If parents, who usually mean the best for their children, actually give children their best, they are likely to be respected and their advice and counsel is likely to be heeded. So far the remarks of Boll.

"These insights offered by Boll are quite fascinating for the Jewish community. They immediately conjure up visions of the re-introduction of the 'shadkhan' into the communal framework. We are no longer immune to divorce as we thought we were and statistically, one could probably make a good argument for the fact that arranged marriages have worked at least as well, if not better than non-arranged marriages. There are dangers, of course, in taking this to an extreme.

"There are many ingredients which go into a good marriage and the love ingredient should not be neglected, but the evidence seems to be that love flowers best in an atmosphere of shared values. Boll's caution against the parents being too concerned about their own positions when sifting out marriage possibilities for their children is a much needed reminder that it is the interests of the children which should be foremost in the minds of parents. Whilst most parents would insist that this is their only concern, it is at times doubtful whether this is the case. The religious leadership of the Jewish community can play a very significant role in discussing publicly with their constituents the matter of how marriages come about within the Jewish community. These days many marriages are the result of accidents—that is, accidental meetings rather than arrangements. To be fair, many of these do work, especially if the accidental meetings take place within a positively oriented Jewish environment; but in general, leaving the future of the Jewish community to happenstance may not be the best procedure. It may be time, therefore, that we reinvestigate the dynamics which lead to the marriage itself. A most important feature demanding emphasis is the responsibility for parents to instill a healthy respect and love in their children, so that when the right time comes, the children will naturally gravitate towards their parents and seek their counsel. This would be a fulfillment of the prophetic promise that the minds of the parents turn back to their children, and the minds of the children back to their parents (Malachi 3:24).

"If the strength of a nation is linked to the strength of the family unit, this applies even more forcefully to the Jewish community. The responsibility to ensure the viability of the Jewish family, and the process through which it is created, cannot be overstated."

Relative to the making of positive proposals, if the *shadkhan* as institution is to make any significant contribution, it must be permeated with honesty and integrity rather than self-serving niceties which too often fall short of the truth. See on this *Hukay HaNashim* of the Ben Ish Hai, p. 37.

29. *Pele Yo'etz* (under the heading *zevug*) suggests that if circumstances limit the choice, one should marry anyone. The *eitzah* (advice) is seemingly *pele* (astounding) yet perhaps can be seen as a suggestion that one lower one's horizons if what one wants is not available.

James McCary, *Freedom and Growth in Marriage,* reports that at the time of marriage, nearly all women felt that their husbands were just the right ones for them. After two years of marriage, only 65 percent of the women felt that way, and after twenty years, only 5 percent felt that way (p. 237).

Regarding perfecting oneself, see Norman Lamm, *A Hedge of Roses,* who argues that for those lacking inner peace and personality integration, hopes for marital harmony are farfetched (p. 32).

30. The age for Bar Mitzvah, as per *Avot* 5:25, is thirteen. "At thirteen one reaches the age of responsibility to fulfill the commandments."

The age for becoming Bat Mitzvah is twelve years old. See *Orah Hayiim* 617:2 and *Hilkhot Shvitat Asor* 2:11. Also *Yoma* 82a.

Relative to thirteen or twelve for commandments not being applied to marriage, see *Helkat Mehokek* to *Even HaEzer* 1:2, who says that since one must study before marrying, and Talmud study commences in earnest at fifteen (*Avot*

5:25), the age for marriage is deferred. This, even though marrying at thirteen is projected as the ideal *mitzvah* (*Even HaEzer* 1:3). *Otzar HaPoskim* to *Even HaEzer* 1:13 (vol. 1, p. 3a), cites Radvaz that the preference for eighteen is because the generative capacity is not properly developed till then. See *Otzar HaPoskim*, ad loc., for a discussion of whether eighteen means at the beginning of the eighteenth year or at the end of eighteen years. The quotation about eighteen years for entry into marriage is from *Avot* 5:25. A wide-ranging discussion of this issue may be found in the very useful volume by Elyokim Ellenson, *HaIshah V'haMitzvot*, vol. 3, *Ish V'Ishto*, pp. 75–89.

Evidence that marriage is deferred is forthcoming in *Song of Songs Rabbah* 7:6. There it is reported by R. Levi that the custom is to marry at thirty or forty. From the context of the Midrash, it is clear that R. Levi is referring to the observant community. One hesitates to read too much into his comment, but that R. Levi says it, and so matter-of-factly, without questioning, should not be taken lightly.

That the age of eighteen is not an unconditional obligation is related to the fact that it takes two, and one may defer marriage in order to wait for the right one (*Bava Kamma* 80a).

31. On the circumstances which justify putting off marriage, *Binyan Aday Ahd* cites various views for how long one may defer marrying in order to study Torah, including that of the Ḥafetz Ḥayyim, who allows deferral till the beginning of the twenty-fifth year (pp. 15–16). Ḥazon Ish to *Yoreh Deah* (152:2) sees twenty as the limit for deferral. See further on for discussion of financial considerations affecting age of marriage. *Birkay Yosef* (*Even HaEzer* 1:9) allows delay of marriage till the age of twenty-four if one has not found the right one, or for other legitimate reasons.

Relative to marrying early, I am aware of the wealth of statistics showing the hazards of marrying early. But not all early marriages fail, and failure relates to the immaturity of those marrying. If the couple is mature, and are capable of handling the burdens of marriage, it is ridiculous to sit and wait for the time that, according to statistics, is most optimal for the marriage to last. See Blood and Blood, *Marriage*, pp. 154–155.

On the merits of marrying early, see the comment of R. Ḥisda (*Kiddushin* 29b) that the advantage he had over his colleagues was attributable to his having married early. *Binyan Aday Ahd* suggests that it is advantageous to fuse together before the personalities harden, when growing together becomes more difficult (p. 18).

Walter Gove and Claire Peterson, in "An Update of the Literature on Personal and Marital Adjustment," report that among surviving never-divorced couples, age at marriage bore no strong relationship to reported marital happiness. The first years of the marriage are critical, and if they can be survived, the outlook leaves room for optimism.

Aside from not joining into marriage prematurely, marriage should not be entered into to escape loneliness or anomie. These are conditions which usually reflect personality rather than situational deficit, and should be resolved before imposing melancholy on an innocent party, the marriage partner.

On not pushing children before they are ready, see *Ḥukay HaNashim*, p. 37. Some of the more likely reasons for children rushing into marriage may be to assert independence, to find themselves, or to attain self-fulfillment. Not rushing into marriage may create other problems, such as that alluded to by *Menorat HaMaor* (*ner* 3, *klal* 1, pt. 1, chap. 1), who cautions that if one delays marriage, care should be given over to controlling one's sensual desires. Obviously, marrying to satisfy sensuality has pitfalls of its own.

32. On the importance of maturity before marriage, see Bulka, "Divorce: The Problem and the Challenge."

Related to the issue of age and maturity, *Binyan Aday Ahd* remarks that the relative age of husband and wife is not critical, that the wife could be older, but the husband should be more mature (p. 23).

Being honest with oneself, the self-awareness dynamic, is also important in marriage; to know where one needs to improve and to have the capacity to adjust.

33. The ability to sustain the spouse as crucial to marrying is evident in *Hilkhot De'ot* 5:11. Rambam says that the way of the wise is to marry only after establishing domicile and sustenance. The fools, he says, marry first. This notion, based on *Sotah* 44a, is not brought in the Codes, suggesting that it may be sound advice but not absolute Halakhah. If it were, the poor would not be allowed to marry. See further the notes of *Yavetz* to *Sotah* 44a, who says that if a poor person comes to marry, the community is obliged to provide him with the basics of rented domicile, food, and clothing; after that he may marry.

On the matter of who is to be the provider, Rabbenu Nissim, to *Kiddushin* 29b, intimates that when the wife works to support the couple, marriage is indicated even if the husband pursues Torah studies afterwards. If the wife does not work, as was the case with Israeli women in talmudic times (as opposed to Babylonian women), then marriage must be deferred.

The essentiality of economic stability is projected by Epstein (*Kuntrus Ha-Zivug V'haBayit*, p. 11), who cites the *Zohar Ḥadash* that marriage should come only after one has a home and an income.

Additionally, *Korban HaEdah* to Yerushalmi *Ketuvot* 4:8 derives from the language of the *ketuvah* (marriage contract), in which the husband undertakes to provide food and sustenance for the wife (*ayzone va'afarnes*), that if he cannot support his wife-to-be, he is prohibited from marrying her.

The income that is required, as Ellenson (*Ish V'Ishto*, vol. 3, p. 76) deftly and correctly points out, is primarily a source of income, and is not to be equated with financial independence. The couple need a source from which to live, not financial independence.

34. On marriage for financial gain being a contemptible abuse, see *Kiddushin* 70a, and the gloss of R. Moshe Isserles to *Even HaEzer* 2:1.

35. Concerning one who has doubts about marrying, see Blood and Blood,

Marriage, p. 116, where it is pointed out that basic uncertainty usually indicates something wrong in the relationship, or with the readiness to marry. It is recommended to hold off till both are sure.

On a rabbi's prerogative to discourage a problematic relationship, see Birner, "Unconscious Resistance to Pre-marital Counseling," p. 21.

36. The matter of too much attention to trivial items prior to the wedding is discussed by G. Naftali, *Iggeret LeHatan V'Hadrakhah LeNasuy*, who criticizes the tendency to focus on trivialities prior to the wedding, such as what to wear, who will be the photographer, what songs to play, are there enough waiters, etc. (pp. 10–11). (By the way, the author of this work is really a Naftali G., who chose to leave his family name a secret, and switched the last and first parts, making his first name appear in the book as a family name. Unlike the author of *Binyan Aday Ahd*, he chose only partial anonymity.)

On the implementation of goals, see ibid. (p. 15), where the author refers to a maximum attributed to the Hazon Ish, who interpreted *"Knay lekha haver"* ("acquire for yourself a friend") as *"Kaneh lekha haver"* ("the pen should be your friend"), a play on words with *knay* and *kaneh*, "acquire" and "pen," from the statement in *Avot* 1:6. The point of the Hazon Ish was that prior to the wedding, one should summarize the past and put down on paper one's aspirations for the future and use these as a personal gauge for how the marriage is evolving.

Soul-searching, for the couple starting a new life, is nothing less than logical, appropriate, and imperative.

The study of ethical tracts should focus on such topics as anger, disparaging talk, verbal abuse, arguing, etc. G. Naftali cites the practice that even when bride and groom may not fast on the day of their wedding, because it is Rosh Hodesh or some other occasion, such as Hanukah, when fasting is prohibited, it is still proper that they have a fast of words, wherein they speak only what is relevant to the ultimate concerns of their marriage (p. 22).

Relative to knowing one's direct responsibilities in marriage, see Shelah (*Shaar Ha'Otiyot, ot kuf*), who insists that one who marries must know all of *Orah Hayyim* 240 and *Even HaEzer* 25 by heart, as well as the seventeenth chapter of *Reshit Hakhmah* (*Shaar Kedushah*), which incorporates the Holy Letter of Ramban with other important passages.

CHAPTER 2

1. On the incompleteness of man without woman, and woman without man, Yerushalmi, *Berakhot* 9:1 states: "Man and woman, each without the other, is impossible, and both without the Godly presence equally impossible."

On man and woman being true equals, see *Kiddushin* 35a, that Scripture equates man and woman regarding laws and admonitions in the Torah. See also Yerushalmi, *Sanhedrin* 3:6.

2. Concerning disparaging remarks about woman, it is useful to compare the apparent attribution of lightheadedness to woman (*Shabbat* 33b) with the

statement that they have more understanding than men (*Nidah* 45b). See on this R. Uzi Kalḥeim, "Al Maamad HaIshah," where the author states that these statements relate to specific circumstances and were not intended to be normative. The statement about lightheadedness really refers to the possibly lower tolerance for affliction, and is certainly not a statement of intellectual ability. See *Megillah* 14a, *Bava Mezia* 59a. Also see Leo Levi, *Man and Woman*, p. 26.

The honor accorded to biblical women is exemplified by the matriarchs, Miriam, Deborah, Ruth, and Esther, among others. That Deborah could reach such a high station, even though admittedly an exceptional instance, indicates that women were recognized for their ability. Had they been seen as lower-class, Deborah would not have been possible. See Tosafot to *Nidah* 50a, "Kol Hakasher," and *Sefer HaḤinukh*, no. 83 (throughout this volume, the numbering of the *mitzvot* in the *Sefer HaḤinukh* follows the Mosad Harav Kook edition by R. Ḥayyim Chavel, 1966).

For a good example of rabbinic sensitivity to the difficulties faced by women, see Eliezer Berkovits, "The Status of Woman within Judaism," in his *Crisis and Faith*, pp. 97–121.

3. The point about so many essentials of Judaism being explicated via woman is made in Rabbenu Baḥya to Exod. 15:20.

4. Pertaining to the exemption of women from observing commandments linked to a specific time, see *Kiddushin* 29a for the basic statement, and later for elaboration.

Among the many reasons suggested for the exemption, Abudarham, in *Seder Tefilot Shel Ḥol* (chap. beginning "Kol Yisrael"), sees this as related to *shalom bayit*, a view which is problematic, since it uses a rabbinic construct of responsibility to the husband to explain a biblical exemption. R. Shimshon Raphael Hirsch, in his commentary to Lev. 23:43, suggests that women need fewer reminders of ultimate responsibility, since they are not as caught up in worldly duties. See also Norman Lamm, *A Hedge of Roses*, who develops the idea that time-oriented commands make one aware of the sanctity of time, but that women already have that time clock through observance of the *Taharat Hamishpaḥah* laws (pp. 76–78). R. Yosef Zvi Weiner, in "Ezer K'Negdo," sees woman's responsibility as boundless, greater than man's, and therefore she is exempted to allow her to actualize the greater responsibility (p. 487). Berman, in "The Status of Women in Halakhic Judaism," posits that the exemption is to ensure no interference with women's home-centered role (p. 9).

5. The proposition that the precepts were given to Israel in order to shape humankind is found in *Genesis Rabbah* 44:1, *Leviticus Rabbah* 13:3.

For more on the view that women do not need all the positive commandments, see my "Woman's Role—Some Ultimate Concerns."

6. For more on the extension of women's exemption to the home situation, see R. Tsvi Travis, *Pirkey Hanhagat HaBayit*, vol. 1, pp. 174–176, where the author enlarges on this theme.

7. Related to the effect of changing conditions on the law regarding women,

see Raphael Patai, *The Jewish Mind,* p. 491, where he asserts that the talmudic emphasis on making the husband attentive and pleasant to his wife was to compensate for the wife's subordinate position in biblical law. This thesis is questionable, since biblical law itself does not mandate subordination; it is possible that through abuse this may have evolved, but this is a personal, not a biblical, failing. If anything, strict biblical law protects the wife against abuse.

The change of women's position relative to their husbands is reflected in *Orah Hayyim* 472:4 regarding reclining on Pesah; all women are in the category of distinguished, and their not reclining is more related to custom than to their being subservient to their husbands.

See also Responsa of Maharsham, 1:45, that the equal control of property in marriage is part of the *tenaim* (conditions) for marriage, and that this may not have been written into that agreement in the time of the Talmud or the writing of the Codes. Its present inclusion is seen by the author, R. Sholom Mordecai Schwadron, as having legal implications.

On the changed position of women in society, see *Yoreh Deah* 84:11, and the *Kreti*, note 19, who cites the difference of view between Maharshal and Ramah relative to the reliability of women concerning certain types of checking which affect kashrut. *Kreti*, in commenting, states that now women are more reliable as inspectors than men.

8. Acknowledgment of women's increased capabilities may be found in R. Shlomoh Wolbe, *Maamaray Hadrakhah LeHatanim*, pp. 18–19.

On the closing of the knowledge gap, see ibid., p. 18, where Wolbe contends that the knowledge gap in TaNakh and Halakhot has more or less disappeared, and in Jewish thought the woman is occasionally more conversant. In *Kuntrus Hadrakhah LeKalot*, written seven years earlier, Wolbe claims that no matter what is the extent of her knowledge, the husband's concentrated Talmud study yields more far-reaching insight. Assuming the validity of Wolbe's observation, it is still not as revelant as the question of how that knowledge is integrated into one's character.

9. On the impact of technology relative to women, see Ruth Neubauer, "The Changing Background of Pre-Marital Counseling," for a discussion of the ramifications of this change.

On the condemnation of idleness and its legal implications, see *Ketuvot* 59b, "Idleness leads to craziness" (emotional depletion), and the husband who forbids his wife's working must grant her a divorce with full *ketuvah* payment. See *Even HaEzer* 80:3, *Hilkhot Ishut* 21:3, and comment of *Maggid Mishneh.*

On the husband's right to coerce his wife to do trivial work rather than atrophy, see ibid., *Even HaEzer* 80:2, and *Hilkhot Ishut* 21:2.

10. That doing nothing is not the norm is clear from Yerushalmi, *Ketuvot* 5:6, that it is not the way of women to sit in idleness.

The Talmud (*Shabbat* 32b–33a) has little good to say of women who live off the fat of the land but do not work.

11. On the attitude of the husband to the wife working, see Daniel Yankelovich, *New Rules*, who reports that in 1938, 75 percent disapproved of a woman earning money if she had a husband who supported her, but by 1978 the percentage went down to 26 percent disapproving (p. 91). The trend to work and its being accepted is widespread. The study of Walter Gove and Claire Peterson, "An Update of the Literature on Personal and Marital Adjustment," indicates that the impact on the home of the wife's working depends less on the fact of her working, and more on the attitudes of the husband and wife to the working. The husband's objections, or the wife's working to escape from the home, have negative connotations. See also *Family and Marriage Newsletter*, vol. 4, no. 1 (1980): p. 2.

Binyan Aday Ahd, p. 144, cautions against the erosion of home life if the wife takes on too much outside the home. In the light of the studies just cited, a more crucial factor for the home is the husband's cooperation and understanding together with the wife's commitment.

12. See further Yehuda Levy, "HaIsh V'haIsha B'Yehadut."

13. Rachel Neriah, "Likrat HaNisuin," p. 233, complains that men today suppress emotions, are not soft and caring.

14. Another insight on the meaning of inner space is suggested by Wolbe (*Kuntrus Hadrakhah LeKalot*, p. 39), who interprets the famous verse about the glory of women being inside (Ps. 45:14) as referring to the world of inner feelings.

The importance of the woman for family vitality is stressed by George Gilder in *Sexual Suicide*. He writes that the woman assumes charge of what are called the domestic values of the community, "its moral, aesthetic, religious, nurturant, social, and sexual concerns. In these values consist the ultimate goals of human life: all those matters that we consider of such supreme importance that we do not ascribe a financial worth to them" (p. 259). Compare with Ashley Montagu, *The Natural Superiority of Women*, who asserts that "It is the function of women to teach men how to be human" (p. 159). See also ibid., p. 216, and further in my "Women's Role—Some Ultimate Concerns."

15. That women do not have to marry is clearly enunciated in *Hilkhot Isuray Biah* 21:26. Compare with *Hilkhot Ishut* 15:16, where Rambam states that women should marry to avoid suspicion. The statement in *Hilkhot Isuray Biah* speaks of women having the right to remain single, so that the two statements of Rambam are not contradictory; the one is a legal statement, the other advice. See *Even HaEzer* 1:13.

The positive climate between men and women is not enhanced by the stance of such as Phyllis Chesler, *Women and Madness*, and Juliet Mitchell, *Psychoanalysis and Feminism*.

On the woman's approach to marrying, R. Epstein, in *Mitzvot HaBayit*, cites the Bet HaLevy that the talmudic comment claiming that a woman would rather have any mate than be alone (*Kiddushin* 7a) is not a statement of fact. The

Talmud is only stating that this can sometimes be the case. Usually, the norm is to be careful in deciding who to marry (vol. 1, p. 376).

16. Erik Erikson, in a speech to the International Psychoanalytical Association, reported in the *New York Times,* August 4, 1979, p. 17, warned of this. He urged that the dangers posed by this repression not be underestimated, and suggested that concern about children in general could be helpful in satisfying the procreative urge. One is tempted to ask why Erikson did not forcefully recommend having children, instead of this dubious concern for "children in general."

17. Some more extreme attitudes relative to the man-woman dialectic are found in Elizabeth Koltun, *The Jewish Woman.*

On the issue of the concern of Halakhah for women, Shlomoh Ashkenazi, *HaIsha B'Aspaklaryat HaYehadut,* claims that equality of men and women was not the worry of Jewish law. Instead, the worry was to promulgate and protect women's rights. This, he says, is most liberal and rational (vol. 2, p. 144).

18. On men and women being equal in laws applying to them, see *Pesaḥim* 43a, *Kiddushin* 35a, *Bava Kamma* 15a.

For an example of the intervention of Halakhah to correct inequity, see Responsa of *Rosh,* 42:1, that the famous edict of Rabbenu Gershom, which disallowed divorce without the wife's consent, served to equalize the power of man and woman.

R. Samson Raphael Hirsch, in his commentary to Gen. 3:16, speaks of the disparate burdens of husband and wife, which are harmonized through the Torah escalating their common commitment to service, akin to that of *Kohanim* (priests).

That equality is rooted in the Torah is reflected in the comment of Hirsch to Gen. 2:28, that *ezer k'negdo* indicates full equality, in mutually complementary positions.

On the similarity of the Hebrew names for man and woman, see Sforno to Gen. 2:18.

19. For further on equality of importance, see *Akedat Yitzḥak* to Gen. 2:23 (*Shaar 8, Perek HaḤibur,* no. 6).

On woman's ability to conceive only from one man at a time, see *Kiddushin* 7a and Yerushalmi, *Yevamot* 5:2.

If a woman were married to more than one man, the paternity of her children would be in doubt. To prevent the child from being in such a precarious state, the woman can have only one man at a time. A man's having many wives, however, leaves no doubt about either paternity or maternity. One may conjecture that this is the main factor behind the biblical allowance of more than one wife for a man, but only one husband for a woman. If reflects biological reality rather than gender preference.

That true encounter is founded on differentness is a point emphasized in Sforno, loc. cit.

20. On the issue of role coherence, see Rachel Neriah, *Happiness in Married Life*, pp. 5–7, where she cites the view of Rudolf Dreikurs regarding the difficulties in unclear roles.

Relative to the matter of whose customs become the family norm, Elyakim Ellenson, *Ha'lshah V'haMitzvot*, cites the Tashbatz, 3:179, who considers the law that the wife must follow the customs of the husband as self-understood. See further the discussion in ibid., pp. 22–24, concerning the views of R. Moshe Feinstein and R. Ovadyah Yosef. See below, Chapter 5, sec. "To Honor One's Husband."

The law on family customs, by the way, does not preclude openness to introducing the wife's customs which actually enhance the family, such as the blessing of children on Sabbath eve. It does not diminish from the letter or the spirit of the regulation if the husband, unaccustomed to this in his own home, adds it to the vocabulary of married life.

21. That the law is geared to creating the proper conditions for *shalom bayit* to evolve is a point stressed by Zev Falk in *Dinay Nisuin* (p. 7).

James McCary, *Freedom and Growth in Marriage*, states that marriages in which there is agreement on the correct roles for each mate are much more likely to succeed than marriages where the couple are in conflict over role expectations (p. 240).

22. Reflected in the *tenaim* (conditions of marriage contractually agreed to by the couple prior to marriage) that they not ignore one another in financial matters, or any other matters.

23. Gove and Peterson, "An Update of the Literature on Marital Adjustment," report that having children is for the modern family a potential crisis in marriage. The child fits well into a transcending environment, but has problems in a self-fulfillment, me-first setting.

24. For more on the woman not being obligated to "be fruitful and multiply," see *Yevamot* 65b, *Even HaEzer* 1:13, *Hilkhot Ishut* 15:2. The husband's *mitzvah* is to have at least one boy and one girl (*Even HaEzer* 1:5, *Hilkhot Ishut* 15:4).

That the *mitzvah* fulfillment is the father's is based on the principle that *mitzvah* fulfillment accrues to the one obliged to actualize the command.

Further elaboration on the woman's link to the *mitzvah* of procreation is found in RaN, to the beginning of the second chapter of *Kiddushin*, who states that the woman, without whom the man cannot have a child, is connected to the *mitzvah* fulfillment of "to be fruitful" as helper in the realization of the commandment. See further discussion in Epstein, *Sefer Mitzvot HaBayit* (chap. 1, "HaIsh V'Ishto"), pp. 81–84. See also Meiri to *Kiddushin* 41a.

25. The rationale for women being exempted from the *mitzvah* of procreation is offered by *Meshekh Hokhmah*, Gen. 9:7. Shlomoh Aviner, *Pirkey Ahavah Bayn Ish L'Ishto*, offers a somewhat weak rationale, that the Torah does not command that which is self-understood and natural (pp. 54–55). One can dispute this thesis, as well as the assumption that women naturally want children.

There are plenty who do not, though it might be contended that this is not natural. Yet the fact it is not automatic leaves Aviner's proposal slightly compromised, at least.

A good treatment of this topic is found in David Shapiro, "Be Fruitful and Multiply."

26. On woman's employing birth control, see the episode of Yehudit, the wife of R. Hiyya, *Yevamot* 65b. See *Shabbat* 111a, *Even HaEzer* 5:11, *Hilkhot Isuray Biah* 16:12.

On the matter of primary responsibility, see *Yevamot* 12b, 100b; *Ketuvot* 39a; *Nedarim* 35b; *Niddah* 45a.

The permissibility of the wife's resorting to birth control without the husband's consent if her health is in jeopardy is from Avnay Nazer (*Responsa Even HaEzer* 1). This, even if the husband has not fully discharged his procreation obligation. R. Moshe Feinstein, in *Igrot Moshe* (*Even HaEzer* 1, 67) allows marriage to a woman who must defer procreation for health reasons. The case there seemed to involve possible further deterioration in the woman's health if she could not marry. Still, the author gave this permission on condition the *heter* not be publicized. *Ziz Eliezer* (9, 51, *Shaar* 2, sec. 6, no. 3) allows temporary contraception if the wife's health and well-being do not presently allow for the raising of more children.

This volume does not propose to treat the issue of birth control in depth. There is ample literature available on the issue, including a quite instructive piece by Herschel Schachter, "Halachic Aspects of Family Planning."

Relative to the point that procreation and conjugal relations are separate matters, *Maggid Mishneh* to *Hilkhot Ishut* 15:1 asserts that this point is obvious.

On the leeway given to the husband, see *Even HaEzer* 76:6; *Hilkhot Ishut*, loc. cit.; this is with the wife's consent.

See *Birkay Yosef, Even HaEzer* 1:2, who postulates that this allows for greater intervals between conjugal visitations, not total abstinence. See further below, note 5 to Chapter 12, for discussion of the *l'erev* concept, which extends the procreation obligation to the later years.

27. Regarding the category of "to inhabit," see Tosafot, *Hagigah* 2b (s.v. *lo . . .*), who states that this obligation rests also on women. *Arukh HaShulhan, Even HaEzer* 1:4, claims that women's relationship to this obligation is the same as to the *mitzvah* of procreation itself; that is, associated but not commanded. Rabbenu Bahya, *Kad HaKemah* ("Hatan B'Bet HaKnesset") sees the *mitzvah* "to inhabit" as applying also to the nations of the world. Effectively, then, it is more than just the underpinning for the "be fruitful" command. R. Bahya thus refutes the later view of the *Arukh HaShulhan* that "to habitate" relates only to one who is obliged in the command to be fruitful. This, of course, is on the assumption that to be fruitful is a command directed only to Israelites. For further on this, see *Yevamot* 62a, *Even HaEzer* 1:7, *Hilkhot Ishut* 15:6, and the discussion in Shapiro, "Be Fruitful and Multiply," specially the bottom of p. 70. See also *Even HaEzer* 1:8 and *Hilkhot Ishut* 15:16.

28. Regarding the wife's noncooperation, *Ziz Eliezer*, 42:4 of vol. 6, states that a woman who sterilizes herself and thus impedes the husband's ability to fulfill the "be fruitful" command, can be divorced by the husband and she forfeits her *ketuvah* settlement.

For more on noncooperation being grounds for divorce, see below, Chapter 3.

On a childless couple not being compelled to divorce, see Gloss of RaMoh to *Even HaEzer* 1:3, where the author states that the practice is not even to interfere in the finalization of a marriage with a woman incapable of having children.

The primacy of marital harmony even in the face of childlessness is posited by R. Moshe Feinstein, *Even HaEzer* 1, 63.

29. On love being independent of procreation, see *Moed Katan* 9b. See also the moving story of a childless couple in *Song of Songs Rabbah* 1:31. *Arukh HaShulhan, Even HaEzer* 154:27, claims that the explanation for why a couple are childless despite all efforts is in the category of "God's secrets." Rivka Levi-Jung, in "HaTaharah, Shaar LeHayay Nisuin Meusharim," argues that it is absurd to forbid the pleasures and fulfillment of marriage simply because of childlessness that is no fault of the couple (vol. 1, p. 367).

CHAPTER 3

1. The marriage ceremony contains no affirmation of love, but the *ketuvah* obligates the husband in *aykor*, which is probably the closest to a statement of love. *Aykor* itself relates to holding dear and precious, honored.

Relevant to the businesslike approach to marriage, Marvin Mitchelson, the well-known palimony lawyer, said of prenuptial contracts, "In nine of ten agreements I've drawn up, the couple eventually got divorced. It might be a wise legal move, but it sure isn't romantic" (*Time Magazine*, October 24, 1983, p. 76).

2. That the *ketuvah* underlines the relationship is a point emphasized by Ben Zion Shereshevsky, in his most useful volume, *Dinay Mishpahah*, p. 111.

After-marriage obligations are a reference to after his or her death, or after divorce. See further.

The rule that the relationship must not continue without the *ketuvah* is found in *Even HaEzer* 66:1, *Hilkhot Ishut* 10:10.

Shereshevsky, in *Dinay Mishpahah*, stresses that the *ketuvah* is not geared to promote the interests of the husband or the wife; it is geared to promote harmony between the couple (p. 96).

Minimizing the *ketuvah* from prescribed norms makes every instance of conjugality in such arrangements an act of harlotry (*Even HaEzer* 66:9, *Hilkhot Ishut* 10:9).

The *ketuvah* contains a settlement of 200 zuz. According to R. Eliyahu Henkin, in his *Edut L'Yisrael*, sec. 45 ("Nisuin"), writing at the time that the United States was on the silver standard, the 200 *zuzim* of the *ketuvah* amount to about $50.

Four *zuzim* equal one shekel, so that the *ketuvah* settlement of 200 *zuzim* is effectively 50 shekels. The shekel itself is about three-quarters of an ounce, so that based on a dollar value of $8 per ounce of silver, the *ketuvah* is worth about $300 (50 × 3/4 × $8 = $300).

Henkin points out that the 200 *zuzim* of the *ketuvah* are *zekukim* (pure silver), worth more than $1,000 U.S. in total; in his time about twenty times the $50 value. With that equation, the value of the *ketuvah* would now be about $6,000 (50 × 3/4 × $8 × 20 = $6,000).

For a further discussion of the value of the *ketuvah*, see Aryeh Kaplan's *Made in Heaven*, pp. 113, 116–118.

3. On the non-negotiability of certain aspects of the marriage relationship, see *Even HaEzer* 69:6 and *Hilkhot Ishut* 12:6.

On the matter of the couple negotiating their arrangement, see for example *Even HaEzer* 92:8. Rambam, *Hilkhot Ishut* 23:1, states that prior arrangement needs no formal procedure, but agreement after the wedding needs formal procedure (*kinyan*).

The notion of freedom within a structure is more fully developed in Appendix 1.

4. For elaboration of the provision for conjugal visitation, see Chapters 10 and 11.

On these ten obligations, see *Even HaEzer* 69:2, *Hilkhot Ishut* 12:2. These are assumed to be operative even if not written out (*Even HaEzer* 69:1, *Hilkhot Ishut* 12:5).

5. The husband's obligation to redeem his kidnapped wife is stated in *Even HaEzer* 69:5. RaMoh, ad loc., adds that this also applies to burial and inheritance; they are not subject to conditions and must be carried out irrespective of either waiving claims. Neither can compromise the good of the other (*Helkat Mehokek*, n. 9).

For when the redemption is necessitated by the wife's negligence, see *Pithay Teshuvah* to *Even HaEzer* 78:1. The language in the text in this volume is to project a difference of opinion on whether the husband is still obliged in such a circumstance of negligence.

6. On the duty to cover medical expenses due to negligence, see ibid. That, too, is a matter subject to difference of opinion.

Relative to the principle that care of the wife not be subject to price limits, see *Even HaEzer* 79:3 and *Hilkhot Ishut* 14:17. Both sources speak of the right of the husband to divorce the wife and give her the *ketuvah* settlement if the medical expenses are great and the husband will lose much money, but that this is not proper because of *derekh eretz* (bad ethics—as per the explanation of *Maggid Mishneh*). Now that divorce against the wife's will is not an option, neither is the husband's bad ethics (See *Bet Shmuel* and *Helkhat Mehokek*, n. 3 and 4 respectively).

7. On postmarital *ketuvah* settlement, see *Even HaEzer* 66:7 and *Hilkhot Ishut* 10:7. See further Shereshevsky, *Dinay Mishpahah*, pp. 98–105.

The obligations of conjugal visitation are spelled out in *Even HaEzer* 76, *Hilkhot Ishut* 14.

8. The obligations for clothing and sustenance are delineated in *Even HaEzer* 70, 73; *Hilkhot Ishut* 12, 13. Rambam, *Hilkhot Ishut* 12:2 indicates these are Biblical obligations. See *Bet Shmuel* to *Even HaEzer* 69:2, note 1.

On the inclusion of personal needs in the obligation to sustain, see *Even HaEzer* 73:3, Hilkhot Ishut 13:4. For more on the extent of this obligation, see *Even HaEzer* 73:4, *Hilkhot Ishut* 12:11, 13:5. See *Even HaEzer* 70:3 and *Hilkhot Ishut* 12:13 regarding the extra money left because the expenses were not as great as anticipated or because the wife tightened the belt regarding her self. In the former case, the money reverts to the husband, in the latter, to the wife. See Shereshevsky, *Dinay Mishpahah*, pp. 119–120.

That marriage only raises the wife's living standard is based on *Ketuvot* 48a, that the wife goes up in standard with her husband and does not have her standards diminished. See *Even HaEzer* 82:3, *Hilkhot Ishut* 21:14; also Shereshevsky, *Dinay Mishpahah*, pp. 117–119.

On the husband's obligation to sustain the wife even if she has her own funds, see Shereshevsky, *Dinay Mishpahah*, pp. 123–124.

On the use of sustenance as a weapon, see *Even HaEzer* 154:3 and *Hilkhot Ishut* 12:11. Rambam ad loc. and *Even HaEzer* 70:2 indicate that if he is poor and cannot support her with the basics, she has a claim to divorce. *Arukh HaShulhan, Even HaEzer* 154:20, suggests that if the husband, after repeated intervention, refuses to maintain his wife, he can be forced to grant a *get*.

9. An extreme case of less than exemplary behavior is *Even HaEzer* 178:18, *Hilkhot Ishut* 24:18.

Relative to what are understandable concerns, see *Even HaEzer* 70:12, 74:10; *Hilkhot Ishut* 13:14. See also *Even HaEzer* 74:12.

10. *Even HaEzer* 74:10 in RaMoh, who mentions that it was customary in such instances to place a reliable person in the house to see who was really the cause of her conflict with the in-laws or other relatives that the husband would like to move into their home.

11. That the husband is not exempt from sustenance even if he leaves the house is evident in *Even HaEzer* 70:5, *Hilkhot Ishut* 12:16.

Concerning excusable circumstances, see *Even HaEzer* 70:3 in RaMoh.

That the husband's obligation extends to maintaining the wife's standard is explained in *Helkat Mehokek* to *Even HaEzer* 70. n. 12, that the husband is so obligated, based on his undertaking to sustain her according to that which befits her station (the word *aykor* is taken to mean "to honor," and ensuring the wife's comfortable sustenance rather than bare subsistence falls into that category).

12. The proper fulfillment of the obligation to sustain is enunciated by Hatam Sofer to *Ketuvot* 70a, who insists that the obligation to maintain one's wife must be exercised personally, and with a cheerful countenance. All this is included in the responsibility.

On eating together, see *Even HaEzer* 70:2 and *Hilkhot Ishut* 12:12. An alternative view to that of the Meḥaber and Rambam is brought by RaMoh, ad loc., in the name of most halakhic authorities, who dispute that the husband may eat separately at all times except Sabbath eve. The majority claim that the husband must eat together with his wife unless she willingly agrees to his eating alone. The point of this is that eating together is part of marital togetherness and should be seen as a priority item for both husband and wife, who should endeavor to adjust their schedules to effect this togetherness.

13. On the wife's earnings belonging to the husband, see *Even HaEzer* 80 and *Hilkhot Ishut* 12:3–4.

On the wife's findings, see *Even HaEzer* 84:1, *Hilkhot Ishut* 21:1.

Concerning the earnings from the wife's property see *Even HaEzer* 85:12, *Hilkhot Ishut* 16:1–2. See the wide-ranging discussion of these matters in Shereshevsky, *Dinay Mishpaḥah*, pp. 152–170. He points out quite perceptively that the general rule that what the wife acquires belongs to the husband is effectively a misnomer. Only the fruits are subject to this rule, but whatever the wife brings to the marriage—the principal—stays in her name, and though the husband has the right to use it during the marriage, the property is hers, and reverts back to her upon divorce.

Related to the husband being her beneficiary, see *Even HaEzer* 69:3, 90:1; *Hilkhot Ishut* 12:3, 22:1.

14. On the wife's right to maintain her economic independence, see *Even HaEzer* 69:4, *Hilkhot Ishut* 12:4, based on *Ketuvot* 58b. See Gloss of RaMoh, *Even HaEzer* 69:4, regarding different views on whether the wife can change her mind and ask that the husband support her. See *Ḥelkat Meḥokek*, n. 6, who indicates that the view which gives the wife the upper hand here would allow her to shift from week to week.

15. *Even HaEzer* 70:4. See Shereshevsky, *Dinay Mishpaḥah*, pp. 172–173.

16. Shereshevsky, *Dinay Mishpaḥah*, pp. 124–125.

17. On the wife's household obligations, see *Even HaEzer* 80:4–10, *Hilkhot Ishut* 21:3–7.

The extent of the wife's exemption based on the husband's ability to pay is extended in *Even HaEzer* 80:9 and *Hilkhot Ishut* 21:15, where both assert that if the wife can show that the husband can afford more household help than he has arranged, such financial capacity exempts her from the work she would have been excused from had the help actually been brought in; it is as if the help were there.

For further on the personal work that remains the wife's obligation, see *Even HaEzer* 80:4–5, *Hilkhot Ishut* 21:3–4; also RaMoh to *Even HaEzer* 80:15. See also R. Yosef Epstein, *Mitzvot HaBayit*, vol. 1, pp. 223–226, 289–295.

18. Concerning the wife's not being obliged to pay for breakage, see *Even HaEzer* 80:17 and *Hilkhot Ishut* 21:9. Rambam mentions that this is not a legal concept, but that if it were not the case, there would be no peace in the home; the wife would refrain from work for fear of breaking anything, and thus fights would erupt.

That the husband was the first to break something is a reference, of course, to the final act of wedding ceremony.

19. The point about contriving evidence is stressed by Shereshevsky, *Dinay Mishpaḥah*, pp. 275–276.

For further on the Jewish marital-stability record, see Immanuel Jakobovits, "Marriage and Divorce," p. 111.

20. The prenuptial agreement recently promulgated by the Rabbinical Council of America will, if endorsed and implemented, go a long way toward correcting some of the outstanding issues related to the husband's noncooperation.

21. On the wife's denying conjugal visitation and her desertion, see *Even HaEzer* 77:2, *Hilkhot Ishut* 14:8. Desertion without just cause effectively prevents conjugal visitation. With just cause and the wife's insistence that she still wants to continue marital relations, it is a different matter.

22. On adultery, see *Even HaEzer* 178:18, 178:17; *Hilkhot Ishut* 24:18; *Hilkhot Sotah* 2:12. See further Tosafot, *Zevaḥim* 2b, s.v. *stam ishah*, and Responsa of *Ketav Sofer*, *Even HaEzer* 99, who allows staying together under very restricted conditions. See also *Even HaEzer* 117:1, specially Gloss of *RaMoh*. See further Shereshevsky, *Dinay Mishpaḥah*, p. 313.

23. *Even HaEzer* 11:1, *Hilkhot Ishut* 24:15. In the language of Rambam, "if the husband desires to divorce her" (ibid.).

24. *Even HaEzer* 115:4, *Hilkhot Ishut* 24:12, 14. See *Bet Shmuel* to *Even HaEzer* 115:4, n. 11.

25. *Even HaEzer* 115:1, *Hilkhot Ishut* 24:11. See further *Even HaEzer* 115:3, *Ḥelkat Meḥokek*, n. 7, and *Bet Shmuel*, n. 7.

26. *Even HaEzer* 117:1, 4, 7–10; *Hilkhot Ishut* 7:7, 4–10.

27. On the wife spoiling the food, see *Gittin* 90a. See *Ḥinukh*, no. 548, where he cites this view, and discourses on the idea of divorce, and rejects the view of some groups in society that husband and wife are stuck with each other, however miserable, even hellish, their life together. Yet the Torah insists on a procedure for divorce, so that separating not be treated casually, and also so that the time it takes for the procedure to be carried out affords an opportunity for second thoughts.

28. This primary mention is in Exod. 10:11.

That the *Beth Din* can elicit a divorce is not to callously ignore the fact that the husband can be nasty and inflict pain, anguish, and feelings of despair on the wife. See above, n. 20.

29. *Even HaEzer* 70:2, 77:1, 154:3; *Hilkhot Ishut* 12:11, 14:6–7. See *Ḥelkat Meḥokek* to *Even HaEzer* 77, n. 1, and *Bet Shmuel*, n. 1, regarding denial of sustenance. See further Shereshevsky, *Dinay Mishpaḥah*, pp. 296–298.

30. On philandering, see *Even HaEzer* 154:1 in Gloss of RaMoh.

On causing a bad name, see *Even HaEzer* 74:3, *Hilkhot Ishut* 13:10.

31. On failure to annul, see *Even HaEzer* 74:4–5; *Hilkhot Ishut* 13:10, 13; 14:6.

On imposed idleness, see *Even HaEzer* 80:3, *Hilkhot Ishut* 21:3.

32. Concerning the husband's ill-treatment, see Gloss of RaMoh, *Even HaEzer* 154:3; also Shereshevsky, *Dinay Mishpahah*, pp. 298–300.

33. On removal of her freedom, see Shereshevsky, *Dinay Mishpahah*, pp. 143–144.

On forced relations during the menstrual period, see Responsa of Radvaz, 3:850 (also listed as no. 407), and *Beer Haytav* to *Even HaEzer* 154:7, n. 22.

See also Ellenson, *HaIshah V'haMitzvot*, vol. 3, p. 150.

34. *Even HaEzer* 154:6–7, *Hilkhot Ishut* 15:8–10. See note of *Be'er Haytev*, op. cit., and Pithay Teshuvah to *Even HaEzer* 154, n. 15.

35. Cigarette smoking falls quite prominently into the category of malodorous. See further *Even HaEzer* 154:1, and note of *Bet Shmuel*, no. 2. See *Hilkhot Ishut* 25:1 and Shereshevsky, *Dinay Mishpahah*, pp. 285–288.

36. See *Avodah Zarah* 13a, and Tosafot, s.v. *lilmod Torah; Even HaEzer* 75:4; *Hilkhot Ishut* 13:20. See also *Pithay Teshuvah* to *Even HaEzer* 75, n. 6. Also Shereshevsky, *Dinay Mishpahah*, p. 147.

37. On *mored*'s link to conjugal visitation, see *Even HaEzer* 77:1, *Hilkhot Ishut* 14:15. See also *Helkat Mehokek* and *Bet Shmuel* to *Even HaEzer* 77, n. 1.

38. On *mored*, see *Even HaEzer* 77:1, *Hilkhot Ishut* 14:15.

On *moredet*, see *Even HaEzer* 77:2, 3; *Hilkhot Ishut* 14:8–13.

Regarding the wife not being compelled to exercise her right, see *Helkat Mehokek* to *Even HaEzer* 77, n. 3; *Bet Shmuel*, ad loc., n. 6; Shereshevsky, *Dinay Mishpahah*, pp. 181–182.

39. See Epstein, *Mitzvot HaBayit*, vol. 2, *Kuntrus HaIshut*, pp. 37–41. Also, *Even HaEzer* 77:2.

40. *Even HaEzer* 76:13. Ritba to *Ketuvot* 48a states that this applies even if the motivation is for modesty. See *Helkat Mehokek* to *Even HaEzer* 76, n. 20.

41. On the wife being a *moredet* even if the husband has not paid his indebtedness, see *Even HaEzer* 77:2, *Hilkhot Ishut* 14:9.

Concerning the wife not being his chattel, *Maharit* 1:5, cited in *Be'er Haytev* to *Even HaEzer* 77, n. 7, asserts that she is not a "prisoner of war to be available to him at all hours."

On the wife not being a *moredet* if she leaves for legitimate reasons, see Shereshevsky, *Dinay Mishpahah*, pp. 188–189.

Related to her leaving yet still being willing to engage in conjugal relations, see Gloss of RaMoh to *Even HaEzer* 80:18.

42. That the intent of Rabbenu Gershom's edict was to effect equality relative to divorce is clearly stated in Responsa of *Rosh*, 42:1.

Rabbenu Gershom, as is known, proscribed having more than one wife at a time and divorcing one's wife without her consent. These two decrees are not unrelated (see Menahem Elon, *HaMishpat Ha'Ivri*, pp. 632–634; he states this but does not elaborate).

Biblically, a man was allowed to be married to more than one woman at a time. The Torah allowed what may be called "economic marriage." It gave the woman the free choice to marry with some measure of material comfort. Some women may have preferred only one husband, of meager means, and a life of struggle. Others may have preferred sharing a husband if that meant fewer financial worries. This free choice was to the woman's advantage. However, the husband who had more than one wife was vulnerable to economic fluctuations. Were he to be obliged to maintain all his wives even when his financial empire collapsed, it would create an impossible situation. Moreover, men who know they are so locked in will not have more than one wife, thus effectively taking away the very choice originally given to women. It is therefore possible, even logical, to see that the biblical legal structure, in allowing for divorce against the will of the wife, was consistent with the best interests of women, even if at times this could create hardship. Rabbenu Gershom, it may be conjectured, grasped with keen insight the Torah's intentions. A combination of societal conditions and general aversion to the practice led to the ban on having more than one wife at a time. This, for all intents and purposes, eliminated the option of economic marriage and erased any legitimate argument for giving the husband the right to divorce against the will of the wife. Thus, the second decree, eliminating divorce by husband's coercion. Rather than seeing the edicts of Rabbenu Gershom as running contrary to biblical law, it is clear from this proposition that the edicts of Rabbenu Gershom were natural statements evolving from a profound understanding of the letter, spirit, and intent of the biblical legislation.

CHAPTER 4

1. Regarding ritual immersion, not only the immersion of the bride but also that of the groom is referred to (See *Hupat Hatanim*, chap. 6).

On the Yom Kippur–like atonement, see *Yevamot* 63b, and Yerushalmi, *Bikkurim* 3:3. See G. Naftali, *Iggeret LeHatan V'Hadrakhah LeNasuy*, who refers to a view attributed to R. Hayyim Vital that the atonement is even for more serious breaches. See also Gloss of RaMoh to *Even HaEzer* 61:1.

An example of customs related to marriage is the emptying of one's pockets and untying of knots, which shows symbolic resolve to start fresh, unencumbered by past failings. Bride and groom wear white, he a white *kitel*, or robe, to symbolize that past black marks have been erased and they can start off renewed.

2. *Deuteronomy Rabbah* 2:22, *Bava Batra* 74b.

3. On the original human having been two forms in one corpus, see *Eruvin* 18a. See also commentary of R. Shimshon Raphael Hirsch to Gen. 2.24.

On togetherness without time limitations, see *Yevamot* 62b that one should marry even in later years.

The oneness and completeness is posited in Gen. 5:2. Sima Basry, in *The*

Challenge of Marriage, suggests that the marriage equation should be $1/2 + 1/2 = 1$, not $1 + 1 = 2$ (p. 14).

For more on the idea of Adam as meaning man and woman together, see R. Samson Raphael Hirsch, *Judaism Eternal,* vol. 2, p. 51.

4. On interconnectedness, R. Shlomoh Wolbe, in *Maamaray Hadrakhah Le-Hatanim,* urges complete sharing of deepest thoughts, with no holding back (p. 16).

In regard to the commitment to common ideals, see the fascinating episode reported by Eliyahu Taharani, *Alufaynu Mesubalim,* vol. 2, pp. 114–115.

"My foot hurts us" is from an episode in Simcha Raz, *A Tzaddik in Our Time,* p. 150.

5. Pertinent to outer appearance, R. Yosef Epstein, *Mitzvot HaBayit,* laments the excessive attention to postwedding accoutrements, covering hair but exposing conceit (vol. 2, Introduction, p. 27).

6. Social scientists refer to the present combination of high rates of marriage and divorce as serial monogamy. People have one spouse at a time, but many, one after another, serial-like. Ira Reiss, in *Family Systems in America,* observes that 75 percent of divorced women and 85 percent of divorced men eventually remarry (p. 343).

John Cuber and Peggy Harroff, in *The Significant Americans,* a study of upper-class Americans, indicated that the most frequent excuse for divorce for these types was that they had found a partner who better suited their needs than the incumbent (pp. 90–92). Indeed, if one looks to the outside, one is always likely to find someone who seemingly fits better. Whether the remarriage is a better fit is another matter.

7. R. Yosef Zvi Weiner, *Neve HaBhirah,* offers a fascinating interpretation to the classic "*matzah* or *motzay*" question (*Berakhot* 8a). If one's wife is found, perceived as a propitious find, a windfall that one does not question, then it will be good (*matzah tov*). If, however, the accent is on *motzay ani* ("I continue to find, to seek"), then one will be continually obsessed with the thought that maybe there is a better mate somewhere. That is *mar mimovet* ("more bitter than death") (pp. 53–55). Indeed, divorce is too often more bitter than death. Death is tragic, divorce is bitter.

Basry, *Challenge of Marriage,* pp. 82–84, aptly suggests that those who are unhappy should search within themselves.

8. On Abraham and Sarah, see Gen. 12:11, *Bava Batra* 16a.

The husband who did not notice his wife's physical deficiency is lauded in *Shabbat* 53b. The Talmud, loc. cit., has two views of this situation, one praising the wife's modesty, the other praising the husband's not staring and instead accepting.

9. On natural devotion, see further the introduction of Rabad to his classic work, *Baaley HaNefesh.* He explains the biblical verse about cleaving to one's wife (Gen. 2:24) as expressing what fits naturally.

A classic example of marital devotion is that of R. Akiva and his wife (*Nedarim* 50a).

The general talmudic advice that "a person's thoughts should be involved with humankind" (*Ketuvot* 17a), interpreted by Rashi to mean that one should be ready to fill the needs and wants of others, applies most appropriately to marriage.

10. On husband and wife being willing to die for one another, see R. Yehiel Yaakov Weinberg, "Nisuin," p. 445.

11. On the breaking of the glass and its relation to the Temple's destruction, see *Orah Hayyim* 560:2, attributed by RaMoh to *Kol Bo*. For more on this, see the excellent recent volume of Maurice Lamm, *The Jewish Way in Love and Marriage*, pp. 228–231.

Concerning the fact that the breaking of the glass comes at the end of the ceremony, it should be noted that in many places in Israel the glass is broken after the placing of the ring and before the reading of the *ketuvah*. That breaking, even though in the middle of the ceremony, also evokes shouts of *Mazal Tov*.

12. The Talmud, *Megillah* 27a (see also *Yoreh De'ah* 270:1 and *Hilkhot Sefer Torah* 10:2), allows for the sale of a Torah scroll to marry, one of the rare instances such sale is permitted. The Torah is the basis of the community, but it is through marriage that community itself becomes a reality.

On shared destiny, see Gen. 29:20. Jacob, about to share a life and destiny with Rachel, sees many years as a few days—the seven years of work relative to a life in the here and now and the fulfillments generated for the future are a few days. When looking at matters from the perspective of present gratification, every day's delay seems like a year. Translating this into present reality need not be a farfetched exercise. The couple who are contemplating marriage, instead of focusing simply on whether each fills the other's immediate needs, should also think very seriously about whether they are suited for each other through the full cycle of life. They cannot be prophets, but they do marry based on thoughts and feelings. These thoughts and feelings should extend beyond the immediate moment.

13. Rabad, in the introduction to *Baaley HaNefesh*, speaks of it being fit and proper to like one's wife as one's own self, and for the husband to watch over her as he would watch over one of his own limbs.

14. This episode, and the implications of shared destiny for marriage, are discussed further in Reuven P. Bulka, "Some Implications of Jewish Marriage Philosophy for Marital Breakdown."

15. Related to the argument that one should try to be happy even in depressing circumstances, see A. A. Girshuni, "HaMafteah L'Osher," p. 643.

On the advice to pray that God improve one's spouse, see *Sefer Hasidim*, 749.

On the advice to accept one's fate, Naftali, *Iggeret LeHatan*, p. 67, reports this advice given by the Hafetz Hayyim to a desperate husband; Tsvi Travis, *Pirkey*

Hanhagat Habayit, vol. 1, p. 127, gives a similar advice; R. Eliezer Papo, *Pele Yo'etz*, "Ahavat Ish V'Ishah," counsels this to the wife plagued with a cruel husband.

On the ultimate benefits of a bad spouse, see R. Papo, *Pele Yo'etz*, loc. cit. The author wryly remarks that by this logic, one who can withstand the difficulties should actually seek out such a mate!

16. Benjamin Schlesinger, "Reflections on Family Breakdown Among Jewish Families," pp. 45–53.

CHAPTER 5

1. The priestly blessing (Num. 6:24–26) concludes with a prayer for peace. The *Amidah* recited thrice daily concludes with a prayer for peace. The six orders of the Mishnah conclude with the observation that God found no better receptacle for blessing than peace (*Uktzin* 3:12). More examples abound, among them the observation in *Midrash Tanhuma* (*Tsav* 7 and *Shoftim* 18) that "peace is great, for even if Israel engages in idolatrous practices but there is harmony among them, the *midat hadin* [Justice] cannot touch them." This Midrash should, of course, not be seen as opening the door to idolatry. The Midrash is merely asserting that *shalom* should have no boundaries, that it should prevail amongst all. See also *Meshekh Hokhmah* to Exod. 14:29.

2. *Avot D'Rabbe Natan* 28—one who establishes harmony in the home is considered by Scripture as having established peace in Israel.

3. Domestic bliss includes harmony, contentedness, love, purposefulness, etc.

On the completeness of opposites, see *Likutei Eitzot* (Jerusalem, 1979), attributed to R. Nahman of Bratslav (*shalom*, n. 10). See also R. Shlomoh Wolbe, *Alay Shur*, that *shalom bayit* is not yet attained when there are no differences. Lack of differences probably indicates the couple have not yet fused their thoughts. *Shalom bayit* is when the couple have successfully bridged their differences (p. 258).

4. A lament echoed by Tsvi Travis, *Pirkey Hanhagat HaBayit*, vol. 1, p. 20.

5. On *shalom bayit* as the obligation of both husband and wife, see *Shevet Musar*, chap. 24, who proposes ten conditions for marital harmony, all of them responsibilities directed to the wife. Travis, *Pirkey Hanhagat HaBayit*, p. 12, and permeating the volume, places the primary onus for *shalom bayit* on the husband. The talmudic statement that "one who likes his wife as himself, honors her more than himself, channels his children in the upright path, and marries them off close to their attaining maturity, on such a man Scripture says 'And you will know that your abode is complete' " (*Yevamot* 62b, and cited in *Hilkhot Ishut* 15:19), seems to support the view that the primary onus for *shalom bayit* is on the husband. *Hilkhot Ishut* 5:20, based on *Kiddushin* 31a, counterbalances with

responsibility directed to the wife. Hence the author's balanced approach, reflecting the balance in talmudic tradition regarding *shalom bayit* responsibility.

On *shalom bayit* being a Godly blessing, see *Sotah* 17a. At the same time, the couple must be worthy, and the language of the Talmud, *Sotah* 17a, points to this conclusion. "If they merit [to go in the upright way—Rashi], then the Divine Presence abides with them." The Godly blessing, then, follows a free-willed decision on the way of life the couple choose.

See further Yedidya Bronsdorfer, *Kedushat Morashah*, p. 39.

On *shalom bayit* being a responsibility each has toward the self, see Sima Basry, "Shalom Bayit," p. 666; *Binyan Aday Ahd*, p. 95. Both correctly argue that *shalom bayit* is the responsibility of each, and not to be demanded of the other.

On being demanding of oneself, see *Avot D'Rabbe Natan* 41. Also, *Sotah* 21b, where the Talmud condemns the practice of making things difficult for others but lenient for oneself.

Relative to taking the initiative, Basry, "Shalom Bayit," advises not to say, "If only my spouse will change, I will then gladly change." Say rather, "If I change, my spouse will not to be able to continue as usual."

One should not underestimate the likelihood that marriage partners can become hostile, or the power of that hostility. See Tosafot to *Taanit* 20a, s.v. *v'natarot*, who offers as one possible explanation of Prov. 27:6 that the hate that evolves from two who previously liked each other is a real hate (true hate).

6. On not provoking, see *Sefer HaMitzvot*, "Lo Taaseh," no. 251; a person should not say things that will anger others. Do not be provoked, easy to anger (*Avot* 2:15). See further *Yevamot* 44a, "Do not introduce strife into your home."

See Gloss of RaMoh to *Orah Hayyim* 250:1, that one should always have the knife sharpened and ready for use, a reference to being ready in time for the Sabbath with that which is necessary for a pleasant Sabbath, and through this you will know that your abode is complete. A knife that does not cut well can lead to recriminations and bad feelings (*Mishnah Brurah*, n. 5.) This, then, is just symbolic of the need to anticipate and prevent strife situations from developing.

7. The principle of being understanding is an application of "Judge all individuals charitably" (*Avot* 1:6).

Regarding being forgiving, one should be "soft as a reed, not hard as a cedar"—*Taanit* 20a, and should not be insistent and unrelenting on one's due— *Megillah* 28a; *Orah Hayyim* 606:1 and *Hilkhot Teshuvah* 2:10.

8. Regarding the avoidance of "no-escape" situations, Travis, *Pirkey Hanhagat Habayit*, recommends having a second suit for the Sabbath always ready, to avoid arguments if the first one is not (vol. 1, p. 179).

On the proper attitude if something breaks or spills, see *Numbers Rabbah* 9:2—if wine spills, be forgiving.

On the proper perspective, see R. Eliyahu Taharani, *Alufaynu Mesubalim*, where he cites and analyzes the famous story of a poor sage who saved his money, bought a beautiful *etrog,* and showed it to his wife, who became enraged that he should spend on an *etrog* when the family was hungry for bread, and broke off the *pitum* (tip), thus invalidating the *etrog.* The sage rushed to close the window so that his red-faced wife would not get sick from the draft blowing on her livid face (vol. 1, pp. 161–163). See also Travis, *Pirkey Hanhagat HaBayit,* vol. 1, pp. 161–163, for a counseling situation concerning a *kugel* controversy.

9. Regarding the primacy of *shalom bayit* in the form of lights, see *Shabbat* 23b, *Orah Hayyim* 263:3, *Hilkhot Hanukah* 4:14. Rambam concludes with "Great is peace, for the entire Torah was given to make peace [completeness] in the world."

On great sages allowing themselves to be humiliated to save a marriage, see *Nedarim* 66b.

On the communal significance of each union, see above, n. 2.

10. Regarding manipulation of the truth, see *Yevamot* 65b. For a wide-ranging discussion of this and other matters related to shalom, see Yosef Epstein, *Mitzvat HaShalom.*

That God manipulated the truth is stated in *Yevamot* 65b, based on Gen. 18:13.

11. Num. 5:11–31. See also *Hinukh,* no. 453.

12. Related to the erasing procedure as no longer in practice, see *Hinukh,* no. 364.

On duty to God not being used as an excuse, see further Travis, *Pirkey Hanhagat HaBayit,* vol. 1, pp. 180–81.

13. On the husband's legal obligation to honor his wife, see *Yevamot* 62b, *Sanhedrin* 76b. See also *Bava Mezia* 59a, *Hilkhot Ishut* 15:19. See also *Menorat HaMaor* (*ner* 3, *klal* 6, pt. 4, chap. 1), who says that "if the wife behaves properly, it is a *mitzvah* for the husband to honor her and make her happy." The language of contingency is problematic, since the obligation of each to honor the other is unconditional, as it so appears from the Talmud and Rambam cited here.

On honor implying salient respect, see Travis, *Pirkey Hanhagat HaBayit,* vol. 1, p. 74, who offers a most insightful interpretation to Rashi on *Yevamot* 62b regarding the obligation to honor the wife more than oneself, to which Rashi adds that disrespect to her is more serious than that directed to him. Travis explains that what would normally not be considered disrespect in regard to others is so in regard to the wife. Neglect of others is not disrespect, neglect of one's wife is. Hence, the honor due to her is escalated beyond normal dictates of honor.

That the wife is the main cause for blessing in the home is enunciated in *Bava Mezia* 59a.

On laxity in honoring one's wife, see Travis, *Pirkey Hanhagat HaBayit,* vol. 1, p. 199.

14. On the dignity of the wife as a person, see R. Shlomoh Aviner, *Pirkey Ahavah Bayn Ish L'Ishto,* where he cautions in strong language against seeing women as baby factories and laments the physical and emotional depletion of women made to have "as many as possible" (p. 52).

Aviner further argues that stereotyping is dangerous, and that many women, by having the freedom to contribute beyond the home, are thus happier and more fulfilled, and consequently better able to take care of the home (p. 54).

Concerning the voicing of appreciation, A. A. Girshuni, "HaMafteah L'Osher," argues that the obligation to honor "more than oneself" implies a special duty to verbalize appreciation (p. 642).

15. Regarding gentle tones, see *Bava Mezia* 59a, *Hilkhot Ishut* 15:19.

Relative to being careful not to embarrass, see *Binyan Aday Ahd*, p. 62, and Taharani, *Alufaynu Mesubalim*, p. 167, for interesting examples of this. See also, for example, *Ketuvot* 72b, regarding the implications of giving one's wife a bad reputation as stingy. See also above, Chapter 3.

On intimate, nonformal language, see *Binyan Aday Ahd*, loc. cit., quoting the Hazon Ish.

16. Regarding inordinate burdens, see *Sotah* 11a–b, *Ketuvot* 72a. Yoel Schwartz, *Ish V'Re'eyhu*, cites the Hazon Ish about the care to be exercised in making requests of others (p. 34). This does not apply to husband and wife, given to helping each other, but taking advantage is also not proper.

On the husband being sensitive not as a mere technique, the obligation to honor the wife *yoter megufo* (*Yevamot* 62b), "more than himself," may also imply honor beyond self-serving motivations.

17. Concerning the prohibition against causing pain, see Lev. 25:17; see also *Hinukh*, no. 341. Its specific application to one's wife is delineated in *Bava Mezia* 59a. See further on this *Netivot Olam* of Maharal (pt. 2, "Ahavat Re'a"). For the extent of application, see Taharani, *Alufaynu Mesubalim*, pp. 172–173.

That pain can be caused by failure to act properly is evident in the instructive talmudic episode of R. Rehumi (*Ketuvot* 62b).

The wife seeks and desires this approbation because the husband is such an important part of her world, not for the reason suggested by Travis (*Pirkey Hanhagat HaBayit*, vol. 1, p. 57).

18. On the obligation to honor the wife more than oneself, see above, note 13.

See *Hilkhot Ishut* 15:19. See also *Hullin* 84b and *Hilkhot De'ot* 5:10. Also interpretation of Rashi to *Sanhedrin* 76b that *yoter megufo*, "more than himself," applies to nice ornaments.

19. For more on the letter and spirit of the "honor" obligations, see Shlomoh Ashkenazi, *HaIsha B'Aspaklaryat HaYehadut*, vol. 1, pp. 36–38.

20. On *shalom bayit* not being a one-sided obligation, see above, n. 5. Compare Travis, *Pirkey Hanhagat HaBayit*, vol. 1, pp. 40–41, who places an almost one-sided onus on the husband.

21. On husband's priority relative to respect, see *Kiddushin* 31a. See further, R. Shlomoh Wolbe, *Maamaray Hadrakhah LeHatanim*, p. 5. See further a problematic responsa of *Bet Yaakov*, no. 147 (paragraph beginning *V'Od*), and the comment thereon in Epstein, *Mitzvot HaBayit*, vol. 1, p. 286.

On coherence and adopting the wife's customs, see above Chapter 2, n. 20.

22. On leading with humility, see further *Megillah* 12b and *Hilkhot Ishut* 15:20.

Ḥukay HaNashim of the Ben Ish Ḥai, p. 43, carries the wife's obligation of honoring the husband to a somewhat unrealistic extent.

Ben Ish Ḥai does admit that this *sefer* is one-sided toward the wife's responsibilities, and says that in another volume he will delineate the husband's responsibilities. In the foreword to the present volume, it is reported that his grandson confirmed that this *sefer* was written but that unfortunately it was lost. Such works as that by Travis, though of a different sort, restore a balance by going to the other extreme and placing extraordinary onus on the husband.

HaMakneh to *Kiddushin* 30b ("Tani") states that though in matters of honor the wife defers to the husband, there is no obligation for the wife to be in "awe" of the husband, and thus not able to sit in his seat, for example.

23. On the wife carrying out the husband's desires, RaMoh, in his Gloss to *Even HaEzer* 69:7, cites the famous and much employed comment of *Tanna D'bay Eliyahu* that "there is no more noble a woman than the one who does her husband's will." *HaMakneh* (see n. 22) insists that this is not a legal obligation. See further the note of *Hagaot Maimoniut* to Rambam, *Hilkhot Ishut* 15:20.

The deeper meaning of the statement in *Tanna D'bay Eliyahu* may be that the noble wife intuitively knows what is her husband's will and does not hesitate to actively enhance her husband. This is a key element in marriage, but certainly not a one-sided dynamic.

Wolbe, *Maamaray Hadrakhah LeHatanim*, advises very strongly against any domineering, bosslike behavior of the husband. The way to gaining respect is by being respectful (p. 20). This is obvious, but even the obvious needs reinforcement.

24. Relative to the wife's tasks, R. Yosef Weiner, *Neve HaBeḥirah*, compares the woman to a levite in Temple times (p. 69, p. 73).

On the wife's slavelike tasks, see *Menorat HaMaor* (*ner* 3, *klal* 6, pt. 4, chap. 2), who suggests the servitude dynamic adopted by the wife as the best way to elicit the equivalent positive response of the husband.

For more on the ill-advisedness of a master-slave relationship in marriage, see Louis Birner, "Unconscious Resistance to Pre-Marital Counseling," p. 26.

The biblical precedent for a master being slave is developed in *Kiddushin* 20a, regarding whoever acquires a slave effectively acquires a master, and the obligations attendant thereto. Travis, *Pirkey Hanhagat HaBayit* (vol. 1, p. 60), urges that the husband should see the relationship with his wife as free of any subservience on her part.

Servitude being the dedication of one part of the body to another is the analogy of Rabad, *Baaley HaNefesh*, in introduction. See also Epstein, *Mitzvot HaBayit*, vol. 1, p. 79.

25. Honor "more than enough" is the language of Rambam, *Hilkhot Ishut* 15:20.

26. On a harmonious couple meriting the Godly presence, see *Sotah* 17a.

The consuming fire is a reference to the aforementioned talmudic comment that if the couple are not meritorious, they will be consumed by fire.

27. On distancing from anger, see for example *Nedarim* 22a–b. Also *Hilkhot De'ot* 2:3.

On anger as on a par with idolatry, see *Shabbat* 105b.

The relation of anger to arrogance is elaborated in *Orhot Zadikim*, "HaKaas."

On anger carrying with it a multitude of sins, see *Nedarim* 22b. Wolbe, *Maamaray Hadrakhah LeHatanim*, claims that the one who acts in anger cannot be a *talmid hakham* (p. 17).

28. On the consequences of anger-induced fear, see *Gittin* 7a.

The benefits of control and calm are stated in *Megillah* 28a; there a connection is made between calm demeanor in the home and longevity (*arikhat yamim*, "length of days"), length of days denoting quality of life.

29. On refraining from anger, see *Hilkhot De'ot* 5:10.

See praise of self-control in time of conflict in *Hullin* 89a. Regarding an understanding response to what may appear as an outlandish request, see *Genesis Rabbah* 71:10. *Haredim* (chap. 4, under "Commandments related to the mouth and the windpipe *midivray kabbalah* and *midivray sofrim*, and able to be fulfilled every day") states that answering softly to one who talks tough (in anger) is a *mitzvah* (no. 5).

30. Concerning the worthwhileness of becoming angry, G. Naftali, in *Iggeret LeHatan*, suggests that getting angry at one's mate should be seen as ridiculous, in the same way as getting angry at the left foot for kicking the right (p. 60). See *Hilkhot De'ot* 6:6. See also Taharani, *Alufaynu Mesubalim*, for some suggestions on how to avoid anger (vol. 1, pp. 24–27).

31. The advice "Do not get angry, and you will not sin" (*Berakhot* 29b) is always timely. See *Hilkhot De'ot* 2:3.

Carol Tavris, in *Anger*, a wide-ranging and incisive study of the topic, disputes the conventional wisdom that "getting it off the chest" helps. Actually, it makes one angrier. She asserts that letting it out has raised the decibel level of noise, but has not solved problems. She adduces evidence that talking it out does not reduce anger, but rehearses it. She recommends reappraisal and trying to understand the behavior of the supposed provoker of the anger, among other suggestions (pp. 120–150).

In the words of Jane Appleton and William Appleton, *How Not to Split Up*, "no one has ever shown that shouting or fighting clears the marital air" (p. 86). The authors advise keeping quiet (they use less subtle language) and putting any response in an anger-provoking situation on hold, to gain time in which to soften the reaction (p. 88).

32. The relation of proper perspective to control of anger probably explains why the one who never becomes angry is one of the types that is beloved by God (*Pesaḥim* 113b). See the episode related by Naftali, *Iggeret LeḤatan*, pp. 151-153.

Among the traditional tracts on the control of anger is *Mesilat Yesharim*. A more recent and useful volume is R. Avraham Yellin's *Erekh Apayim*. Also available and an excellent sourcebook is R. Zelig Pliskin's *Gateway to Happiness*.

Resolve to be extrascrupulous about losing control is recommended in *Hilkhot De'ot* 2:3.

33. The statement about not engaging in excessive idle chatter with women is in *Avot* 1:5. Further elaboration of its implications can be found in my *As a Tree by the Waters*, pp. 28–29.

34. Bronsdorfer, *Kedushat Morashah*, recommends that the wife not strive to know the inner feelings of her husband (p. 47), questionable advice to say the least.

That the husband should be forthcoming about his activities is stated in a letter of Ḥazon Ish, printed for the first time in Wolbe's *Maamaray Hadrakhah LeḤatanim*.

The husband should be careful not to relate matters which will lower the wife's respect for him (*Avot D'Rabbe Natan* 7), and does this best by not becoming involved in such matters.

35. For the legal implications of sharing and consulting, see Ben Zion Shereshevsky, *Diney Mishpaḥah*, pp. 144–145.

The talmudic advice, "If your wife is short, bend down to listen to her" (*Bava Mezia* 59a), points to a true one-to-one relationship. One can listen to someone shorter without bending down; the bending down is a symbolic concept of perceiving the relationship as that between two respecting equals.

36. Aviner, in *Pirkey Ahavah Bayn Ish L'Ishto*, claims that two good people can have a difficult time together (p. 85). That may be true, but the more good they are, the less this is likely.

37. On tender communication, see *Hilkhot Ishut* 15:19. Even concerning *mitzvah* fulfillments, it is mandated that any instructions be conveyed in soft tones (*Shabbat* 34a, *Oraḥ Ḥayyim* 260:2).

38. Relative to proper admonition, it is posited that "love without admonition is not true love" (*Genesis Rabbah* 54:3).

On the difficulties involved in admonition, see *Arakhin* 16b. When done with sensitivity and caring, it can actually enhance the relationship, it "leads to love" (*Genesis Rabbah* 54:3).

39. On warmth in communication, see Prov. 15:17.

Related to doing nice things, there is no nicer thing one can do for the other than extending a cheery, loving disposition (*Avot D'Rabbe Natan* 13). See Epstein, *Mitzvot HaBayit*, where the author suggests that if one wants to buy his wife a gift but cannot afford it, he should tell her of his desires, and indicate that he looks forward to improved conditions when he will be able to buy the desired item (vol. 1, p. 355).

40. On each having no better a friend, see R. Eliezer Papo, *Pele Yoetz* ("Aizah"). The author makes the suggestion, then quickly rescinds it. His argument for rescinding is weak, so the suggestion remains.

Statements about the plus side of the relationship can be found, for example, in *Shabbat* 24b and *Bava Batra* 145b; the minus side, for example, in *Bava Batra* 145b.

41. See further on this *Shabbat* 118b; also *Yevamot* 63a, the discussion of *ezer knedgo*, and comment of Maharsha.

CHAPTER 6

1. Marriage works if it is worked at. See further R. Shlomoh Aviner, *Pirkey Ahavah Bayn Ish L'Ishto*, p. 2.

2. The verse referred to, in its entirety, reads as follows: "And I will betroth you unto Me forever; and I will betroth you unto Me with righteousness and justice, and with loving-kindness and mercifulness. And I will betroth you unto Me with faithfulness, and you shall know the Lord" (Hos. 2:21–22). See further on this Norman Lamm, *A Hedge of Roses*, pp. 13–14.

3. Yedidya Bronsdorfer, *Kedushat Morashah*, p. 41, recommends never talking, except in a counseling situation, about internal house matters.

4. R. Eliyahu Dessler, in *Mikhtav M'Eliyahu* (pt. 1, p. 39), states that when the couple falls into the demand syndrome, their happiness is behind them.

5. See Tsvi Travis, *Pirkey Hanhagat HaBayit*, vol. 1, p. 79; Sima Basry, *The Challenge of Marriage*, pp. 100–101.

6. Basry, *Challenge of Marriage*, pp. 37, 43.

7. On happiness and marriage, it is asserted that one of the deficits for a person who does not marry is that of having a life without true happiness (*Yevamot* 62b); see also Gloss of RaMoh to *Even HaEzer* 1:1, and comment of the GRA, no. 3.

R. Nahman of Bratzlav, in *Likutay Eitzot*, says that it is a great *mitzvah* to be in a happy frame of mind always, and one must muster all one's resources to thrust off depression and melancholy and to always be only happy (p. 184). He perceptively realizes the difficulty in this advice and recommends even acting silly as a way to become happy.

8. See the classic reaction of Elkanah to the depressed feeling of his wife Hannah (1 Sam. 1:8).

9. Concerning being forgiving, one may find in more comprehensive prayer books a preamble to the regular nightly Shma before retiring, which includes a statement absolving all individuals who may have caused one harm or who caused one to become angry (see, for example, Rabbi Yitzhak Bernfield's edition

of *Siddur Ḥatam Sofer* [Bnai Brak: Zikhron Meir, 1980]; also *Siddur Minḥat Yerushalayim* [Jerusalem: 1972], ed. Rabbi Y. A. Dvorkes).

See Bronsdorfer, *Kedushat Morashah*, p. 40, for a further elaboration of the notion of *vatranut* (not standing on ceremony, deferring, accepting).

See further R. Shlomoh Wolbe, *Kuntrus Hadrakhah LeKalot*, pp. 23–25; R. Eliyahu Taharani, *Alufaynu Mesubalim*, vol. 1, pp. 20–28.

10. Hillel's statement is in *Avot* 1:14. See the famous response of the same Hillel to the one who demanded to be taught the entire Torah while standing on one foot (*Shabbat 31a*). The balance of concern for the self and reaching out to others in the Mishnah presently under discussion may be seen as an elaboration of the verse which is at the root of that response (Lev. 19:18).

11. Reuven P. Bulka, *As A Tree By the Waters*, pp. 42–43.

12. Maimonides' views are found in *Guide for the Perplexed*, pt. 3, chap. 49.

13. See further Reuven P. Bulka, "Divorce: The Problem and the Challenge."

14. See on this the talmudic lament (*Shabbat* 32b–33a).

15. This operative dynamic is helpful in overcoming times of argument and conflict, since a framework of concern has been established. See further G. Naftali, *Iggeret LeḤatan V'Hadrakhah LeNasuy*, p. 53.

On the meaning of transcendence in life, see Viktor E. Frankl, *Man's Search for Meaning*, p. 175.

16. On not expecting reward, see *Avot* 1:3.

On the importance of expressing gratitude, see, for example, *Berakhot* 7b.

17. On appreciativeness even in taxing circumstances, see *Yevamot* 63a–b. *Sefer Ḥaredim*, in "Positive commandments *medivray kabbalah* and *medivray sofrim* that are related to the heart and can be fulfilled every day," includes in that category the duty to be grateful to anyone who has performed a kindness to you, and even a small kindness should be viewed as a large kindness. One should never be ungrateful (chap. 1, no. 23).

18. See R. Eliezer Papo, *Pele Yo'etz* ("Ahavat Ish V'Ishah"). Also Travis, *Pirkey Hanhagat HaBayit*, vol. 1, p. 116.

Under normal circumstances, marital benefits are always forthcoming (*Bava Mezia* 59a).

19. For more on *taharat hamishpaḥah*, see Chapter 10.

20. R. Akiva Eiger writes that he often would argue with his wife on matters related to "awe of God" for half the night (*Mikhtivay Rabbe Akiva Eiger* [Petaḥ Tikvah, 1969], p. 149).

21. See R. Shlomoh Wolbe, *Maamaray Hadrakhah LeḤatanim*, p. 9, where the author cautions patience with interruptions that are likely to interfere, usually related to household matters.

22. See R. Yosef Epstein, *Mitzvot HaBayit*, vol. 1, pp. 95–96, 96–105; also his *Mitzvat HaEitzah*, pp. 363–367.

23. On differentness, see *Sanhedrin* 38a. On differences and marriage, see Wolbe, *Kuntrus Hadrakhah LeKalot*, p. 23.

24. A. A. Girshuni, "HaMafteaḥ L'Osher," contends that if either of the partners can find no instance of having deferred, forgiven, helped the other, or changed a personality trait, it is a sign that all is not right (p. 648).

25. "Make sure you are okay and do not worry about the other. Then almost naturally the other will also be okay" (Aviner, *Pirkey Ahavah Bayn Ish L'Ishto*, p. 69).

26. The natural extension of "not appeasing in time of anger" is that one should choose a propitious moment (see *Avot* 4:23).

27. See *Binyan Aday Ahd*, p. 77, where the author cites a statistic that a woman usually is ready forty-seven minutes later than the time agreed upon for an engagement. Women, in fairness, do not have an exclusive hold on lateness.

28. One cannot extricate oneself from one's own prison (*Berakhot* 5b).

29. Naftali Kover, "Drakhehah Darkhey Noam," suggests that every couple have such a person agreed upon even before marriage (p. 650).

30. See *Taanit* 22a and comment of R. Ḥananel on the merit of specialists in making peace among parties in conflict. See also *Iggeret HaTeshuvah* of Rabbenu Yonah (2nd day, no. 14) that it is obligatory to appoint specialists to bring peace between husband and wife, people who are themselves happy and content. See Epstein, *Mitzvot HaBayit*, vol. 1, pp. 418–419.

31. See Epstein, *Mitzvat HaEitzah*, p. 10.

32. Relative to the context for pleasure, the Talmud states that the Godly presence resides not in depression but in happiness, but the happiness that is praiseworthy is that which is connected to *mitzvah*, to fulfillment of a higher meaning (*Shabbat* 30b).

Further discourse on psychology and humility is found in Epstein, *Mitzvat HaEitzah*, pp. 49–58.

On the differing perspectives of "mental health" and Torah tradition, see Norman Linzer, *The Jewish Family*, pp. 43–48.

On the track record of psychology, see further James McCary's *Freedom and Growth in Marriage*, where he laments the sorry state of affairs in marriage counseling (p. 357). Gerald Gurin, Joseph Veroff, and Sheila Feld, in *Americans View their Mental Health*, found that only a quarter (25 percent) of those who went to marriage counselors felt they were helped a lot, with about two-thirds (67 percent) feeling that the counseling did not help at all. Clergymen, by the way, scored well, but there may be reasons other than counseling ability involved (pp. 314–324).

For a further critique of psychological services, see Martin Gross, *The Psychological Society*. All this is not to condemn wholesale, it is to urge extreme caution when contemplating counseling.

33. Epstein's critique (*Mitzvat HaEitzah*, p. 49) that true respect by the

clinician for the person in trouble is lacking is well taken, but it is unfair to make of this an across-the-board generalization. A good clinician will not see the client as a springboard to wealth, and will certainly be respectful. There are others who might be aloof or abrupt (Lacan) but may do so in the best interests of the client. And then there are those who are a discredit to their profession. That, unfortunately, can be said of almost any profession.

Aviner (*Pirkey Ahavah Bayn Ish L'Ishto*, p. 62) expresses a negative view about going to psychologists, and attributes the same view to R. Moshe Feinstein (*Igrot Moshe, Yoreh Deah* 2, 57). This is a misreading of the responsum. R. Feinstein's responsum deals with clinicians who have an antireligion posture, not with all clinicians. Travis (*Pirkey Hanhagat HaBayit*, vol. 1, p. 21) also lashes out at those whose personal ethics and morals are wanting, yet dispense advice to others on how to live. McCary (*Freedom and Growth in Marriage*, p. 363) actually attributes the ineffectiveness of marriage counselors partly to the fact that they have marital or personal problems of their own.

34. An example of a value-oriented psychology is the logotherapy of Viktor Frankl, a concise presentation of which may be found in his *The Doctor and the Soul*. For more on the adaptability of that approach to Judaism, see my *The Quest for Ultimate Meaning*.

On Jewish "cultural baggage," see, for example, Gerald Zuk, "A Therapist's Perspective on Jewish Family Values."

An excellent treatment of many of the issues that are posed in the Judaism-psychology interface is Moshe HaLevi Spero's *Judaism and Psychology*.

35. The Ben Sira debate is in *Sanhedrin* 100b.

36. See Leon Hankoff, "Psychotherapy and Values."

37. Moshe HaLevi Spero, "On the Relationship between Psychotherapy and Judaism."

38. Jacob Mermelstein, "Halachic Values and the Clinical Practice of Psychotherapy."

39. On the demise of behaviorism, see Sigmund Koch, quoted in Michael Mahoney and Diane Arnkoff, "Cognitive and Self-Control Therapies," p. 689.

On behavior change and modification of thinking, see Donald Meichenbaum, *Cognitive Behavior Modification*.

40. *Hilkhot De'ot* 1:7.

41. On the spiritual orientation of logotherapy, see further Viktor Frankl's incisive volume, *The Unconscious God*.

42. See *Ḥagigah* 15b relative to taking the essence but discarding the shell. See further my "Psychology and Judaism—Retrospect and Prospect," from which much of the present analysis is excerpted.

43. On husband and wife helping each other, see R. Eliezer Papo, *Pele Yo'etz* ("Eitzah").

Epstein's claim that going to an outsider entrenches that there is a wall between the couple (*Mitzvat HaEitzah*, p. 361) is a weak argument. First, the going does not create a wall. Second, the willingness to go indicates an awareness that there is a problem. Third, the going itself, when accompanied by the resolve to overcome rather than merely to satisfy a demand of the spouse, quite likely will destroy the wall, if the counselor is a capable person.

CHAPTER 7

1. *Avot* 5:19.

2. See my *As a Tree by the Waters*, pp. 216–217.

3. "True love is bound to the covenant" (Aviner, *Pirkey Ahavah Bayn Ish L'lshto*, p. 8).

4. See commentary of Rambam to *Avot* 1:6, where he speaks of three types of relationship: (1) liking that suits purposes (*to'elet*), (2) liking that contains contentedness (*menuḥah*), and (3) exalted liking, a valuational fusion in which each will do anything for the other. See also Meiri to Prov. 9:8—that love is closeness of thought and fusion of desire. *HaKtav V'HaKabbalah* to Gen. 4:1 ("Yadeh") sees love as a union of wills (*ratzon*), effected through knowing (*da'at*). His view is akin to that of Meiri. These are all generalized descriptions, but do not get at the heart of the emotion itself, which is just about an impossible task.

5. Theodor Reik, in *A Psychologist Looks at Love*, spoke of love as a necessary illusion. The Ḥazon Ish is reported to have remarked that what others call love, we call extinction (*karet*) (R. Shlomoh Wolbe, *Maamarary Hadrakhah LeḤatanim*, p. 1).

Reik, in *Jewish Wit*, further suggested that in the traditional Jewish home, the marriage may have been happy even though the couple were not in love in the classical (?) sense (p. 98). See also Norman Lamm, *A Hedge of Roses*, p. 15.

6. In gematriac calculations, *ahavah* ("love") totals 13; and *eḥad* ("one") also totals 13. Love, therefore, is oneness.

7. "As of one piece" (*Akedat Yitzhak* to Gen. 2:21, *Shaar* 8, *Perek HaḤibur*, no. 4). See also *Mikhtav M'Eliyahu*, pt. 1, p. 36.

8. See Malbim to Deut: 24:1, that love evolves after, not before the wedding.

Love as the holy of holies is a reference to Song of Songs, considered to be the Holy of Holies of Scripture (*Yadayim* 3:5). Song of Songs expresses the love relationship between God and Israel in the language of the love of marital partners. See *Bava Batra* 99a, regarding the cherubim, male and female, on the Holy Ark which, facing each other, expressed the vitality of the Israel-God bond. See also Jer. 2:2.

9. On marriage bereft of love, Yeḥiel Asher, in "Halshah HaZeirah," brands the marriage of a young girl to one who is rich, but who will never love her, a heinous crime (p. 461).

Love enables the couple to overcome; hence, the famous observation that when love is strong, two can sleep on the edge of a blade; when love wanes, the widest bed is not big enough (*Sanhedrin* 7a).

Relative to love enabling the couple to realize their personal aspirations, compare "In the mutual surrender of love, in the giving and taking between two people, each one's own personality comes into its own" (Viktor Frankl, *The Doctor and the Soul*, p. 117).

Eliezer Papo, in *Pele Yo'etz* ("Ahavat Ish V'Ishah") asserts that it is imperative that there be a strong love between husband and wife. It may be obligatory, but it cannot spring up on its own. Obligatory implies that one can strive toward fulfilling the obligation. That comes from work. In other words, true love evolves from what each of the partners gives to the other.

10. The first seven days are referred to as the *shivat yemay mishteh* (seven days of feasting), in which, if there is a meal with a *minyan* (quorum) including *panim hadashot* (new faces), the seven blessings recited under the *hupah* are recited again at the conclusion of the festive meal, following the *Birkhat HaMazon* (Blessing after the Meal), hence the name given to these meals is *Sheva Berakhot*. See *Even HaEzer* 62:6–7; *Hilkhot Berakhot* 2:9. See a most eloquently expressed rationale for the *Sheva Berakhot* concept and practice in Maurice Lamm, *The Jewish Way in Love and Marriage*, p. 235.

On the obligation to focus attention exclusively on the bride, see *Ketuvot* 7a; *Even HaEzer* 64:1, *Hilkhot Ishut* 10:12.

That the seven days are not observed the way they should be is the lament of R. Shlomoh Luriah in *Yam Shel Shlomoh* to *Ketuvot* (chap. 1, no. 12). See further on this R. Yosef Epstein, *Mitzvot HaBayit*, vol. 1, p. 161.

11. Relative to the work prohibition in the first seven days, see *Even HaEzer* 64:1; *Hilkhot Ishut* 10:12. Hida, in *Hayyim Shaal*, pt. 2, sec. 38, no. 60, indicates that the prohibition extends even to light work.

On irretrievable work, see Hida, loc. cit. Also, R. Ovadyah Yosef, *Yabea Omer*, vol. 4, *Even HaEzer* sec., pt. 8, no. 3. Both argue that if the wife agrees, the husband can do work that is allowed in intermediate days of festivals as *davar haavad* (work which if not done causes irretrievable loss), as is the case in the search for income. See further *Yabea Omer*, loc. cit., no. 7, that the wife too can do necessary work at home with her husband's consent. The major obligation to gladden in these seven days rests with the husband, so that the conditions for the wife working are not as restrictive as for the husband.

On the anxiety related to the first conjugal experience, R. Barukh Yashar, *LeBat Yisrael B'Gil HaNisuin*, observes that there is some psychological difficulty for a young couple immediately consummating. They may need a few days of getting used to one another before they can properly and completely achieve consummation. He explicitly allows for this adjustment period, provided, of course, that no bleeding has occurred or has been induced (p. 107).

It should be noted that not merely through abstention from work does the groom fulfill the dictates of the first seven days. From the sources of the tradition, the work prohibition is somewhat akin to the work prohibition on the Sabbath, which on the Sabbath makes possible the true experience of the joy of

Sabbath, and in the seven days of wedding-like joy, makes possible the extending of full attention to the wife. Just as on the Sabbath one does not fulfill the *mitzvah* just by merely making it possible to observe the Sabbath—indeed one must actively enjoy the Sabbath—so too the groom does not fulfill his obligation simply by being there if needed. He must actively use the time made available by the work proscription to share, with his wife, her thoughts and feelings, setting her at ease and making her glad. The mere discussion of whether either can waive the claims of attention is also noteworthy, for the marriage itself is bigger than either of them alone, and what is at stake in these seven days is not merely personal satisfaction; also at stake is the stability of one of the communal building blocks (see *Ḥelkat Meḥokek* to *Even HaEzer* 64, n. 2, who offers a different rationale).

This matter of whether the right to undivided attention, the wife's responsibility, can be waived for the bride by the groom, clearly shows that the wife too is an important partner in this gladdening process, even though the primary onus is on the husband.

12. The first seven days condense, with great intensity, the pattern of embrace—distance that prevails through the marriage; hence, the absolute importance of these seven days.

13. Concerning the ecstasy of the wedding, the wedding itself is referred to in the Talmud as *hillula* (see, for example, *Berakhot* 30b). This carries with it the connotation of praise (*hallel*) and levity (*hollelut*). The wedding in fact strides between the two, combining seriousness and celebration, conveying the idea that marriage is a serious ecstasy.

On the role of others in making the couple feel happy, R. Ḥayyim David HaLevy, in *Mekor Ḥayyim,* suggests that the reason why the community is obliged to share in extended joy with the bride and groom is to make them forget all the complexities of life that await them after the wedding (p. 50). Somehow, that theory does not sit well. *Sheva Berakhot* is not an escape from reality, it is a mood-setter to be able to better handle reality. See further *Ketuvot* 16b–17a, *Even HaEzer* 65:1.

14. One of the seven blessings asks that the bride and groom be as happy as Adam and Eve in the Garden of Eden (see *Ketuvot* 8a, *Even HaEzer* 61:1, *Hilkhot Berakhot* 2:11, *Hilkhot Ishut* 10:3). For Adam and Eve, there was no one else in the community (i.e., no other people) to help them. They had to make it on their own, with God's help. For the present bride and groom, the community helps, but the responsibility is theirs.

15. The exemption and the reason for it are found in Deut. 24:5. See Elyakim Ellenson, *Ish V'Ishto,* p. 195, and n. 18. See also Ramban to Deut. 24:5.

16. If this is true of marriage in Israel, it is even more pertinent outside Israel, where the battle against internal erosion is even more critical.

17. On the husband's being there, see Deut. 24:5, *Ḥinukh,* no. 549. See also *Sefer HaMitzvot* of Rambam, *Mitzvat Aseh* no. 214.

The intent of the *mitzvah* is clear from the *Ḥinukh*, loc. cit. He sees the *mitzvah* as directed to acclimatize the husband and wife to each other so that involvement with any other person of the opposite sex will seem strange. The solidity of the family and the community is at issue in this *mitzvah*, and even the wife's allowing the husband to leave does not give the husband license to go for more than a few days.

Ellenson, *Ish V'Ishto*, reads in *Ḥokhmat Adam* 129:19 that even being away only one night is wrong (p. 196).

The last sentence of the paragraph in the text resolves the question raised by Ellenson (ibid., p. 197) about absence enhancing love, and here Halakhah ostensibly demands presence for an entire year.

18. See Responsa of Radvaz, 1:238, who allows leaving for the good of the home, to gladden his wife who is despondent over having nothing to eat.

One can see the issue of leaving on a continuum. The lower limit is established by the prohibition, forbidding going to war, or leaving for protracted periods (see *Ḥinukh*, no. 591). The upper limit is achieved via "Clear he should be to his house" (see *Ḥinukh*, no. 549). For that, there is no limit, and the more he is home and attentive to his wife (see above, n. 11), the better.

19. See *Sotah* 44a; see *Binat Adam* to *Ḥokhmat Adam* 129:19.

20. The pattern of living that a couple establishes at the beginning of their marriage usually becomes their lifelong pattern together, and it is for this reason that married couples should begin the process of adjustment early, when each is strongly motivated to make the marriage succeed (James McCary, *Freedom and Growth in Marriage*, p. 245). Quite without intent, this is an uncannily accurate reflection of the Torah concern in the *mitzvah* of the first year. See *Ḥinukh*, no. 549.

21. See Abarbanel to Deut. 24:5.

22. On bride and groom as royalty, see *Pirke D'Rabbe Eliezer* 16, *Semaḥot* 11. See also *Ketuvot* 17a.

See *Yalkut Shimoni* (Gen. 79) on why the matriarchs had difficulty bearing children, including a suggestion dealing with marital closeness.

23. Concerning the vulnerability in the first year, see further Ernest Burgess and Paul Wallin, *Engagement and Marriage*, pp. 617–618; Judson Landis and Mary Landis, *Building a Successful Marriage*, pp. 280–287.

Relevant to the obligation of always making the other happy, on the word *v'semaḥ*, to make happy one's wife, the *Baal HaTurim* (Deut. 24:5) observes that its numerical equivalent is 364, an allusion to the 364 days of the year that conjugality, according to biblical law, can be fulfilled, the only day biblically prohibited being, of course, Yom Kippur. See further Tsvi Travis, *Pirkey Hanhagat HaBayit*, vol. 1, p. 79.

On the requirement to buy the wife new clothes for each festival, see *Oraḥ Ḥayyim* 529:2, *Hilkhot Yom Tov* 6:18. See further Epstein, *Mitzvot HaBayit*, vol. 1, pp. 320–324; also *Mishnah Brurah* to *Oraḥ Ḥayyim* 240:1, n. 7, and *Shaar HaZiyon*, n. 3.

24. On the communal obligation to praise, see *Ketuvot* 16b–17a, *Even HaEzer* 65:1. See also *Bava Mezia* 87a, where the Talmud indicates that the *malakhim* (angels) responded as they did to Abraham in order to make Sarah more dear to him.

25. See *Zohar* to Gen. 9:1, that a guest should leave a present for the wife upon leaving and should give it to the husband for her, to increase the husband's affection for his wife.

See some enlightening episodes relative to not interfering with family harmony in R. Eliyahu Taharani, *Alufaynu Mesubalim*, vol. 1, pp. 160–161, 168; vol. 2, pp. 56–58. The last-mentioned relates that the Hafetz Hayyim married his stepfather's daughter, a few years older than he was, in order not to disturb the relationship between his mother and stepfather, who would have been upset had he not married the daughter, and the Hafetz Hayyim feared the upset would spill over into his mother's marriage. This, of course, is not what one would call an ordinary occurrence. But, on the other hand, the Hafetz Hayyim was not an ordinary man.

26. On the relation between deficient unions and deficient children, see *Nedarim* 20b, *Orah Hayyim* 240:3, *Hilkhot Isuray Biah* 21:12–13.

27. See *Menorat HaMaor* (*ner* 3, *klal* 6, pt. 6, chap. 4). Also *Siddur Bet Yaakov* of R. Yaakov Emden (*Hanhagat Leyl Shabbat, Heder MaMitot, Mitot HaKesef*, chap. 6).

See Meiri to *Kiddushin* 82b, that the statement of the Talmud regarding happiness or woe with one's children relates to deficiency in the children. See also *Kallah*, toward the end, that the well-being of one's children results from fulfilling the desires of Heaven and the desires of one's wife.

CHAPTER 8

1. See the commentary of R. Ovadyah to *Avot* 1:1, where he sees the notion of God as the souce of ethics as the inherent message of the first statement in the tractate.

On emulation of God, see Chapter 1, and note 8 in that chapter.

2. The quotation is from *Avot* 3:13. See further my *As a Tree by the Waters*, pp. 117–118.

3. See Prov. 3:6, *Berakhot* 63a, Mic 6:8, *Sukkah* 49b, *Makkot* 24a.

4. See R. Eliyahu Taharani, *Alufaynu Mesubalim*, vol. 1, pp. 155–156, where he discusses the tendency to take liberties within the family. See John Gottman et al., *A Couple's Guide to Communication*, where the authors observe that people tend to say mean, insulting things primarily to members of their own household (p. 45).

5. On assisting those who need help, see *Hinukh*, no. 536.

On doing that which is upright and good, see *Hinukh*, no. 608.

Ibn Ezra to Deut. 5:16 stresses that the essential purpose of all the commandments is to straighten out the heart. Focusing on the strict legalities stultifies, rather than expanding the heart in the right direction. But true service of God demands the heart (see Deut. 6:5–6, 10:12).

6. On being careful not to cause pain to one's wife, see *Bava Mezia* 59a.

7. Relative to the importance of that which pertains to everyday life, see the introduction of the Hafetz Hayyim to his classic work, *Mishnah Brurah*.

8. *Avot* 1:2.

9. Ibid., 1:3.

10. Ibid., 1:5.

11. Ibid., 1:6.

12. Ibid.

13. Ibid., 1:10.

14. Ibid., 1:12.

15. Ibid., 1:14.

16. Ibid., 1:15.

17. Ibid.

18. Ibid., 1:17.

19. Ibid., 1:18.

20. Ibid., 2:1.

21. Ibid.

22. Ibid.

23. Ibid., 2:5.

24. Ibid.

25. Ibid., 2:6.

26. Ibid.

27. Ibid., 2:8.

28. Ibid., 2:13.

29. Ibid., 2:15.

30. Ibid.

31. Ibid., 2:16.

32. Ibid., 2:17.

33. Ibid.

34. Ibid., 2:18.

35. Ibid., 2:20.

36. Ibid., 2:21.

37. Ibid., 3:1.

38. Ibid., 3:3.

39. Ibid., 3:12.

40. Ibid., 3:13.

41. Ibid., 3:16.

42. Ibid., 3:17.

43. Ibid., 3:19.

44. Ibid., 3:21

45. Ibid., 4:1.

46. Ibid.
47. Ibid.
48. Ibid.
49. Ibid., 4:2.
50. Ibid., 4:4.
51. Ibid., 4:20.
52. Ibid., 4:23.
53. Ibid., 5:10.
54. Ibid.
55. Ibid., 5:13.
56. Ibid., 5:14.
57. Ibid., 5:19.
58. Ibid., 5:20.
59. Ibid., 5:27.
60. See Ramban, Lev. 19:17, and further *Targum Yonatan ben Uziel*, ad loc. Also *Shabbat* 31a.
61. On communication of praise, see *Hilkhot De'ot* 6:3. See also *Ḥinukh*, no. 219.

On being concerned about others, see *Hilkhot Avel* 14:1. The language of the Talmud (*Shabbat* 31a), reflected in *Ḥinukh* (219), indicates being careful with what accrues to others. The Rambam in *Hilkhot Avel* sees in the *mitzvah* an active duty to help, but more as a fulfillment *(kiyum)* than an obligation *(ḥiyuv)*.

62. The notion of desiring for community is reflected in Ramban, Lev. 19:17. See also *Sefer HaMitzvot* of Rambam, *Mitzvot Aseh* 206.

63. On liking your neighbor as a great principle of Torah, see Yerushalmi, *Nedarim* 9:4. See also *Hilkhot Avel* 14:1.

On this being a *mitzvah* without boundary, see Ramban, Lev. 19:17. See also R. Yosef Epstein, *Mitzvat HaMusar*, p. 230.

64. See *Berakhot* 23a, *Ketuvot* 66a, *Menahot* 93b, *Bekhorot* 35b, for examples related to husband and wife being as one.

65. Related to seeing the other before marriage, see *Kiddushin* 41a. See *Sefer Ḥasidim* (389), that the woman must also see the prospective groom.

On not marrying an unfit partner, see Tosefta, *Sotah* 5:6.

Concerning the dignity of the other, see *Niddah* 17a, on conjugal relations in daylight.

Regarding not thinking about another possible mate, *Baal HaTurim* to Lev. 19:18–19 comments that the proximity of *v'ahavta* to the commands relating to admixture of diverse species teaches that the husband, who must love his wife, should not engage in conjugal relations with her and have his mind on another woman.

On not being deterred by an undesirable feature, see A. A. Gershuni, "HaMafteaḥ L'Osher," p. 640, for an allusion to this.

A further extension of "Like the other as yourself" is a comment of R. Baḥya, in *Kad HaKemah* ("Shavuot—Mitzvot Lo Taaseh"), who derives from the identification of wife with *re'ah* ("friend," as in *V'ahavta l're'akha*, "Love your friend") that one must never divorce one's wife.

66. As per the talmudic analogy of finding one's missing link (*Kiddushin* 2b). See also *Yevamot* 62b.

67. The comment about deeds shaping character is per the well-known view of the *Hinukh*, no. 20, that the deeds make the person.

CHAPTER 9

1. See R. Eliyahu Dessler, *Mikhtav M'Eliyahu*, pt. 1, p. 39.

2. See my "Some Implications of Jewish Marriage Philosophy for Marital Breakdown."

3. See further Bob Blood and Margaret Blood, *Marriage*, pp. 547-557.

4. See *Sanhedrin* 6b, that one must confront a conflict situation in the early stages, before it gets out of hand. Much of the marriage difficulties that fall into the laps of counselors could probably be prevented if the couple were alert to the first signs of deterioration in the relationship and did not let the slippage extend even further.

5. The observation that most marriages are failures is from Norman Lamm, *A Hedge of Roses*, pp. 11–12.

6. The talmudic source is *Bava Mezia* 59a—strife in the household is caused primarily by matters relating to sustenance.

See Blood and Blood, *Marriage*, pp. 523–544. Lloyd Saxton, in *The Individual, Marriage and the Family*, estimates that for 98 percent of all households in the United States there will never be enough money (p. 547). This leads to the suspicion that we may be dealing more with a matter of attitude than with legitimate financial difficulties, as Saxton himself implies. This factor is important, since studies such as that of Philip Blumstein and Pepper Schwartz, *American Couples*, indicate that disappointment with the amount of money the couple has is linked with marital disappointment in general (pp. 67–68).

7. On the primary onus for sustenance, see above, Chapter 3.

Regarding the resentments that may develop, see Blood and Blood, *Marriage*, p. 523.

8. A point stressed by R. Yosef Epstein, *Mitzvat HaEitzah*, p. 388.

9. On the matter of who should control the finances, R. Shlomoh Wolbe, *Kuntrus Hadrakhah LeKalot*, argues that the husband should control the finances (p. 15). Tsvi Travis *Pirkey Hanhagat HaBayit,* argues that the wife should be in control of the finances (vol. 1, p. 193).

Joint management is reflected in the wording of the *tenaim* (conditions of the engagement) that they "exercise equal control over their property." On the *tenaim,* and its use today, see the helpful few pages in Maurice Lamm, *The Jewish Way in Love and Marriage,* pp. 176–179. Even R. Shlomoh Wolbe urges that the couple have a joint account (*Maamaray Hadrakhah LeHatanim*, p. 11). Blumstein and Schwartz, *American Couples*, in their survey, found that couples who feel they have equal control over expenditures have a more tranquil relationship (p. 89).

On trusting the other, see R. Eliezer Papo, *Pele Yo'etz* ("Ahavat Ish V'Ishto").

Regarding the sharing of how the money was spent, see Ben Ish Hai, *Hukay HaNashim*, p. 44. It should be added that normal, level pitch dialogue is called for, not accusatory or suspicious tones.

10. This is not only good financial advice, it is good marital advice. See also Wolbe, *Kuntrus Hadrakhah LeHatanim*, p. 11.

11. On giving one's wife what she needs, *Shevet Musar* (chap. 16) recommends that one be affirmative to all requests made by the wife.

Relative to the importance of trusting one's wife, it is obvious that trust breeds trust, and creates a climate of respect. See Prov. 27:19. And, extend respect to your wife in order to be enriched (*Bava Mezia* 59a).

Travis, *Pirkey Hanhagat HaBayit*, recommends that the husband not go into the store when the wife goes clothes shopping (vol. 1, pp. 196–197). This may reflect more on his clientele than on what is advisable. Here, as in most such situations in marriage, the rule is not to have rules, but that each couple do what it feels is mutually comfortable.

12. Regarding support in times of crisis, *Shevet Musar*, in the third and fourth of his ten conditions for women in marriage (chap. 24), places this onus almost one-sidedly in the lap of the wife. He does, at the end of the ten-point program, indicate that his conditions, where relevant, apply equally to the husband. That point is specially pertinent concerning the issue presently under discussion, the need for each to be supportive in extra doses during a crisis.

For more on the proper approach to the financial situation, see the study of Richard Galligan and Stephen Bahr, "Economic Well-Being and Marital Stability," to the effect that the level of family income is not as central to marital stability as the wisdom with which the couple spends the money, and translates income into assets.

The talmudic observation that "whoever remains happy in the midst of trying circumstances brings salvation to the world" (*Taanit* 8a) expresses in lucid terms the idea that maintaining resolve and spirit is critical to managing one's problems. One who is overcome by the circumstances becomes depressed, creates a sour mood, and almost guarantees failure. Salvation, the capacity to fight, and the will to overcome, result from keeping proper perspective, and remaining happy. The talmudic observation is at once an ultimate truth and a sound principle for daily life.

13. See Robert Blood and Donald Wolfe, *Husbands and Wives*, pp. 247–248.

14. See Hope Leichter and William Mitchell, *Kinship and Casework*. Also, Gerald Leslie, *The Family in Social Context*. The former, in regard to Jewish families (p. 46), and the latter, in general (p. 244), see the wife–mother–in–law situation as the more likely to be problematic.

15. R. Yaakov Emden, in *She'elat Ya'avetz* (1:32) disputes the prevailing view that wife and daughter-in-law do not get along. He insists this is only true when they are living in the same abode. See further Harvey Locke, *Predicting Adjustment in Marriage*, pp. 119–123. He reports from surveys that living with in-laws is problematic for marriage, but living in close proximity is not.

16. Ruth 2:11.

17. On equal respect for parents and parents-in-law, see *Yoreh Deah* 240:24. *Sefer Haredim* (chap. 4, "Positive commandments related to the mouth and windpipe and able to be fulfilled every day"), in the beginning of the chapter, states that since husband and wife are now as one, the father and mother of the one are like the father and the mother of the other.

See Yerushalmi, *Bikurim* 3:3, regarding the custom of R. Yehuda b. Hiyya to visit his father-in-law, R. Yannai, every *erev Shabbat*, grateful for the wife to whom he was privileged to be married.

See Ben Ish Hai, *Hukay HaNashim*, p. 49, for an extreme example of gratitude to in-laws in spite of seemingly justified complaints.

See also *Moed Katan* 26b, *Yoreh Deah* 240:4 and 374:6, *Hilkhot Avel* 2:5 and 8:5. The issue is whether one must tear garments upon the passing of a parent-in-law. Whilst the talmudic statement indicates that this indeed is the case, not because of legal obligation but because of the honor due to one's spouse who is in mourning, the prevailing custom, as it has evolved, is to desist from such show of mourning.

18. See Landis and Landis, *Building a Successful Marriage*, who report that the happier a marriage is, the less likely it is that there will be in-law problems (pp. 331–332). This is hardly surprising, since the two are mutually reinforcing, the husband-wife and parent-child relationships.

19. James McCary, in *Freedom and Growth in Marriage*, suggests that if the couple who are marrying maintain an awareness that they too will eventually become in-laws, the in-law problems could possibly be avoided (p. 257).

The capacity to see the other side, and what might be going through their mind, is also a healthful approach for husband-wife relations.

See *Sefer Hasidim* 563 and 564, regarding the obligation of the husband to stand by his wife when she has problems with his contentious parents.

20. See the next chapter, which discusses the impact of *taharat hamishpahah* on the excitement factor in marriage.

21. On manna and spices, see *Yoma* 75a.

I remain unimpressed with the fact that the modern gurus of the bedroom, William Masters and Virginia Johnson, in *Human Sexual Response*, p. 265, suggest that a major contributor to the waning interest of one's partner is the lack of care about personal appearance. Unimpressed because it is ill-advised to make them the standard by which to operate. Their first books treated conjugality almost exclusively as a biological act, and only in *The Pleasure Bond* did such elements as fidelity and commitment enter their vocabulary. Even here, what they suggest these imply is a far cry from our understanding of these terms. As will become clear in the next two chapters, and is already seen in the matter presently under discussion (spices with manna), Judaic tradition has shown a sensitivity to these issues and its approach has stood the test of time. That is impressive.

22. On perfumers, see *Bava Kamma* 82b. Ezra was following in the tradition of the manna (*Yoma* 75a).

23. See *Shabbat* 140b, *Taanit* 23b, *Moed Katan* 8b, for some examples of this principle.

24. Concerning adornments, see *Midrash Tanhuma, Vayishlah* 5, that ornaments were given for wearing in the house. See the *Orhot Yosher* of R. Yitzhak Molkho, chap. 8 ("Azharat Nashim"), for an interesting discourse on this theme.

Related to abstaining from that which repulses, see advice of R. Hisda to his daughters (*Shabbat* 140b). Also, the advice of *Shevet Musar* (chap. 24, 1st and 9th conditions).

On dress, see Shabbat 64b, *Yoreh Deah* 195:9, *Hilkhot Isuray Biah* 11:19, that this applies, for the wife, even during the menstrual period.

25. What is herein proposed may sound simplistic. Mature individuals should understand. But the point here is that it is ill-advised for either of the partners to assume that the other will tolerate self-neglect. That is part of a behavior syndrome which could include a host of undesirable expressions. Each could feel free to let loose a temper tantrum here and there, hurl an insult now and then, be oblivious and insensitive on occasion, because the other will understand. And if the other really does understand, the "now and then" could escalate into a more regular pattern. The rest is almost predictable. The sanctity and inviolability of the relationship, as *kiddushin*-cum-*nisuin* ("holy toward uplifting"), asks that each not rely on the other's tolerance, but on their own good sense, to establish in their minds that the mate is absolute priority, and each will be at their best, in their best material and emotional uniforms, for the other.

CHAPTER 10

1. See *Siddur Bet Yaakov* of R. Yaakov Emden (*Hanhagat Leyl Shabbat, Heder HaMitot, Mitot Hakesef,* chap. 7, 3:17), where he observes that the chapter regarding conjugal relations is 240, or *RaM* in Hebrew. *RaM* backwards is *MaR*. In Hebrew, *RaM* means "exalted," *MaR* means "bitter." Good conjugality is exalted, bad conjugality makes things bitter.

2. Relative to conjugality as ultimate closeness, this is the way the *Hinukh,* no. 166, describes conjugality.

Regarding *shalom bayit,* see *Shabbat* 152a, and Rashi, *"Mishum shalom bayit,"* that conjugality is actually referred to as a *shalom bayit* instrumentality.

3. See Ramban's *Iggeret HaKodesh* (chap. 2), where he writes that when the union is for the sake of Heaven, there is nothing more holy or pure.

4. See Rambam, *Guide for the Perplexed* 2:36; also *Hilkhot Isuray Biah* 21:9. But

see *Hilkhot Shabbat* 30:14, where Rambam states clearly that this is part of Sabbath delight.

See beginning of chap. 2 of *Iggeret HaKodesh*. Also Maharal, *Be'er Hagolah* (*Be'er* 5), that there is no shame or disgust in creation, only glory. Any shame comes from the way a person uses or abuses the body.

5. On conjugality as holy as holies, see R. Moshe Hayyim Luzzatto, "Inyan HaZivug," in *Yalkut Yediot HaEmet*, vol. 2. See also Ramban, *Iggeret HaKodesh*, chaps. 2 and 5.

6. On the human generative organ, see Ramban to Gen. 2:9. Also, *Reshit Hokhmah* of R. Eliyahu Vidas (*Shaar HaKedushah*, chap. 16).

See RaDak to Gen. 3:7, that after the Garden of Eden episode the sensual lust was born in them, and the embarrassment was that an organ of the body was not under their control.

7. On being inspired by the beauty of one's mate, see *Yoma* 74b, where the Talmud exalts this more than the conjugal act itself.

On conjugality and souls, see *Siddur Bet Yaakov*, loc. cit., chap. 7, 2:6; Ramban, *Iggeret HaKodesh*, chap. 1.

Relevant to the Yom Kippur reading, see further Norman Lamm, *A Hedge of Roses*, pp. 27–28.

8. On preparatory expressions, see R. Moshe Sternbukh, *HaHalakhah B'Mishpahah*, p. 119, par. 7. At the back of that volume, p. 122, one can find the moving prayer composed by Ramban to be said before conjugal relations.

See also *Mishnah Brurah* to *Orah Hayyim* 240:15, n. 54.

On recitation of a blessing, see *Siddur Bet Yaakov*, in the notes to the *Shema* recited before retiring. Here R. Yaakov Emden suggests that the words *t'hay mitati shlema* ("may my bed be complete") were intended to also be a blessing over the pleasures of conjugality. David Feldman, in his otherwise excellent volume, *Marital Relations, Birth Control, and Abortion in Jewish Law*, overlooks this in his discourse on whether a blessing is said (p. 71).

Relative to knowing thoroughly the Halakhah for conjugality, *Shelah* (*Shaar HaOtiyot, ot kuf*), recommends knowing *Orah Hayyim* 240 and *Even HaEzer* 25 by heart. See above, Chapter 1, n. 36.

Related to the two works cited, R. Zerahiah HaLevi, in *Sela HaMahloket*, a response to Rabad's *Baaley HaNefesh*, says of the *Shaar Kedushah*, in which Rabad speaks of conjugal union, that it is "all nice and pleasant, pure of thought." On all other sections he has no shortage of rebuttals.

These two works by Ramban and Rabad, by the way, form the basis of R. Yaakov Emden's discourse on this theme in his *Siddur Bet Yaakov* (see *Siddur Bet Yaakov, Hanhagat Leyl Shabbat, Heder MaMitot, Mitot HaKesef*, chap. 7, 3:13). To be sure, there is some doubt as to whether Ramban is indeed the author of *The Holy Letter*.

Regarding the reliability of modern advice, one can refer, for example, to George O'Neill and Nena O'Neill, who in *Open Marriage* recommended that marriage in its traditional sense restricts growth, and open marriage, with acceptance by each partner that the other can share love with others, indicates a mature relationship (pp. 256–259). The philosophy of the O'Neills is absurd, and clinically it was a disaster. In *The Marriage Premise*, Nena O'Neill resurrected fidelity. The dangers of playing with grandiose theories are obvious, and jumping onto every fad, as indeed the O'Neills' theory was in the 1970s, invites disaster. Families and communities are not built by O'Neill types.

9. It does not really matter, but it is interesting that David Shope and Carlfred Broderick, in "Level of Sexual Experience and Predicted Adjustment in Marriage," using the Adams Marital Happiness Prediction Inventory, compared eighty girls who had no sexual experience before marriage with eighty who did. Overall scores revealed that girls with no previous sexual experience scored significantly higher in terms of predicted marital happiness, and the pattern was the same for predicted marital adjustment. So much for the idea that one needs to know all aspects of the partner before marriage.

But it really does not matter, because the Jewish approach to conjugal relations is not contingent on findings which reinforce the theory. The Jewish approach is of an unconditional, uncompromising nature. And it works.

10. For more on *yetzer* as energy, see R. Shimshon R. Hirsh's commentary to Gen. 6:5. An excellent treatment of the subject is found in Moshe HaLevi Spero's *Judaism and Psychology*, pp. 76–81.

On *yetzer hara* and creation, see Gen. 1:3, *Genesis Rabbah* 9:9.

See further my "Logotherapy as a Response to the Holocaust," pp. 138–145.

11. On serving God with the two *yetzer* tendencies, see *Berakhot* 54a.

12. On enjoying of God's bounty, see *Genesis Rabbah* 9:9.

13. See *Niddah* 13a–b, *Even HaEzer* 23:1, *Hilkhot Isuray Biah* 21:18. The condemnation in *Niddah* 13a–b is sweeping and uncompromising. *Even HaEzer* 23:1 calls it the gravest of all sins.

14. On conjugality and pregnancy, see the interesting comment in *Sefer Hasidim* (380) that by rights conjugality during pregnancy should be prohibited, but it would be too trying for both the husband and the wife and may have adverse consequences.

Rabad, in *Baalay HaNefesh* (*Shaar HaKedushah*), considers conjugality during pregnancy as potentially the second most exalted level of conjugality.

On relations with a wife incapable of having children, see Gloss of RaMoh to *Even HaEzer* 23:5. See further Feldman, *Marital Relations, Birth Control, and Abortion in Jewish Law*, pp. 65–71.

On sensuality without spirituality, *Sefer Haredim*, "Prohibitive commandments of the Torah connected to the reproductive organ" (chap. 7, no. 19), refers to masturbation as adultery without a partner.

Related to the times when conjugal relations are by custom enjoined, see *Hokhmat Adam* 128:19, cited in *Mishnah Brurah* to *Orah Hayyim* 240:1, n. 7. If the conjugal relations is in order to prevent spillage, *Hokhmat Adam* refers to such relations, even on Rosh Hashanah, as *mitzvah gedolah* ("a great *mitzvah*").

15. On killing desire, see Rabad, *Baaley HaNefesh* (*Shaar HaKedushah*), to-

ward the end. On abstinence, see *Taanit* 11a, *Nedarim* 10a, *Nazir* 19a, for examples. See *Even HaEzer* 76:13, that even insistence on wearing clothing during conjugal relations is grounds for divorce.

16. Conquering desire is from *Avot* 4:1.

Subordinating instincts to the spiritual is the meaning of serving God with the two *yetzer* components (*Berakhot* 54a).

The last statement of the paragraph is an allusion to "Whoever is greater than the other has a greater *yetzer*" (*Sukkah* 52a).

17. The left-right dialectic is from *Sotah* 47a.

R. Levi Yitzhak of Berditchev said that one whose passion for his wife is that of a bodily urge does not like his wife at all; instead he likes only himself (cited in G. Naftali, *Iggeret LeHatan*, p. 134).

In the customs around the wedding is included the throwing of nuts at the groom on the Sabbath before the wedding when he is called to the Torah (*Aufruf*). "Nut" in Hebrew is *egoz*, which is the numerical equivalent of *het* ("sin"), 17. Also, *tov* (good) is equivalent to 17. Aside from the reason suggested, that the groom is forgiven his sins, it may be that the intent is to tell the *hatan* that what would previously have been a sin, now, through marriage, becomes good. (See further, Naftali, *Iggeret LeHaton*, p. 137; Maurice Lamm, *The Jewish Way in Love and Marriage*, p. 190.)

The custom of throwing nuts is mentioned in *Berakhot* 50b; see *Orah Hayyim* 171:4 and *Hilkhot Berakhot* 7:9.

18. See *Hilkhot Mikvaot* 11:12; also R. Barukh Yashar, *LeBat Yisrael B'Gil HaNisuin*, pp. 9–10. See also the incisive piece by Norman Lamm, "Jewish Mothers," *The Royal Reach*, pp. 291–302.

19. See *Yoreh Deah* 201:3, *Hilkhot Mikvaot* 4:12.

See further N. Lamm, *A Hedge of Roses*, pp. 84–89. Also Aryeh Kaplan, *Waters of Eden*, pp. 45–46.

20. That separation is to recreate the wedding excitement is the precise notion of R. Meir (*Niddah* 31b). R. Meir is quite assertive in his language, and there is no need to mitigate its impact or lessen its significance (see Leo Levi, *Man and Woman*, p. 10).

On spices and perfumes, see p. 104.

Relative to routinization, see N. Lamm, *A Hedge of Roses*, p. 55. Jane Appleton and William Appleton, *How Not to Split Up*, in speaking of marital boredom, claim that one of the leading causes of the boredom is clinging to rigid routine (p. 13).

That the menstrual laws make possible a more intense intimacy has its parallel in the Sabbath restrictions. See Appendix 1. John Gottman et al., *A Couple's Guide to Communication*, observe that in a good relationship there are cycles of closeness and apartness. The couple need some breathing room, separateness, and independence. A perpetually intense intimacy is unrealistic (p. 147).

21. On problems that may arise because of adherence to *taharat hamishpahah*,

see Norman Fertel and Esther Feuer, "Treating Marital and Sexual Problems in the Orthodox Jewish Community." Also, Ruben Schindler, "Counseling Hassidic Couples."

That *mikveh* takes precedence over building a shul or writing a Torah is the ruling of the Ḥafetz Ḥayyim in *Sefer Bet Yisrael*; see R. Menaḥem Zaks, ed., *Kol Kitvey Ḥafetz Ḥayyim HaShalem*, vol. 1, pp. 25–26.

22. See R. Shimshon R. Hirsch to Lev. 20:18. In later years the sensuality may not be as intense, but it is there. See Chapter 11, n. 22. This is implicit in Eccles. 11:6. See also *Yevamot* 62b and *Moed Katan* 9b.

23. The gist of this idea is found in Raphael Patai, *The Jewish Mind*, pp. 502–504.

24. Relative to conjugal relations in the menstrual period, see Simone de Beauvoir, *The Second Sex*, pp. 27–29. Also, Rachel Neriah, *Happiness in Married Life*, pp. 21–26.

On the need for emotional intimacy, see further Aryeh Kaplan, *Made in Heaven*, p. 46.

R. Shimshon R. Hirsch, on Lev. 20:18, speaks of times when husband and wife are like brother and sister.

25. In places such as Tunisia and Morocco, the night of immersion was indeed a celebration, including a wedding-like festive meal.

26. See *Nidah* 7b, where *onah* is used to denote "time." The term can also refer to "his time," as in *onah shel talmiday hakhamim* ("the *onah* of scholars") (*Ketuvot* 62b). It is his time that must be shared with the wife.

See Ramban to Exod. 21:10, who sees the entire verse as related to conjugality—*she'er* is "intimacy," *ksut* is "bed linen," and *onah* refers to the relations. See also *Ketuvot* 48a. By this view, the obligation for maintenance is rabbinic rather than biblical. See also *Even HaEzer* 69:2, *Hilkhot Ishut* 12:2.

Sefer Ḥaredim ("Positive commandments from the Torah and related to the reproductive organ," chap. 7, n. 8) sees the *onah* obligation also as a positive command, based on Deut. 24:5; *v'semaḥ*, "to make her happy," is the obligation, or positive fulfillment, to carry out the *onah* duty, even when the wife is pregnant. See also *Sefer Mitzvot Katan*, 285.

27. Vows made by either to cut off conjugal visitation are ineffectual. See *Yoreh Deah* 234:67, *Hilkhot Nedarim* 12:9. See further Chapter 3.

28. On *onah* as debt, see *Even HaEzer* 25:2, *Oraḥ Ḥayyim* 240:1; also R. Yosef Epstein, *Mitzvot HaBayit*, vol. 2, "Mishpat HaIshut," p. 59; also R. Moshe Feinstein, *Igrot Moshe, Even HaEzer*, 3, 28.

On the extent of the husband's responsibility, see *Pesaḥim* 72b, Oraḥ Ḥayyim 240:1.

29. On the transgression for causing her pain, see *Even HaEzer* 76:11, *Hilkhot Ishut* 14:7. The accent is on "in order to cause her pain." Allowances are understandably made if he is sick and therefore cannot carry through his obligation. The transgression refers to Exod. 21:10.

On subjugating desire, see *Mishnah Brurah* to *Oraḥ Ḥayyim* 240:1, n. 6.

On agreeing to moderate, see *Even HaEzer* 25:2. See Rabad, *Baaley HaNefesh, Shaar HaKedushah,* who states that the primary *onah* obligation is when it is evident that the wife is desirous. See *Orah Hayyim* 240:1.

On waiving *onah* claims, see *Even HaEzer* 76:6, *Hilkhot Ishut* 15:1; also *Mishnah LeMelekh* to *Hilkhot Ishut* 6:10, *v'od.* With regard to the husband's waiving and whether he can retract, see Ben Zion Shereshevsky, *Dinay Mishpahah,* pp. 110–111.

See further *Ketuvot* 62a; Rashi, ad loc., *"urhah d'milta."* See also *Bet Shmuel* to *Even HaEzer* 76:4, n. 7.

30. The language of the Talmud is, "One is obligated to make one's wife happy via the conjugal command" (*Pesahim* 72b). This is an obligation applicable beyond the first year. See also *Igrot Moshe, Even HaEzer* 3, 28.

31. See Responsa of Maharam M'Lublin, no. 53, that the *mitzvah* includes not merely the consummation, but all forms of intimacy. See *Yoreh Deah* 184:10, and notes of Shakh (27) and TaZ (14). Also *Hilkhot Ishut* 15:17.

Conjugal relations is not an end in itself, but the by-product of genuine love.

32. The night of immersion is obligatory to such an extent that the custom of refraining from conjugality on Rosh Hashanah, the first night of Pesah and Shavuot, and the night of Shmini Atzeret does not apply if that coincides with immersion at the conclusion of the postmenstrual counting. See *Mishnah Brurah* to *Orah Hayyim* 240:1, n. 7.

Even HaEzer 76:4; *Sefer Haredim* ("Positive commands *medivray kabbalah* and *medivray sofrim* related to the reproductive organ," chap. 7, no. 1) considers conjugal visitation prior to embarking on a journey as a *mitzvah medivray kabbalah.*

See further the Gloss of RaMoh to *Yoreh Deah* 184:10. See also Rabad, loc. cit.

33. See Rashi to *Pesahim* 72b (*"L'sameah et ishto"*), who says that *onah* applies when he sees she is desirous. See above, no. 29.

On the legal minimum, see *Orah Hayyim* 240:1, *Hilkhot Ishut* 14:1.

The onus leans heavily on the husband. If it were a dual responsibility, each could legitimately argue they are waiting for the other. Cooperation and mutuality are not hereby eliminated, but neither are matters left to chance.

The Talmud (*Yevamot* 62b) states that "whoever knows that his wife is God-fearing and does not 'remember' her is considered a sinner." The idea is clear, but the text problematic. Since when is the husband's obligation to "remember" his wife contingent on whether the wife is God-fearing? There is here a subtle but potent message. The husband is less likely to ignore his wife when she makes obvious overtures. However, a God-fearing wife might not want to cause trouble, and may refrain from putting the husband in an uncomfortable position. She may really want, but her God-fearing uprightness prevents her from making her wishes known. The husband who knows that his wife is God-fearing, and thus is reluctant to make overtures, may conveniently ignore the real wishes of his wife, knowing full well that she will not complain. This, says the Talmud, is taking unfair advantage and is considered sinful.

34. See *Orah Hayyim* 240:1, *Even HaEzer* 76:1, 2; *Hilkhot Ishut* 14:1. The starting point is conjugal visitation every day, and the frequency is diminished based on the work conditions of the husband. *Sefer Mitzvot Katan* 285 states that the categories of lesser frequency because of hard work or travel conditions, i.e., *hamar* or *sapan,* are not relevant since so rare.

A regular worker in the city has a twice-weekly minimum; if the work is outside the city, the minimum is once per week.

See *Igrot Moshe, Even HaEzer* 3, 28, that present travel conditions are much easier in that one can fly long distances in short hours, thus mitigating the travel exemption.

The man of leisure who is healthy is in the category of everyday frequency. See Epstein, *Mitzvot HaBayit,* vol. 2, "Mishpat HaIshut," pp. 69–71, where he conjectures concerning the possibility that one who teaches children and gains pleasure from it is in the everyday category. See discussion in *Ketuvot* 62a–b.

35. See *Even HaEzer* 76:5, *Hilkhot Ishut* 14:2.

36. See *Even HaEzer* 76:11, *Hilkhot Ishut* 14:7, which allows for a six-month hiatus if the husband is not well. Elyakim Ellenson, *HaIshah V'haMitzvot,* vol. 3, p. 185, cites authorities who restrict this only to couples who have been married for a while, but for one whose potency is compromised at the very outset, the wife can ask for a divorce.

As to the general abstention from conjugality in time of famine (*Taanit* 11a), see *Orah Hayyim* 240:12, 574:4; *Even HaEzer* 25:6; *Hilkhot Taaniyot* 3:8. The general view is that on the night of immersion and also in the situation of not having fulfilled the procreative obligation, this abstention rule is waived. Tosafot (*Taanit* 11a, "*Asur*") states that this is not a law, but a matter of piety. See the lengthy discussion of this issue in Epstein, *Mitzvot HaBayit,* vol. 2, pp. 51–55.

On excessive conjugality, see *Even HaEzer* 25:2. See *Sukkah* 52b, where the Talmud observes that man has a small organ which if he underindulges will be satisfied, but if he overindulges will be hungry. The argument is that quality is more important than quantity.

See further *Gittin* 70a, *Orah Hayyim* 240:14, *Hilkhot De'ot* 4:19, that conjugality is one of a number of things which are good in limited doses but cause difficulty when done to excess.

37. On Sabbath eve conjugality, see *Ketuvot* 62b, *Orah Hayyim* 240:1, *Even HaEzer* 76:2, *Hilkhot Ishut* 14:1; Ramban, *Iggeret Hakodesh,* chap. 3. Also *Menorat HaMaor, ner* 3, *klal* 6, pt. 6, chap. 2.

Igrot Moshe, Even HaEzer 1, 102, says that it is self-evident that all who have a once-a-week frequency should choose the Sabbath. See *Baal HaTurim* to Exod. 21:10, who observes that the word *onatah* ("her *onah*") is written without a *vav,* the numerical equivalent of 6. He reads in this a hint that the main *onah* is not in the six, but in the seventh, the Sabbath. Further on, in the discussion of the Sabbath in Exod. 31:17, he notes that *biah,* the Hebrew word for "conjugality," is spelled out by the first letters of the words in the phrase *bnay yisrael ot he* ("it is a sign for the children of Israel"), which in the biblical text refers, of course, to the Sabbath.

See Rambam, *Hilkhot Ishut* 14:1, relative to the prowess of the talmudic scholar, who gives as the reason for the reduced frequency the fact that intensive study enervates.

38. *Hokmat Adam*, 128:19, cites a view that endorses twice a week for Talmud scholars. He says that each situation must be taken individually, and therefore he refrains from adjudicating on frequency. *Igrot Moshe, Even HaEzer* 3, 28, endorses the twice-a-week formula, since the present generation desires conjugality more, so that it becomes part of the husband's duty to be alert to the increased desires of his wife.

39. *Onah* then, the letter and the spirit, is worthy of special attention by *hatan* and *kallah* before they enter married life.

CHAPTER 11

1. See *Siddur Bet Yaakov, Hanhagat Leyl Shabbat, Heder HaMitot, Mitot HaKesef*, chap. 6, n. 10.

2. Viktor Frankl, in *Man's Search for Meaning*, says that love is not a mere side effect of sex; rather, sex is a way of expressing the experience of the ultimate togetherness we call love (p. 177). It is the unique language of love.

3. See Tsvi Travis, *Pirhey Hanhagat HaBayit*, pt. 2, pp. 26–29. The author's stress on extra attentiveness prior to Sabbaths and festivals appears as an approach which will before long be seen by the benefacted mate as contrived.

4. Regarding proper eating, this advice goes not only for the night of conjugal relations, but for life in general. Because of the obligations to each other, aside from the general obligation to take care of oneself (Deut. 4:15), each should strive to be in good shape, with abundant vigor, to please the other. Bodily vigor, in the words of the Talmud, is the best of blessings (*Yevamot* 102b).

See further Ramban's *Iggeret HaKodesh*, chaps. 3 and 4. Also *Orah Hayyim* 240:15, *Hilkhot Deot* 5:4.

Relative to drunkenness, see *Nedarim* 20b. Also *Even HaEzer* 25:9, *Hilkhot Isuray Biah* 21:12. See tractate *Kallah*, where the language of the text is illuminating. There it states that engaging in relations when drunk leads to "impotence of the heart." Each abuses the other, and does not express heartfelt feelings, aware thoughts, during the relationship. This pattern leads to emotional paralysis.

On excessive passion, see Ramban, ad loc. He explains the talmudic advice to have the conjugal bed between north and south as a euphemism for between cold and hot; that is, in moderation.

5. The comment about avoiding repulsive habits is per the advice of R. Hisda to his daughters (*Shabbat* 140b). Also, conjugality is ill-advised immediately after a visit to the privy (*Gittin* 70a, *Hilkhot Deot* 4:19).

On receptive spirit, see *Eruvin* 100b and *Nedarim* 20b regarding being enticed by one's wife, a response which is less likely to be self-serving sensuality, and more likely to be meaningful conjugality.

6. See *Even HaEzer* 25:3, *Oraḥ Ḥayyim* 240:7, *Hilkhot Isuray Biah* 21:10.

See *Mishnah Brurah* to *Oraḥ Ḥayyim* 240:7, note 34. Also *Hilkhot Deot* 5:4, where it seems that the middle-of-the-night preference relates to moderation. It is after the fullness of supper and before the morning hunger.

7. On verbal expression prior to conjugal relations, the Talmud (*Nedarim* 20b) refers to conjugality as talking. See Rashi ad loc., "*Ayno m'saper.*" See also *Eruvin* 100b, about wooing before conjugality. See too *Even HaEzer* 24:2, *Hilkhot Ishut* 15:17. Ramban (*Iggeret HaKodesh*, chap. 6) recommends words of passion combined with awe of Heaven.

On physical embrace, see *Siddur Bet Yaakov*, loc. cit., chap. 7, 2:2, 2:6.

8. From *Eruvin* 100b it is obvious that affection needs to continue after consummation.

See *Gittin* 70a, that one who gets up immediately following conjugal relations is considered closer to death than to life. Aside from the physical intent of the statement, it may also project the idea that one who has just experienced ultimate closeness should savor the moment, cherish it, embrace it, rather than leave it. It implies spiritual deficiency (closer to death) to perform and go. This reduces the act to a biological exercise. See *Siddur Bet Yaakov*, loc. cit., 2:8, that conjugality should be followed by falling asleep together.

9. On reasons and causes, see Viktor Frankl, "Self-Transcendence as a Human Phenomenon."

10. See Ramban to Deut. 22:27, that relations without an adequate prior intimacy is an affliction, painful.

11. On the husband's needing to be aroused, see *Yevamot* 53b. Also *Hilkhot Isuray Biah* 1:9.

12. On relations without the wife's willingness, see *Nedarim* 20b, *Oraḥ Ḥayyim* 240:10, *Even HaEzer* 25:2, *Hilkhot Isuray Biah* 21:12, *Hilkhot Deot*, 5:4. Travis, *Pirhey Hanhagat HaBayit*, vol. 2, p. 89, calls it prostitution.

See on this Rabad, *Baalay HaNefesh*, *Shaar HaKedushah*.

13. On coercion, see *Mishnah Brurah* to *Oraḥ Ḥayyim* 240:3, n. 14.

Relative to the desired union, see *Hilkhot Ishut* 15:17.

The husband's license is on the assumption of the wife's agreement. It is in this context that one must read *Even HaEzer* 25:2 and *Hilkhot Isuray Biah* 21:9. This applies to the act and all that pertains to it.

The talmudic warning against becoming involved with a boor (*am ha'aretz*) (*Pesaḥim* 49a–b), who is like a devouring lion, and attacks rather than woos his wife, is a warning against sensuality without human feeling.

14. See *Eruvin* 100b regarding encore.

On correlation of desires, see Ramban, *Iggeret HaKodesh*, chap. 6. See *Siddur Bet Yaakov*, loc. cit., 3:21, where it is contemplated that the sin of Adam was that he did not wait for the right time for conjugal relations, the right time being the Sabbath.

15. On modest dress, see *Shabbat* 53b, 140b.

Modest speech refers even to words of Torah (*Sukkah* 49b).

On modest behavior, see ibid. Also *Sotah* 47b, that one who behaves arrogantly (lack of modesty) will not be accepted in that person's household. See further Eliyahu Kitov, *The Jew and His Home*, pp. 72–78.

16. Relative to modesty applying equally to men and women, see *Orah Hayyim* 1:1.

On staring, see *Nedarim* 20a, *Orah Hayyim* 240:4. But see *Even HaEzer* 25:2 and *Hilkhot Isuray Biah* 21:9. The accent is on staring, which has a significantly different connotation then simply looking. See on this *Ezer Mekodesh* to *Even HaEzer* 25:2.

17. See *Nidah* 16b, 17a. Also *Orah Hayyim* 240:11, *Even Haezer* 25:5, *Hilkhot Isuray Biah* 21:10.

18. See *Eruvin* 100b. See also the dispute of Rashi and Ramban on Gen. 3:16. Also, *Sefer Hasidim* 516, that the husband who anticipates a direct request should ask first.

19. *Sotah* 11b. In their merit Israel was redeemed. See also Rashi to Exod. 38:8.

20. Concerning the active role of women, see *Shabbat* 140b for the technique suggested by R. Hisda to his daughters, to show the attraction but hide the place of passion. See Rashi, "*Margenesa*," who, using explicit language, indicates that the upper part of the body should be shared, but the place of consummation should not be readily available; this in order to arouse passion and amorous desire. This can hardly be termed a passive exercise. See *Ezer Mekodesh* to *Even HaEzer* 25:2, who also states that the wife should not hesitate to indicate to the husband that his approach in conjugality leaves something to be desired, and is not pleasant for her.

Relative to conjugality on demand, see Viktor Frankl, "The Depersonalization of Sex," where he reports on an experiment dealing with demand. From a species of fish whose females habitually swim coquettishly away from desirous males, one was trained to do just the opposite, to forcefully approach the male. The result was a complete incapacity on the part of the male to carry out the sexual act (p. 11). Demands turn off, whereas true love inspires automatically.

21. See Maharal (*Netzah Yisrael*, chap. 47) that the prophetic statement about God being called "my *ish*," not "my *baal*" (Hos. 2:18), indicates that in a relationship between *baal* (master) and *ishah* (woman) there is disparity, the one doing to the other. In an *ish* (man) and *ishah* (woman) relationship, they are equal, and that is the ideal.

22. On the importance of conjugality, see *Sefer Hasidim*, no. 509, who interprets the verse "One who find a wife finds good" (Prov. 18:22) as referring to a conjugally compatible partner.

There is also great danger in overemphasizing conjugality in marriage. Ira Reiss, in *Family Systems in America,* claims that general marital satisfaction is the more compelling factor generating conjugal satisfaction, not the reverse (pp. 282–283).

Michael Gordon, in "From an Unfortunate Necessity to a Cult of Mutual Orgasm," speaks of the societal emphasis on achieving the peak together (pp. 53–77). This can be to the detriment of the warm feeling of intimacy which is crucial to conjugality.

Marcia Lasswell and Norman Lobsenz, in "The Intimacy That Goes Beyond Sex," warn that technique in marital relations is overemphasized compared with the total marriage (pp. 347–354). Companionship is crucial to marital happiness (see Margaret Marini, "Dimensions of Marriage Happiness").

Billie Ables, in *Therapy for Couples,* claims that bedroom problems alone do not destroy a marriage. Instead, general interactional dysfunction pervades the entire relationship, and sex therapy will not solve the couple's problem (pp. 313–315).

John Scanzoni's *Opportunity and the Family* revealed that matters related to conjugal relations were the first area of disagreement among less than 1 percent of a study, with close to 40 percent naming money and close to 20 percent naming children as the first area of difficulty and conflict (p. 157).

Conjugality is vital, then, but it is part of a context, the context of the marriage as a whole, rather than an independent category on its own.

On conjugality evolving over the years, see Bob Blood and Margaret Blood, *Marriage,* who report that with an increase in the years of marriage comes an increased responsiveness and pleasure in conjugal relations (p. 200). A woman's desire usually increases in her thirties and forties and maintains itself to the sixties. Remaining in good shape and sensitive to the increasing desire of one's mate is thus particularly vital for the husband. Quality of conjugality also seems to be affected positively by the less rushed, more content approach in later years.

23. See Rabad, *Baalay HaNefesh, Shaar HaKedushah.* Also *Orah Hayyim* 240:1, *Even HaEzer* 25:2, *Hilkhot Isuray Biah* 21:9.

Angus Campbell, "The American Way of Mating," found, with other researchers, a U-shaped pattern to marital happiness. Happiness, in his survey, was high at the outset, dipped during the child-rearing years, and went up again when the children left home (pp. 37–43). This pattern reflects on an unhealthy narcissistic trend to self-growth and self-centeredness, a trend sometimes so entrenched that the afflicted couple may have trouble functioning as a team (see Jane Appleton and William Appleton, *How Not to Split Up,* p. xvi).

Some fall apart and divorce, others endure the trials and tribulations caused by the invasion of new people into their lives. And this, when such sharing of the self and the couple with this new generation should and could be a source of joy, contentedness, and meaning.

24. See Rabad, *Baalay HaNefesh, Shaar HaKedushah.*

25. On self-serving conjugality, see *Pesaḥim* 49b; see also above, no. 13.

R. Elyah Lopian is reputed to have said that one who says he loves fish is indulging in deception. He hooks, kills, cooks, and eats the fish, and cares nothing about the welfare of the fish. What he really loves is himself (see *Binyan Aday Ahd*, p. 120). The analogy to marriage is obvious.

On the husband's obligation to extend his wife's pleasure, see *Pesaḥim* 72b.

See *Tomer D'vorah* (chap. 6), quoting and elaborating on the *Zohar* that man's sensual desire was created specifically for his wife. Yet he is open to pleasure himself. See further *Menorat HaMaor* (*ner* 3, *klal* 6, pt. 6, chap. 5).

On pleasure from giving, see *Siddur Bet Yaakov*, loc. cit., 3:17.

Maharal, in *Netivot Olam* (*Netiv HaAvodah*, chap. 16) states that in the ideal conjugal act, each receives from the other. As to the notion that one should minimize one's pleasure in conjugality (see, for example, *Oraḥ Ḥayyim* 240:1), *Derekh P'Kudekha al Taryag Mitzvot HaTorah* states that this does not apply to the act itself, in which it is impossible to avoid pleasure (*Mitzvah* 1, *Ḥelek HaDibbur*, no. 5).

In an unsigned letter from one of the *gedolay hador* (giants of the generation), *Iggeret Kodesh Me'Et Gedolay HaDor* (Jerusalem, 1968), the author rejects piety if it compromises what is the biblical obligation. The author rejects the "quick and finished" conjugality which does not benefit the wife and leaves her hurt and embarrassed. This makes such eminent sense that one wonders why this forceful letter was not signed.

For more on the giving process as crucial to marriage, see further my "Philosophical Foundations for Marriage Counseling."

26. On verbal expression, see *Siddur Bet Yaakov*, loc. cit., 2:6.

On talking during the conjugal act, see *Nedarim* 20a. Also *Even HaEzer* 25:2, *Oraḥ Ḥayyim* 240:9. Also, *Siddur Bet Yaakov*, loc. cit., 2:3.

27. On not being in a hurry, see Ramban, *Iggeret HaKodesh*, chap. 6.

In the mutuality, each one's thoughts are not oblivious to the other; mutuality means that "your wife's intentions correlate with yours" (Ramban, *Iggeret HaKodesh*, chap. 6). See also *Siddur Bet Yaakov*, loc. cit., chap. 6, 6:10. Heavy breathing is a telltale sign of arousal. Proper breathing, by the way, breathing out fully so that air automatically gets taken in, is an important body energizer.

The mutuality paradigm is *Nidah* 71a, where the Talmud praises content, intimate embrace and delay of emission of seed so that the wife can reach satisfaction first. Staying tightly together, in the view of the Talmud, with the husband controlling his rapid movements in anticipation of his wife's peak pleasure, is the ideal. This pleasures the wife and enables the husband to fulfill his sacred obligation to make his wife happy. See further Travis, *Pirkey Hanhagat HaBayit*, vol. 2, pp. 92–95.

28. See Paul Gebhard, "Factors in Marital Orgasm," who indicates from studies that the longer the intromission prior to consummation, the more likely is the wife to experience peak pleasure. Less than one minute is insufficient;

many women respond to intromission ranging from one to eleven minutes, and twelve or more minutes raises the likehood of the wife's satisfaction significantly (pp. 172–173). And that, of course, is *the mitzvah*. See further Th. Van de Velde, *Ideal Marriage*, who quotes a view that "the purpose of circumcision is probably the prolongation of coitus, as the exposed gland takes longer to reach the summit of stimulation than the covered" (p. 200).

The matter of positions at the peak moment differs, of course, from changing positions prior to consummation.

See *Reshit Hokhmah*, that part of the sanctity of the peak union is that the couple be face-to-face, not face-to-back (*Shaar HaKedushah*, chap. 16). See *Be'er Haytev* to *Orah Hayyim* 240:5, n. 15.

Reshit Hokhmah, ad loc., claims that face-to-back interferes with procreation and is thusly condemned. See further on this *Even HaEzer* 25:2 and *Hilkhot Isuray Biah* 2:19. The concern for waste of seed is a critical issue.

29. See *Orah Hayyim* 240:5.

30. On free expression, see *Nedarim* 20b, *Even HaEzer* 25:2, *Hilkhot Isuray Biah* 21:9. On the importance of consent not only for the act but for the dynamics of it, see Rabad's *Baaley HaNefesh*, loc. cit.

See *Hupat Hatanim* (*Hilkhot Zniut*, par. 6) that the wife-on-top position is not prohibited outside the night of immersion. See also *Sefer Hasidim*, 509. *Shelah*, who heartily recommends knowing *Orah Hayyim* 240 and *Even HaEzer* 25 by heart before marrying (see above, Chapter 1, n. 36), excludes learning about the permission to "turn the tables" to the wife-on-top position (*Even HaEzer* 25:2), which he insists is not allowed. See further R. Shlomoh Aviner, *Etzem MaAtzamay, Banekha Kishtelay Zaytim*, who discusses this issue and concludes that since conjugality can affect the marriage, this type of expression is permitted, especially when it increases the likelihood of attaining peak pleasure, thus bringing the couple closer together.

The statement about the standing position is from R. Zvi Shapiro, *Derekh P'Kudekha Al Taryag Mitzvot Hatorah, Mitzvah* 1, *Helek HaMaaseh*, no. 11. See *Orah Hayyim* 240:15, *Hilkhot Deot* 4:19.

31. See *Hokhmat Adam* 128:3.

32. The observation about one who has a little bit of a good thing wanting more is from *Ecclesiastes Rabbah* 1:13.

"Pleasure, as a rule, ensues automatically and simultaneously with the reaching of a goal. Pleasure is a sequel, not an aim in itself; it must occur, but it cannot be endeavored. It is effect, but not intention; it can be effectuated, but not intended. Whenever it is intended, it will always fail. This becomes particularly evident in sexual neuroses; there, man fails just at the moment when he is trying consciously to attain pleasure as a goal" (Viktor Frankl, "Logos and Existence in Psychotherapy," pp. 13–14).

Helen Singer Kaplan, in *The New Sex Therapy*, indicates that fear of failure is perhaps the greatest immediate cause of impotence, and also to some extent of orgastic dysfunction (p. 127). Excessive demand and excessive need to please the partner both interfere with the naturalness of the experience (pp. 129–132).

33. The shift of focus toward the partner is the de-reflection technique used in logotherapy. A fascinating presentation of this technique can be found in Viktor Frankl, *The Unheard Cry for Meaning*, pp. 150–158. See also ibid., pp. 114–150, on the application of paradoxical intention.

34. *Berakhot* 62a.

35. See *Igrot Moshe, Even HaEzer* 1, 102, who allows study of books on conjugal relations just prior to marriage. The question, of course, is, which books? The only book of its kind presently on the market is Travis, *Pirkey Hanhagat HaBayit*, reference to which has been made on occasion in this volume. Travis is explicit, but the book is too didactic, and addresses itself to a very specific clientele.

By the way, to his great credit, the venerable sage R. Yaakov Kaminetsky saw fit to give a hearty endorsement to Travis's book. Yet in places like Bnai Brak it is unavailable because of a *herem* (ban). It is a loose *herem* whose exact source cannot be pinpointed. Yet for all its limitations, books like that of Travis are needed.

36. Parents, good and capable parents, are usually better than books, however good. "Something goes wrong when the consciousness attempts to regulate acts which normally take place, so to speak, without thought" (Viktor Frankl, *The Doctor and the Soul*, p. 127). Rollo May, in *Love and Will*, claims that the new emphasis on technique in sex and love-making backfires. "It often occurs to me that there is an inverse relationship between the number of how-to-do-it books perused by a person or rolling off the presses in a society and the amount of sexual passion or even pleasure experienced by the persons involved. Certainly nothing is wrong with technique as such. But the emphasis beyond a certain point on technique in sex makes for a mechanistic attitude toward love-making, and goes along with alienation, feelings of loneliness, and depersonalization" (p. 43).

To this critique one should add that the Jewish approach to conjugality is unique, and works within a much different philosophical orientation than do the textbooks. Hence good, sound teachers are preferable to books.

CHAPTER 12

1. On death being most keenly felt by the spouse, see *Sanhedrin* 22b, *Ruth Rabbah* 2:7. That the world blackens is from *Sanhedrin* 22a.

2. On the left-right dialectic, see *Sotah* 47a.

3. On re-marrying in one's later years, see *Yevamot* 62b.

4. The obligation of remarriage is linked to the passage "In the morning plant your seed, and toward evening do not let your hand relax" (Eccles. 11:6). The implication is that in later years (toward evening) one tries to continue what was started in the early years (morning). This inference is homiletic discourse, not halakhic derivation.

5. On remarrying, see *Even HaEzer* 1:8, *Hilkhot Ishut* 15:16, *Hilkhot Isuray Biah* 21:26.

On the binding nature of the *l'erev* (not to desist from procreation in later years) obligation, see the dispute between R. Zerahyah HaLevi (*HaMaor HaGadol*) and Ramban (*Milḥamot HaShem*) in Alfasi to *Yevamot* 62b. The former sees *l'erev* as a rabbinic obligation; the latter sees it as a recommended way of living, but not as a rabbinic obligation. Rambam (*Hilkhot Ishut* 15:1) allows the wife's waiving of the *onah* obligation once the husband's procreation obligations have been fulfilled. Rambam (*Hilkhot Ishut* 15:7) allows a man to marry a woman who is incapable of having children on the proviso that he has already fulfilled the procreation obligation. These two views of Rambam would appear to support the view of Ramban. See on this the critique of *Bet Shmuel* (*Even HaEzer* 1:1) and the defense of *Birkay Yosef* (*Even HaEzer* 1:2). *Birkay Yosef* explains that *l'erev* simply means that one should not ever totally detach from the procreation imperative; instead, once the *mitzvah* has been fulfilled, intervals are permitted, and one can wait for the propitious moment.

See *Igrot Moshe* (*Even HaEzer* 3, 24), where in allowing contraception for a woman who is not well and would be adversely affected by a pregnancy, R. Moshe Feinstein conjectures that once the husband has fulfilled the *mitzvah* of procreation, it is logical to assume that the wife who is not well can permanently forego procreation. R. Yitzhak Yaakov Weiss (*Minḥat Yitzhak* 5, 113) likewise allows contraception via the pill for reasons of weakness, tiredness, or being on edge, and likewise only when the husband has already fulfilled the *mitzvah* of "Be fruitful and multiply," but this is only for a limited time. These two halakhists, though they differ somewhat in their halakhic pronouncements, nevertheless see the *l'erev* obligation as of lesser legal significance, apparently leaning to the Rambam-Ramban view.

On the fulfillments from second marriage, the Talmud notes that "one does not find real contentedness save with one's first wife" (*Sanhedrin* 22a).

On first marriage being a once-in-a-lifetime experience, the Talmud observes that "there is a replacement for everything, except the wife of one's youth" (*Sanhedrin* 22a).

6. Regarding divorce as avoidable, see Newton Berry, "Portrait of a Family Conservationist," where it is claimed that at least one out of ten divorces should never have taken place, this based on the general feelings of both the former spouses months after the divorce had been finalized (pp. 10–13).

See further the useful presentation of Ira Reiss, *Family Systems in America*, where, based on his wheel theory of love, Reiss endeavors to explain how a couple may grow apart. Reduced self-revelation due to an argument may affect dependency and intimacy need-fulfillment processes, in turn weakening the rapport process, and lowering self-revelation levels even further, starting a potentially disruptive downward spiral (p. 128). Small deviations can have great consequences.

Billie Ables, in *Therapy for Couples*, written in collaboration with Jeffrey

Brandsma, expresses her continued amazement at the ease with which therapists decide whether a couple should divorce (p. 304).

The general prediction is from Robert Weiss, *Marital Separation*, p. 12.

The prediction for Jewish marriage is from Benjamin Schlesinger, "The Jewish Family in the 1980's."

7. Morris Rosenberg, *Society and the Adolescent Self-Image*, sees a low-self-esteem problem in children of divorce (pp. 88–90). Admittedly, there are many other factors which can damage a child's self-esteem, including a conflicted household where the parents do not divorce. The concern is not with divorce per se, but with the conditions that result in unhappiness, and possibly also in divorce.

8. On Jewish tradition as accepting of divorce as a legitimate possibility, see Deut. 24:1, Exod. 21:11. See *Even HaEzer* 119:3, *Hilkhot Gerushin* 10:21. See Ben Ish Hai, in *Hukay HaNashim*, who has harsh things to say about anyone who would destroy an existing husband-wife relationship (p. 23). See above, Chapter 8, n. 65.

On no-fault divorce, see Ben Zion Shereshevsky, *Dinay Mishpahah*, pp. 275–276.

The change in attitude to divorce is reflected in Abigail Van Buren, *The Best of Dear Abby*, where the author was asked why she used to counsel couples to do all they could to save their marriages, but now gives the impression that divorce could be the answer. Her response was that it is more important to save people than to save marriages. Sometimes, she says, in an effort to save a marriage not worth saving, people have destroyed themselves and each other (p. 22). The writer may not be an authority to be quoted in a scholarly work, but she is a good barometer of prevailing conditions and social currents.

9. *Gittin* 90b. The Talmud seems to project a greater tolerance if divorce occurs in a second marriage (see *Sotah* 2a, *Gittin* 90b). Also *Even HaEzer* 119:3, *Hilkhot Gerushin* 10:21.

10. The Hebrew for "sacrifice," *korban*, links to the word *karov*, "near." The sacrifice has as its purpose to draw the person near, more near to God. See R. Shimshon R. Hirsch to Lev. 1:2.

11. What is really meant by this is that they are blessed by God (see *Yevamot* 63a, *Sotah* 17a).

12. Be patient in choosing your mate (*Yevamot* 63a).

13. See Jane Appleton and William Appleton, *How Not to Split Up*, who offer some good advice in this regard.

14. *Binyan Aday Ahd* counsels that a couple contemplating divorce should be sure that the cure is not worse than the disease (p. 104). See also Rudolf Dreikurs, *The Challenge of Marriage*, who suggests that the second choice of the same mate may be more fortunate and urges trying to rediscover the present mate (p. 98).

15. Relative to divorce as unnatural, it should be remembered that the

couple were, after all, as one, and the legal complexities in divorce are the halakhic equal of a Siamese section.

16. On conjugal relations after having decided to divorce, see *Gittin* 90a, *Nedarim* 20b, *Oraḥ Ḥayyim* 240:3, *Hilkhot Isuray Biah* 21:12.

On household duties, see Meiri to *Gittin* 90a.

17. On the command to love one's neighbor, see for example *Ketuvot* 37b, *Sanhedrin* 52b, where the verse "Love your neighbor as yourself" (Lev. 19:18) is used to justify showing kindness in administering the death penalty to one convicted of a capital crime. "Choose for him a dignified death" is the operating principle. If one views the divorce as the death of the marriage (which it is), then the operating principle should be "Choose for the other a dignified divorce."

On decency in divorce, the statement "In a place where there are no people, strive to be a person" (*Avot* 2:6) is pertinent. Divorce is certainly a place where too often there is a shortage of decency and decent people. Here is the challenge to be a *mentsch* in trying circumstances.

18. Examples of sensitive treatment of one's former mate are found in *Genesis Rabbah* 17:3; *Leviticus Rabbah* 34:14.

Benny Don-Yechiya, *Mishpaḥah B'Mishpat*, offers some useful, practical parameters for facilitating the divorcing couple's task (pp. 182–183). The usefulness of all his advice is contingent on the couple's ability to agreeably work things out. This is not always the case, and the author also discusses the more complicated scenarios.

See Shereshevsky, *Dinay Mishpaḥah*, pp. 112, 276–285.

19. On "within the boundary of the law," see Appendix 1.

Relevant to being oblivious to one's own flesh, see Yerushalmi, *Ketuvot* 11:3, that "To your own flesh be not oblivious" (Isa. 58:7) applies to one's divorced partner. Having been married, they are not suddenly total strangers after marriage terminates.

Shereshevsky, *Dinay Mishpaḥah*, pp. 338–340, cites tendencies in the Israeli rabbinical courts to grant support payments to the wife and give her the residence, even though by strict Halakhah these do not accrue to her.

20. They are caught in between, and have great difficulty respecting either parent. They can easily carry the mistrust into their own adult lives, thus extending the effects of divorce far beyond its original boundaries.

21. On hatred, see *Yoma* 9b, where the Talmud declares that wanton hatred is the equal of idolatry, adultery, and murder in gravity of offense. This derivation relates to the reason for the destruction of the First and Second Temples, the second having been destroyed because of hatred. That hate can destroy a community has already been proven. That it should not again destroy a community must be assured.

Another answer to the question "Who is mighty?" (*Avot* 4:1) is found in *Avot D'Rabbe Natan* 23. There, the answer is "one who makes of an enemy a friend." In divorce, the enmity between the couple indicates weakness rather than strength, since they probably started out as friends. The couple are, via the response in *Avot D'Rabbe Natan*, called upon to be strong after the divorce, strong by making the other feel less enmity and more friendliness. This may sometimes seem unrealistic, but this does not mitigate from it being desirable.

See *Even HaEzer* 119:8, Gloss of RaMoh, and comment of *Ḥelkat Meḥokek*, n. 25.

CONCLUSION

1. *Avot D'Rabbe Natan* 41.

2. Charles Liebman, in "Orthodox Judaism Today," tries to extract from Orthodoxy what makes it click and give it to the rest of the Jewish community, but the feeling is that extraction can hardly work. It is a package, and that is equally true of the theme presently under discussion.

3. It is realized that what has been proposed in this volume may be seen by some as too idyllic, as too far removed from reality. That it may be far removed from reality is probably correct, but then reality too is far removed from the ideal. Insofar as its being idyllic, to that one can only respond by saying that marriage is intended to be idyllic.

This volume should not be seen as a problem-solver. There are many marriages with complicated situations, personality and interactional conflicts that need careful attention. Books do not usually solve problems.

But books can sometimes prevent problems, because approaching situations with the proper philosophy can go a long way toward realizing meaningful achievement. Herein, it was proposed that marriage works best when each goes into the marriage with the commitment to give, unconditionally. This one sentence covers many chapters, the full gamut of life between husband and wife, the couple and their parents, the couple and their children, the couple and their community. When this is the approach, even if at first it is done as play-acting, the couple are drawn closer to each other, the love intensifies, and the marriage is—idyllic. When marriage is not approached with the giving commitment, and is even a demand relationship, the couple is courting potential difficulties.

Gordon Allport, in "Comments on Earlier Papers," observed that sometimes an acquired world outlook (philosophy) may constitute the central motive of a life, and if it is disordered, may be the ultimate therapeutic problem (p. 97). The feeling is that much of what goes wrong in a marriage falls into the Allport scenario.

Couples who bring childhood problems or later developing problems to the marriage would be much better off going beyond themselves, into the "giving" dimension. To a woman who complained of depression, Alfred Adler once said, "Every morning for the next two weeks, in the first half hour after waking up, think of ways you can help others. Your depression will then go away." Fixation on the self can bring with it negative feelings which may sour a relationship.

Devotion to the other, even adopted initially merely as a technique, soon brings significant enough results (usually) to reinforce the technique and make it almost a self-generating pattern. That, in a word, is the Torah for marriage.

4. On prayer related to marriage, *Hupat Hatanim*, for example, has a prayer to find the right partner (in *Dinay Zivug*), a prayer by the groom and the bride on the day of the wedding (in sec. 6, *B'Yom HaHupah*), and a prayer before immersion (loc. cit.), as well as a prayer for a woman entering her ninth month (last page of end supplement, Mekor of Jerusalem edition).

Regarding prayer for what is considered important, see my *Torah Therapy*, where this theme is more fully developed (pp. 97–98).

APPENDIX 1

1. Ramban, *Sefer HaMitzvot, Mitzvah* 1. Much of what follows originally appeared in Reuven P. Bulka, "The Role of the Individual in Jewish Law."

2. Relative to the post-Sinai experience, there is a sarcastic comment attributed to R. Meir Premishlan, who notes that on the verse "and there Israel encamped before the mountain" (Exod. 19:2), Rashi comments, "As one man and with one mind, but all their other encampments were made in a murmuring spirit and in a spirit of dissension." R. Meir explains that unity prevailed before the giving of the law, but after the law was given, each individual looked upon it as his own, insisting on the validity of his own approach.

3. Martin Buber, letter to Franz Rosenzweig, in Franz Rosenzweig, *On Jewish Learning*, p. 111.

4. See Walter S. Wurzburger, "Covenantal Imperatives," pp. 3–12, where the author attempts to find a place for the individual in Judaism. "Covenantal imperatives" is conceived as a construct outside the framework of law. The author proposes the term "to denote the kind of religious obligation which cannot be said to derive its sanction from a general norm or law" (p. 8). Here we attempt to find the place of the individual inside the law.

5. Ibid., p. 8.

6. On *lifnim meshurat hadin*, see *Berakhot* 7a, 45b; *Ketuvot* 97a; *Bava Kamma* 99b–100a; *Bava Mezia* 24b, 30b.

7. Viktor E. Frankl, *The Doctor and the Soul*, p. 61.

8. The derivation is in *Bava Kamma* 100a.

9. Samuel Belkin, *In His Image*, pp. 190–191.

10. *Makkot* 24a. Regarding R. Safra, see further in Rashi. For more about R. Yishmael b. R. Yose, see *Ketuvot* 105b.

11. *Lifnim meshurat hadin* is applied mainly in social situations, such as property rules, when one should return property even though not required by law. An exception is *Berakhot* 45b, where it is stated: "If three persons have been eating together, one breaks off to oblige two, but two do not break off to oblige one. But do they not? Did not R. Papa break off for Abba Mar his son, he and

another with him? R. Papa was different because he went *lifnim meshurat hadin*." Whilst this deals with the question of *zimun*, which is not in the category of social law, nevertheless the matter of two waiting for one, or breaking off for one, is really a question of social ethics, so that even here *lifnim meshurat hadin* is a social expression. For a more thorough and insightful treatment of the notion of *lifnim meshurat hadin*, see Shubert Spero, *Morality, Halakhah, and Jewish Tradition*, pp. 166–200.

The comment about the destruction of Jerusalem is from *Bava Mezia* 30b. See Tosafot, ad loc., who questions this from another talmudic statement attributing the destruction to wanton hate. He answers that both were causes. One could also suggest that wanton hate and strict application of the law are related and interwoven with each other. The lack of feeling for another is often masked in mercilessly applying strict law, with no demonstration of kindness.

12. *Midot hasidut* is in *Shabbat* 120a, *Bava Mezia* 52b, *Hullin* 130b.

Lazet yeday shamayim is in *Shabbat* 120a; *Gittin* 53a; *Bava Kamma* 56a, 98a; *Bava Mezia* 37a.

V'aseeta hayashar v'hatov is in Deut. 6:18; *Bava Mezia* 16b, 108a; *Avodah Zarah* 25a.

L'maan telekh b'derekh tovim is in Prov. 2:20, *Bava Mezia* 83a. See Rashi, who equates this with *lifnim meshurat hadin*.

13. As a note of caution, whilst this dimensional picture is true to some extent, it should be borne in mind that every *bayn adam lahavero* ("between man and his fellowman") law has an element of *bayn adam LaMakom* ("between man and God") in it, and every *bayn adam LaMakom* command has potential feedback into the social situation.

14. Frankl, *The Doctor and the Soul*, p. 61.

15. This may be the message in the famous rabbinic statement that " 'remember' and 'keep' [*zakhor* and *shamor*] were spoken in a single utterance" (*Rosh Hashanah* 27a). There would be no purpose to the restrictedness of *shamor* without the fulfillment in freedom of *zakhor*; hence *shamor* could not have existed, philosophically, even one second without *zakhor*. Similarly, the fulfillment of *zakhor* would have been impossible without the bounded guidelines established by *shamor*; hence *zakhor* could not have existed, philosophically, even one second without *shamor*. Thus, one utterance, or mutual dependency. See Erich Fromm, *The Forgotten Language*, pp. 242–249, where the author develops an understanding of the Sabbath in many ways superior to some Jewish apologetics.

16. The quote is from *Ta'anit* 16a.

Isa. 58:5–7. "Is such the fast that I have chosen? The day for a man to afflict his soul? Is it to bow down his head as a bulrush, and to spread sackcloth and ashes under him? Will you call this a fast, and an acceptable day to the Lord? Is not this the fast that I have chosen? To loose the fetters of wickedness, to undo the bands of the yoke. . . . Is it not to deal your bread to the hungry, and that you bring the poor that are cast out to your house?"

17. Concerning fasting as an ultimate, reference can be made to R. Elimelekh of Lizhensk, who, when asked to explain why the Baal Shem Tov fasted, replied that when the Baal Shem Tov was young he would go into seclusion for an entire week with six loaves of bread and water. Upon interrupting his meditation on Friday to return home, he would lift up his sack, and, not understanding why it was so heavy, would be surprised to find his loaves still there. Such fasting, said R. Elimelekh, is allowed. See Martin Buber, *Tales of the Hasidim*, p. 45.

18. The term normally used is "negative commandments," but the word "negative" has negative connotations. "Prohibitive" would seem to better project the intent of the laws in this category.

19. The quotation is from *Berakhot* 28b. See ibid., 29b.

20. The first quotation is from *Kiddushin* 31a–b.

On the differentiation at the beginning of the paragraph, see Tosafot, *Kiddushin* 31a. The second quotation is from *Sukkah* 49b.

21. *Kiddushin* 40a.

22. On *v'anvayhu*, see *Shabbat* 133b, *Sukkah* 11b, *Nazir* 2b.

On *hidur mitzvah*, see *Bava Kamma* 9b. See Rashi, who identifies this with *v'anvayhu*.

On *hivuv mitzvah*, see *Pesahim* 68b, *Sukkah* 41b, *Sotah* 13a. *Kiddushin* 33a.

The concept of *lishmah* is found throughout the Talmud and the Codes. Some examples are *Pesahim* 38b, 50b; *Sukkah* 9a; *Gittin* 20a; *Avodah Zarah* 27a.

For *kavanah*, a few examples of a much-discussed concept will suffice: *Berakhot* 5b, 13a, 31a; *Eruvin* 95b; *Pesahim* 114b; *Megillah* 20a.

On *zerizut*, see *Pesahim* 89b, *Yoma* 84b, *Menahot* 43b.

23. The quotation is from *Sotah* 21b.

24. On *averah lishmah*, see *Nazir* 23b, "A transgression performed with good intention is as good as a precept performed for an ulterior motive."

On "live thereby," see Lev. 18:5. See further *Yoma* 85b; also *Pesahim* 8a and *Hullin* 10a for discussion of the prohibition against letting oneself into dangerous situations.

Concerning the exceptions mentioned at the end of the paragraph, see *Sanhedrin* 74a.

25. Bernard Weinberger, "The Growing Rate of Divorce in Orthodox Jewish Life," p. 13.

APPENDIX 2

1. On "sheep for each household," see Exod. 12:3. See the commentary of R. Shimshon R. Hirsch on that verse, which amplifies this point.

That nothing be left over is from Exod. 12:10.

On the dedicated wives, see *Song of Songs Rabbah* 8:5.

2. The projections found herein are from Paul Glick and Arthur Norton, "Marrying, Divorcing and Living Together in the U.S. Today."

3. On marital stability and having fewer children, see Nathan Drazin, *Marriage Made in Heaven*, where this point is heavily stressed.

4. On the statistics for divorce, see Chaim Waxman, "The Threadbare Canopy," p. 473, and Bernard Weinberger, "The Growing Rate of Divorce in Orthodox Jewish Life," p. 9. See also Judith Lang, "Divorce and the Jewish Woman," p. 220. Also, Bernard Postal, "Postal Card," *Jewish Week*, March 11, 1979, and Boris Smolar, "Easy Marriages Bring Easy Splits: Jews in the 1 in 3 Divorce Scene," *New Brunswick Jewish Journal*, March 8, 1979.

The Canadian statistics are in Leo Davids, "Jewish Marriage Breakdown in Canada." The statistics for New York are from Saul Hofstein, "Perspectives On the Jewish Single-Parent Family," p. 230.

5. Weiss's comments are in Robert Weiss, *Marital Separation*, pp. 8–10.

The analysis of Orthodox Jewish divorce is in Weinberger, "The Growing Rate of Divorce in Orthodox Jewish Life," p. 10.

6. Benjamin Schlesinger, "Reflections on Family Breakdown Among Jewish Families."

7. Herbert Hendin, "The Ties Don't Bind."

8. F. J. Fowler, *1975 Community Survey*, p. 13. To be sure, outside factors, such as education and career are involved, but they all relate to placing family in the background, as less of a priority than other, "more important" fulfillments.

9. The Boro Park High School statistics are from Gershon Kranzler, "The Changing Orthodox Jewish Family," p. 29.

The prediction is one of the many by Dr. Alvin Schiff, widely reported in the Jewish media, and found in the *Family and Marriage Newsletter*, 7, no. 2 (Spring–Summer 1983).

For the demographers' predictions, see Glick and Norton, "Marrying, Divorcing and Living Together in the U.S. Today."

10. Richard Farson, "Why Good Marriages Fail." Parts of what follows originally appeared in the *Family and Marriage Newsletter*, 2, no. 3 (Summer 1978).

11. It should be noted that in traditional Jewish families all the ingredients mentioned, in varying degrees, were present in the marriage.

The idea that having does not satisfy but, rather, increases one's desire is best expressed in the famous midrashic statement that one who has one hundred wants two hundred and one who has two hundred wants four hundred (*Ecclesiastes Rabbah* 1:34). The idea of being content with what one has seems to be inconsistent with a capitalistic ethic, if indeed there is such a thing as a capitalistic ethic. Concerning the fact that marriage was never intended to provide for all human needs, it should be noted that the notion of shared destiny, which does not involve demands but, rather, common investment in the community, brings with it, almost automatically, all those things which, if demanded, will not be delivered. The problem is not so much that marriage cannot fulfill these areas, but that if they become needs which provoke demands, they lessen the prospects of the demands being met. Spontaneity beings better results.

12. This may be a case of a little knowledge being dangerous or of ostensibly well-educated people jumping to conclusions based on half the facts. Perhaps the most important lesson implicit in the prohibition against coveting a neighbor's wife is the idea that one should not assume the grass is greener on the other side, that what another person has is better. Instead, one should always assume that one's own situation is the most appropriate for oneself, so that coveting becomes impossible.

13. Again, what appears on the surface is the absence of a destiny model. Instead one has a demand situation which is doomed to collapse by the very nature of the relationship. When there is nothing to carry the marriage except need gratification, the pressure to be constantly responsive can become unbearable.

14. We have here the prototype of excessive demands leading to failure. It is a situation of stretching human resources beyond the limit, of expecting superhuman responsiveness. Sexual fulfillment is not easily realized when it is focused upon and demanded. In fact, it is this very type of attitude which leads to impotence. Instead, sexual fulfillment is best realized as a by-product of true love.

15. Rather than seeing marriage as an end in itself, Judaism sees it as a vehicle toward the higher values of life. As such, the focus is not on the marriage but on the values, the sum total of which add up to Jewish destiny.

16. There is a basic trust in a good relationship. Ironically, trust works out of an honest framework but does not demand honesty. Where the trust is intrinsic to the relationship, there are very few things left to hide. Common commitments are the best way to avoid uncommon problems.

The figures were suggested by Farson in 1971, when his piece originally appeared in the October 1971 issue of *McCall's*. One must assume that the figures have jumped appreciably since then.

17. Here perhaps one may apply the famous talmudic dictum that blessing only resides in that which is hidden from the eye (*Ta'anit* 8b). That which is obviously good is, in fact, obviously problematic.

18. Marriage seen in an introverted self-gratification concept contains the seeds of its own destruction. Particularly in the aspect of children does the traditional marriage context in Judaism shine forth as a model for efficacy. The birth and raising of a child involve the fulfillment of a sacred obligation and are part of the shared destiny which should be the impetus for the marriage in the first place. In such an atmosphere, the switching of emotions toward the child is not only understandable, but expected and natural for father and mother. Anything less would be disappointing, rather than the reverse.

Farson suggests that if we could digest the idea that it is possible to leave a marriage because it is good, then separation would not be as painful and acrimonious. Indeed, separating spouses would be grateful for the head start into life that has been granted them through the marital experience they lived.

This is good insofar as divorce counseling is concerned. It should be emphasized that this very notion is most vital for marriage itself. If indeed some are contemplating divorce, it would be quite helpful to make them aware of how good their marriage is and thus possibly forestall an unnecessary separation. The Midrash says that "good" refers to life, "very good" refers to death (*Genesis Rabbah* 9:12). In this seemingly incongruous remark, it posits the idea that expecting too much out of life brings its very termination. What is true of life in general has been more than adequately shown by Farson to be true of marriage. The focus is better honed not on blissful, unrealistic mirages; instead, it is better directed toward establishing good, fundamentally solid, value-oriented unions.

19. On what occupies the attention of the American couple, see Philip Blumstein and Pepper Schwartz, *American Couples*, pp. 45–46.

The quotation is from ibid., p. 46.

20. The quotation is from ibid.

Glossary

Words set in SMALL CAPS are defined elsewhere in the Glossary.

AMIDAH. Main body of prayer, including eighteen plus one blessings.

AUFRUF. Call to the Torah of groom on SABBATH before the wedding.

AVERAH LISHMAH. Transgression performed with good intentions.

AYZONE VA'AFARNES. Will provide food and sustenance (obligations of husband assumed at marriage and included in the KETUVAH).

BAAL TESHUVAH. Person engaged in the process of repentance.

BAR MITZVAH. Age of responsibility for males to observe the commandments (*mitzvot*); thirteen years old.

BAT MITZVAH. Age of responsibility for females to observe the commandments (*mitzvot*); twelve years old.

BAYN ADAM LAHAVERO. Between the person and a friend.

BAYN ADAM LAMAKOM. Between the person and God.

BEN-SIRA. Author of Ecclesiasticus.

BET AVOT. Patriarchal household.

DEREKH ERETZ. Respectfulness; way of the world.

EREV SHABBAT. Friday afternoon before SABBATH.

ETROG. Citron, part of observance on SUKKOT involving four species: palm branch, citron, myrtles, and willows.

EZER K'NEGDO. Lit., "help by his side;" reference to wife.

GAN. Garden; reference to Garden of Eden.

GEHINNOM. Hell.

GET. Jewish divorce.

GITTIN. Talmudic tractate dealing mainly with divorce; alternatively, the plural form for GET.

HAFTORAH. Concluding Prophetic reading on Sabbaths, Festivals, and fasts, following the Biblical reading.

HALAKHAH. Jewish law applied to life.

HALAKHIC. Related to HALAKHAH (Jewish law).

HALAKHOT. Laws.

HAMAR. Driver of beasts of burden; lit., "ass-driver."

HANUKAH. Eight-day festive period commemorating Maccabee victory and rededication of the Temple.

241

HAREDI. Lit., "one with anxious reverence;" a reference to a type of Jew perceived to be more intensely religious.

HASHKAFAH. Philosophy of purpose; outlook on life and its meaning.

HASID SHOTEH. Foolish pietist.

HATAN. Groom.

HAVDALAH. Separating prayer, signaling end of SABBATH or festival.

HESED. Kindness.

HETER. Permission.

HIDUR MITZVAH. Beautifying the commandments.

HIVUV MITZVAH. Love of the commandments.

HOTZA'AT ZERA L'VATALAH. Wasteful emission of seed.

HUPAH. Canopy under which marriage ceremony takes place.

IMITATIO DEI. Emulation of God.

ISH. Man.

ISHAH. Woman.

KALLAH. Bride.

KASHRUT. Jewish dietary regulations.

KAVANAH. Single-mindedness in fulfilling the commandments; concentration.

KETUVAH. Marriage contract.

KIDDUSH. Sanctification prayer ushering in the SABBATH or festivals.

KIDDUSHIN. Talmudic tractate dealing mainly with marriage; alternatively, sanctification toward marriage, or betrothal.

KINYAN. Formal, legally binding act of agreement.

KIYUM HAMITZVAH. Fulfillment of the commandment.

LAZET YEDAY SHAMAYIM. To fulfill the desires of Heaven.

L'EREV. Lit., "toward evening"; metaphorically, in later stages of life; talmudically, the obligation not to desist from procreative activity in later years.

LEVITE. Member of the tribe of Levi who ministered in the Holy Temple.

LIFNIM. Inside.

LIFNIM MESHURAT HADIN. Within the boundary of the law.

LISHMAH. The pure intent for fulfilling the obligation.

L'MA'AN TELEKH B'DEREKH TOVIM. Lit., "in order that you walk in the path of good people."

MANNA. Food from Heaven which sustained Israel in their forty-year trek through the wilderness.

MATZAH OR MOTZAY. Found or find.

MATZAH TOV. Lit., "has found good."

MAZAL. Luck.

MAZAL TOV. Good luck; congratulations.

MEDIVRAY KABBALAH. Deriving from post-Mosaic tradition.

MEDIVRAY SOFRIM. Deriving from the scribes.

MEHABER. Literally, author; usually a reference to R. Yosef Karo, author of SHULHAN ARUKH, the Code of Jewish Law.

MENTSCH. Genuine human being; of high ethical and moral stature.

MENTSCHLICHKEIT. Authentic, genuine humanness.

MIDOT ḤASIDUT. The way of the pious.

MIDRASH. Rabbinic exegesis in the form of homily.

MIKVEH. Ritual bath.

MISHNAH. Basic test of law which is basis for ensuing discussion and debate, all together forming the TALMUD.

MITZVAH (pl. MITZVOT). Commandment.

MORED. Rebellious husband.

MOREDET. Rebellious wife.

MOTZAY ANI. "I find."

NISUIN. Marriage.

OLAM HABA. World-to-come.

OMNIPRESENT. A reference to God.

ONAH. Lit. "her time;" conjugal obligations.

PANIM. Face.

PESAḤ. Festival of freedom (Passover), commemorating the exodus from Egypt.

PITUM. Crown of ETROG.

PNIM. Interior.

RABBENU GERSHOM'S EDICT. Rule that the husband cannot divorce his wife against her will.

ROSH HASHANAH. Holy day of beginning of year.

ROSH ḤODESH. Beginning of the month, celebrated as a semifestival.

SABBATH. Seventh day of the week, celebrated as a day of rest and spiritual reinvigoration, from Friday before sundown to Saturday after sunset.

SAPAN. Sailor.

SHADKHAN. Matchmaker.

SHALOM. Peace, harmony.

SHALOM BAYIT. Domestic bliss.

SHAMOR. Obligation to keep from trespassing SABBATH regulations.

SHAVUOT. Festival of Weeks, commemorating acceptance of the Torah.

SHEVA BERAKHOT. Seven blessings recited at wedding and at festive meals in the week following the wedding.

SHLEMUT. Completeness.

SHEMA. Basic prayer of faith affirmation recited twice daily.

SHMINI ATZERET. Eighth day of assembly, the festival following the seven days of SUKKOT.

SHTETL. Small city, a reference to the integrated, intimate Jewish communities of yesteryear.

SHULḤAN ARUKH. Code of Jewish Law, compiled by R. Yosef Karo (16th century).

SUKKOT. Festival of Tabernacles.

TAHARAH. Purity.

TAHARAT HA'ISHAH. Purity of the woman.

TAHARAT HAMISHPAḤAH. Purity of the family; usually a reference to observance of laws related to menstruation and incumbent upon husband and wife.

TALMID ḤAKHAM. TORAH scholar.

TALMUD. Tractates containing explication of the TORAH by the rabbinic sages; *see also* MISHNAH.

TA'MAY. In a state of ritual limbo.

TANAKH. *Torah, Nevi'im, Ketuvim*; or TORAH, Prophets, and Scriptures, together comprising the twenty-four books of the Holy Scriptures.

TEFILIN. Phylacteries, boxes with parchment scrolls within; wrapped around arm and head during weekday morning prayers.

TESHUVAH. Repentance.

TORAH. Specifically, the Five Books of Moses; more generally, a reference to the Scriptures, the TALMUD, and commentaries thereon.

TOV. Good.

TRACTATE. Volume of the TALMUD.

TVILAH. Immersion.

V'AHAVTA. "And you shall like."

V'ANVAYHU. "To adorn the precepts."

V'ASEETA HAYASHAR V'HATOV. "And you shall do that which is upright and good."

V'SEMAḤ. "And should make happy, or gladden."

YASH-HENNA. Banishing, relating.

YETZER. Propensity, creative capacity.

YETZER HARA. Capacity to generate energy for actualizing the bad.

YETZER TOV. Capacity to generate energy for actualizing the good.

YIḤUS. Family pedigree.

YOM KIPPUR. Day of Atonement.

YOTER MEGUFO. "More than himself."

ZAKHOR. Positive obligation to observe the SABBATH.

ZERIZUT. Eagerness to actualize.

ZIMUN. Summons to recite grace in company of three or more.

ZUZ. Coin.

Bibliography

Primary Jewish Sources

The following is a partial list of primary Jewish sources consulted and cited in this book. Works which are commentaries of more primary texts are indented under the more primary text. Dates (in centuries) for authored works cited are given for texts which are not relatively contemporary.

1. Torah and Commentaries

The *Torah*, *Nevi'im* (Prophets), and *Ketuvim* (Scriptures).
    Abarbanel. R. Yitzhak Abarbanel (15th cent.).
    Akedat Yitzhak. R. Yitzhak Arama (15th cent.).
    Ba'al HaTurim. R. Yaakov ben Asher (14th cent.).
    HaKtav V'haKabbalah. R. Yaakov Zvi Meklenburg (19th cent.).
    Ibn Ezra. R. Avraham ibn Ezra (12th cent.).
    Meshekh Hokhmah. R. Meir Simhah HaKohen.
    RaDak. R. David Kimhi (12th–13th cent.).
    Ramban. R. Moshe ben Nahman (13th cent.).
    Rashi. R. Shlomoh Yitzhaki (11th cent.).
    Sforno. R. Ovadyah Sforno (16th cent.).
    Shimshon Raphael Hirsch's *Commentary on the Torah* (19th cent.).
    Targum Yonatan. R. Yonatan ben Uziel (7th cent.).

2. Midrash

Midrash Rabbah.
Midrash Tanhuma.
Yalkut Shimoni.
Zohar.

3. Talmud and Commentaries

The Babylonian Talmud with *Rashi* (11th cent.) and *Tosafot* (medieval French and German talmudists) on all standard editions of the Talmud.
    HaMakneh. R. Pinhas HaLevi Hurwitz (18th cent.).
    Maharsha. R. Shmuel Edels (16th–17th cent.).

Meiri, *Bet HaBhirah.* R. Menahem HaMeiri (13th cent.).
Yam Shel Shlomoh. R. Shlomoh Luria (16th cent.).

The Jerusalem Talmud.
Korban HaEdah. R. David Fraenkel (18th cent.).

Tosefta.

4. Codes and Commentaries

Alfasi (Rif). R. Yitzhak AlFasi (11th cent.).
HaMaor HaGadol. R. Zerahiah HaLevi (13th cent.).
Milhamot HaShem. R. Moshe ben Nahman (13th cent.).

Mishneh Torah. R. Moshe ben Maimon (12th cent.)
Maggid Mishneh. R. Vidal of Tolosa (14th cent.).
Mishneh L'Melekh. R. Yehudah Rozanes (17–18th cent.).

Hinukh. *Sefer HaHinukh.* R. Aharon HaLevi of Barcelona (14th cent.).
Sefer HaMitzvot. R. Moshe ben Maimon (12th cent.).
Ramban, *Hasagot haRamban.* R. Moshe ben Nahman (13th cent.).
Sefer Mitzvot Katan. R. Yitzhak of Corbeil (13th cent.).

Shulhan Arukh. R. Yosef Karo (16th cent.), with Glosses of *RaMoh*, R. Moshe
Isserles (16th cent.).
Arukh HaShulhan. R. Yehiel Mikhel Epstein (19th cent.).
Be'er Haytav. R. Yehudah Ashkenazi (18th cent.) on *Orah Hayyim* and *Even
Ha'Ezer.* R. Zekharia Mendel of Belz (18th cent.) on *Yoreh De'ah* and
Hoshen Mishpat.
Bet Shmuel. R. Shmuel ben Uri (17th cent.).
Birkay Yosef. R. Hayyim Yosef David Azulai (18th cent.).
Ezer MiKodesh. R. Avraham David of Buczacz (19th cent.).
Hazon Ish. R. Yeshayahu Karelitz.
Helkat Mehokek. R. Moshe of Brisk (17th cent.).
Hokhmat Adam. R. Avraham Danzig (18th–19th cent.).
Binat Adam. R. Avraham Danzig (18th–19th cent.).
Kreti U'Fleti. R. Yonatan Eybeshitz (18th cent.).
Mishnah Brurah. R. Yisrael Meir HaKohen.
Otzar HaPoskim.
Pit'hay Teshuvah. R. Avraham Zvi Eisenstadt (19th cent.).
Siftay Kohen (ShaKh). R. Shabtai HaKohen (17th cent.).
Toray Zahav (TaZ). R. David HaLevi (17th cent.).

5. Responsa

Avney Nezer. R. Avraham Bornstein.
Edut L'Yisrael. R. Eliyahu Henkin.

Ḥatam Sofer. R. Moshe Sofer (19th cent.).
Ḥayyim Shaal. R. Ḥayyim Yosef David Azulai (18th cent.).
Igrot Mosheh. R. Moshe Feinstein.
Ketav Sofer. R. Avraham Sofer (19th cent.).
Maharam M'Lublin. R. Meir ben Gedaliah (16th–17th cent.).
Maharit. R. Yosef of Trani (16th–17th cent.).
Maharsham. R. Shalom Mordecai Shwadron (19th cent.).
Minḥat Yitzḥak. R. Yitzḥak Yaakov Weiss.
Radvaz. R. David ben Shlomoh ibn Zimra (16th cent.).
Rosh. R. Asher ben Yeḥiel (13th–14th cent.).
She'elat Yaavetz. R. Yaakov Emden (18th cent.).
Yabea Omer. R. Ovadyah Yosef.
Ziz Eliezer. R. Eliezer Waldenberg.

6. Philosophical and Ethical Works

Ba'aley HaNefesh. R. Avraham ben David (12th cent.).
  Sela HaMaḥloket. R. Zeraḥiah HaLevi (13th cent.).
Be'er HaGolah. R. Yehudah Loew (16th–17th cent.).
Derekh P'kudekha al Taryag Mitzvot HaTorah. R. Zvi Elimelekh Shapira.
Guide for the Perplexed (Moreh Nevukhim). R. Moshe ben Maimon (12th cent.).
Ḥukay HaNashim. R. Yosef Ḥayyim ben Eliyahu Al Ḥakam (Ben Ish Ḥai) (19th cent.).
Ḥupat Ḥatanim. R. Rafael Meldola (18th cent.).
Iggeret HaKodesh. R. Moshe ben Naḥman (13th cent.).
Iggeret Teshuvah. R. Yonah ben Avraham Gerondi (13th cent.).
Kad HaKemaḥ. R. Baḥya ben Yosef ibn Paquda (11th cent.).
Likutay Eitzot. R. Naḥman of Bratslav (18th–19th cent.).
Menorat HaMaor. R. Yitzḥak Aboab (14th cent.).
Mesilat Yesharim. R. Moshe Ḥayyim Luzzatto (18th cent.).
Mikhtav M'Eliyahu. R. Eliyahu Dessler.
Netivot Olam. R. Yehudah Loew (16th–17th cent.).
Netzaḥ Yisrael. R. Yehudah Loew (16th–17th cent.).
Orḥot Yosher. R. Yitzḥak Molkho (17th cent.).
Orḥot Zadikim. (15th cent.).
Pele Yo'etz. R. Eliezer Papo (19th cent.).
Reshit Ḥakhmah. R. Eliyahu de Vidas (16th cent.).
Sefer Ḥaredim. R. Eliezer Azikri (16th cent.).
Sefer Ḥasidim. R. Yehudah HaḤasid (12th–13th cent.).
Shelah (Shnay Luḥot HaBrit). R. Yeshayahu Horowitz (17th cent.).
Shevet Musar. R. Eliyahu HaKohen Ittimari (17th–18th cent.).
Shmonah Perakim. R. Moshe ben Maimon (12th cent.).
Tomer Dvorah. R. Moshe Cordovero (16th cent.).

7. Works on Prayer

Abudarham. R. David ben Yosef (14th cent.).
Siddur Bet Yaakov. R. Yaakov Emden (18th cent.).
Siddur Hatam Sofer. R. Moshe Sofer (19th cent.)—edited from his works.
Siddur Minhat Yerushalayim. R. Yeshayahu and Yehoshua Dvorkes.

English and Recent Hebrew Sources

Ables, Billie. *Therapy for Couples.* San Francisco: Jossey-Bass, 1977.
Allport, Gordon. "Comments on Earlier Papers." In *Existential Psychology*, ed. Rollo May, pp. 93–98. New York: Random House, 1961.
Appleton, Jane, and William Appleton. *How Not to Split Up.* New York: Berkley Books, 1979.
Asher, Yehiel. "HaIshah HaZeirah." In *Bet Yisrael. HaMishpahah HaYehudit*, ed. Yehezkel Rottenberg, pp. 466–467. Bnai Brak: Netzah, 1981.
Ashkenazi, Shlomoh. *HaIsha B'Aspaklaryat HaYehadut.* Tel Aviv: Zion, 1979.
Aviner, Shlomoh. *Etzem Ma'Atzamay, Banekha Kishtelay Zaytim.* Jerusalem: Privately printed, 1984.
———. *Pirkey Ahavah Bayn Ish L'Ishto.* Jerusalem: Privately printed, 1983.
Basry, Sima. *The Challenge of Marriage.* Jerusalem: HaKtav Institute, 1982.
———. "Shalom Bayit." In *Bet Yisrael. HaMishpahah HaYehudit*, ed. Yehezkel Rottenberg, pp. 663–667. Bnai Brak: Netzah, 1981.
Belkin, Samuel. *In His Image.* New York: Abelard-Schuman, 1960.
Berkovits, Eliezer. *Crisis and Faith.* New York: Sanhedrin Press, 1976.
Berman, Saul. "The Status of Women in Halakhic Judaism." *Tradition* 14, no. 2 (Fall 1973): 5–28.
Berry, Newton. "Portrait of a Family Conservationist." *Marriage and Family Living* 60, no. 10 (October 1978): 10–13.
Binyan Aday Ahd. Jerusalem: Dvar Yerushalayim Publications, n.d.
Birner, Louis. "Unconscious Resistance to Pre-Marital Counseling." In *Pre-Marital Counseling: A Guide for Rabbis*, ed. David Feldman, pp. 19–26. New York: Commission on Synagogue Relations, Federation of Jewish Philanthropies of New York, 1974.
Blood, Bob, and Margaret Blood. *Marriage.* New York: Free Press, 1978.
Blood, Robert, and Donald Wolfe. *Husbands and Wives: The Dynamics of Married Living.* Glencoe, Ill.: Free Press, 1980.
Blumstein, Philip, and Pepper Schwartz. *American Couples: Money, Work, Sex.* New York: William Morrow, 1983.
Boll, Eleanor. "Should Parents or Cupid Arrange Marriages?" In *Marriage Today: Problems, Issues and Alternatives*, ed. James De Burger, pp. 199–203. Cambridge, Mass.: Schenkman, 1977. Reprinted from *New York Times Magazine*, December 13, 1959.
Bronsdorfer, Yedidya. *Kedushat Morashah.* Tel Aviv: Privately printed, n.d.

Buber, Martin. Letter to Franz Rosenzweig. In Franz Rosenzweig, *On Jewish Learning,* p. 111. New York: Schocken Books, 1955.

———. *Tales of the Hasidim: The Early Masters.* New York: Commentary Classics, 1958.

Bulka, Reuven. *As a Tree by the Waters—Pirkey Avoth: Psychological and Philosophical Insights.* New York: Philipp Feldheim, 1980.

———. "Divorce: The Problem and the Challenge." *Tradition* 16, no. 1 (Summer 1976): 127–133.

———. "Logotherapy as a Response to the Holocaust." In *The Quest for Ultimate Meaning: Principles and Applications of Logotherapy,* pp. 138–145. New York: Philosophical Library, 1979.

———. "Philosophical Foundations for Marriage Counseling." In *Logotherapy in Action,* ed. Joseph Fabry, Reuven Bulka, and William Sahakian, pp. 138–145. New York: Jason Aronson, 1979.

———. "Psychology and Judaism—Retrospect and Prospect." *L'Eylah* 1, no. 10 (Fall 1980): 23–26.

———. *The Quest for Ultimate Meaning: Principles and Applications of Logotherapy.* New York: Philosophical Library, 1979.

———. "The Role of the Individual in Jewish Law." *Tradition* 13–14, nos. 4–1 (Spring–Summer 1973): 124–136.

———. "Some Implications of Jewish Marriage Philosophy for Marital Breakdown." *Pastoral Psychology* 30, no. 2 (Winter 1981): 103–112.

———. *Torah Therapy: Reflections on the Weekly Sedra and Special Occasions.* New York: Ktav, 1983.

———. "Woman's Role—Some Ultimate Concerns." *Tradition* 17, no. 4 (Spring 1979): 27–40.

———, ed. *Dimensions of Orthodox Judaism.* New York: Ktav, 1983.

———, ed. *Family and Marriage Newsletter.* New York: Rabbinical Council of America Family and Marriage Committee. (Published semiannually since 1977.)

Burgess, Ernest, and Paul Wallin. *Engagement and Marriage.* Chicago: Lippincott, 1953.

Campbell, Angus. "The American Way of Mating: Marriage Si, Children Only Maybe." *Psychology Today* 8, no. 12 (May 1975): 37–43.

Chavel, Hayyim, ed. *Sefer HaHinukh.* Jerusalem: Mosad HaRav Kook, 1966.

Chesler, Phyliss. *Women and Madness.* New York: Avon Books, 1973.

Cuber, John, and Peggy Harroff. *The Significant Americans: A Study of Sexual Behavior among the Affluent.* New York: Appleton-Century, 1965.

Davids, Leo. "Jewish Marriage Breakdown in Canada: Some Plain Facts." *Family and Marriage Newsletter* 5, no. 2 (Winter 1981): 1–4.

de Beauvoir, Simone. *The Second Sex.* New York: Alfred A. Knopf, 1953.

Don-Yechiya, Benny. *Mishpahah B'Mishpat: Madrikh L'Dinay Ishut.* Tel Aviv: Hok U'Mishpat, 1983.

Drazin, Nathan. *Marriage Made in Heaven*. London and New York: Abelard-Schuman, 1958.

Dreikurs, Rudolf. *The Challenge of Marriage*. New York: Duell, Sloan & Pearce, 1946.

El HaMekorot. Bnai Brak, 1982.

Ellenson, Elyakim. *HaIshah V'haMitzvot*. Jerusalem: World Zionist Organization, 1981. Especially Vol. 3 (*Ish V'Ishto*).

Elon, Menahem. *HaMishpat Ha'Ivri*. Jerusalem: Magnes Press, 1973.

Epstein, Yosef. *Mitzvat HaEitzah*. New York: Torat Ha'Adam Institute, 1983.

———. *Mitzvat HaMusar*. New York: Torat Ha'Adam Institute, 1973.

———. *Mitzvat HaShalom*. New York: Torat Ha'Adam Institute, 1969.

———. *Sefer Mitzvot HaBayit*. New York: Torat Ha'Adam Institute, 1975.

Falk, Zev. *Dinay Nisuin*. Jerusalem: Mesharim, 1983.

Farson, Richard. "Why Good Marriages Fail." In *Marriage Today: Problems, Issues and Alternatives*, ed. James De Burger, pp. 250–56. Cambridge, Mass.: Schenkman, 1977.

Feldman, David. *Marital Relations, Birth Control, and Abortion in Jewish Law*. New York: Schocken Books, 1974.

Fertel, Norman, and Esther Feuer. "Treating Marital and Sexual Problems in the Orthodox Jewish Community." *Journal of Psychology and Judaism* 5, no. 2 (Spring–Summer 1981): 85–94.

Fowler, F. J. *1975 Community Survey: A Study of the Jewish Population of Greater Boston*. Boston: Combined Jewish Philanthropies of Greater Boston, 1977.

Frankl, Viktor. "The Depersonalization of Sex." *Synthesis* 1 (Spring 1974): 7–11.

———. *The Doctor and the Soul: From Psychotherapy to Logotherapy*. New York: Bantam Books, 1967.

———. "Logos and Existence in Psychotherapy." *American Journal of Psychotherapy* 7 (1953): 8–15.

———. *Man's Search for Meaning: An Introduction to Logotherapy*. New York: Washington Square Press, 1963.

———. "Self-Transcendence as a Human Phenomenon." *Journal of Humanistic Psychology* 6, no. 2 (Fall 1966): 97–106.

———. *The Unconscious God: Psychotherapy and Theology*. New York: Simon & Schuster, 1975.

———. *The Unheard Cry for Meaning: Psychotherapy and Humanism*. New York: Simon & Schuster, 1978.

Fromm, Erich. *The Forgotten Language*. New York: Grove Press, 1957.

Galligan, Richard, and Stephen Bahr. "Economic Well-Being and Marital Stability: Implications for Income Maintenance Programs." *Journal of Marriage and the Family* 40, no. 2 (May 1978): 283–290.

Gebhard, Paul. "Facters in Marital Orgasm." In *Handbook of Sex Therapy*, ed. Joseph Lo Piccolo and Leslie Lo Piccolo, pp. 167–174. New York: Plenum Press, 1978.

Gilder, George. *Sexual Suicide.* New York: Bantam Books, 1975.

Girshuni, A. A. "HaMafteaḥ L'Osher." In *Bet Yisrael: HaMishpahah HaYehudit*, ed. Yeḥezkel Rottenberg, pp. 638–648. Bnai Brak: Netzaḥ, 1981.

Glick, Paul, and Arthur Norton. "Marrying, Divorcing and Living Together in the U.S. Today." *Population Bulletin* 32, no. 5 (October 1977): 36–37.

Gordon, Michael. "From an Unfortunate Necessity to a Cult of Mutual Orgasm: Sex in American Marital Education Literature, 1830–1940." In *Studies in the Sociology of Sex*, ed. James Henslin, pp. 53–77. New York: Appleton-Century-Crofts, 1971.

Gordon, Suzanne. *Lonely in America: A Portrait of Americans—Young, Old, Married, Single, in Groups and Alone.* New York: Simon & Schuster, 1976.

Gottman, John, Cliff Notarius, Jonni Gonso, and Howard Markham. *A Couple's Guide to Communication.* Champaign, Ill.: Research Press, 1976.

Gove, Walter, and Claire Peterson. "An Update of the Literature on Personal and Marital Adjustment: The Effects of Children and the Employment of Wives." *Marriage and Family Review* 3, nos. 3–4 (Fall–Winter 1980): 63–96.

Gross, Martin. *The Psychological Society: A Critical Analysis of Psychiatry, Psychotherapy, Psychoanalysis and the Psychological Revolution.* New York: Random House, 1978.

Gurin, Gerald, Joseph Veroff, and Sheila Feld. *Americans View Their Mental Health.* New York: Basic Books, 1960.

HaLevy, Ḥayyim David. *Mekor Ḥayyim: LeHatan Lekallah Ul'Mishpaḥah.* Tel Aviv, 1979.

Hankoff, Leon. "Psychotherapy and Values: Issues, Conflicts, and Misconceptions." *Journal of Psychology and Judaism* 4, no. 1 (Fall 1979): 5–14.

Hendin, Herbert. "The Ties Don't Bind." *New York Times*, August 26, 1976, p. 33.

Hirsch, Samson Raphael. *Judaism Eternal.* London: Soncino Press, 1956.

Hofstein, Saul. "Perspectives on the Jewish Single Parent Family." *Journal of Jewish Communal Service* 54, no. 3 (Spring 1978): 229–240.

Iggeret Kodesh Me'Et Gedolay HaDor. Jerusalem, 1968.

Jakobovits, Immanuel. "Marriage and Divorce." In *Woman*, vol. 3 of *The Jewish Library*, ed. Leo Jung, pp. 101–121. London: Soncino Press, 1970.

Kalkheim, Uzi. "Al Maamad HaIshah." In *HaIshah V'Ḥinukhah*, ed. Ben Zion Rosenfeld, pp. 77–89. Kfar Saba: Amanah, 1980.

Kaplan, Aryeh. *Made in Heaven.* New York: Maznaim, 1983.

———. *Waters of Eden: The Mystery of the Mikveh.* New York: National Conference of Synagogue Youth, Union of Orthodox Jewish Congregations of America, 1976.

Kaplan, Helen Singer. *The New Sex Therapy: Active Treatment of Sexual Dysfunctions.* New York: Brunner/Mazel, 1974.

Kirkendall, Lester. *Premarital Intercourse and Interpersonal Relations.* New York: Julian Press, 1961.

Kitov, Eliyahu, *The Jew and His Home.* New York: Shengold, 1963.

Koltun, Elizabeth, ed. *The Jewish Woman: New Perspectives*. New York: Schocken Books, 1976.

Kover, Naftali. "Drakhehah Darkhey Noam." In *Bet Yisrael: HaMishpahah Ha-Yehudit*, ed. Yehezkel Rottenberg, pp. 649–652. Bnai Brak: Netzah, 1981.

Kranzler, Gershon. "The Changing Orthodox Jewish Family." *Jewish Life*, Summer–Fall 1978, pp. 23–36.

Lamm, Maurice. *The Jewish Way in Love and Marriage*. San Francisco: Harper & Row, 1980.

Lamm, Norman. *A Hedge of Roses: Jewish Insights into Marriage and Married Life*. New York: Philipp Feldheim, 1966.

———. *The Royal Reach: Discourses on the Jewish Tradition and the World Today*. New York: Philipp Feldheim, 1970.

Landis, Judson, and Mary Landis. *Building a Successful Marriage*. Englewood Cliffs, N.J.: Prentice-Hall, 1968.

Lang, Judith. "Divorce and the Jewish Woman. A Family Agency Approach." *Journal of Jewish Communal Service* 54, no. 3 (Spring 1978): 220–228.

Lasswell, Marcia, and Norman Lobsenz. "The Intimacy That Goes Beyond Sex." In *The Changing Family: Making Way for Tomorrow*, ed. Jerald Savells and Lawrence Cross, pp. 347–354. New York: Holt, Rinehart & Winston, 1978.

Leichter, Hope, and William Mitchell. *Kinship and Casework: Family Network and Social Intervention*. New York: Teachers College Press, 1978.

Leslie, Gerald. *The Family in Social Context*. New York: Oxford University Press, 1979.

Levi, Leo. *Man and Woman: The Torah Perspective*. Jerusalem: Ezer LaYeled, 1979.

Levi-Jung, Rivka. "HaTaharah, Shaar LeHayay Nisuin Meusharim." In *Bet Yisrael: HaMishpahah HaYehudit*, ed. Yehezkel Rottenberg, pp. 364–369. Bnai Brak: Netzah, 1981.

Levitz, Irving. "Crisis in Orthodoxy: The Ethical Paradox." In *Dimensions of Orthodox Judaism*, ed. Reuven Bulka, pp. 380–386. New York: Ktav, 1983.

Levy, Yehuda. "HaIsh V'haIsha B'Yehadut." In *El HaMekorot*, vol. 2, pp. 213–219. Bnai Brak, 1982.

Liebman, Charles. "Orthodox Judaism Today." In *Dimensions of Orthodox Judaism*, ed. Reuven Bulka, pp. 106–120. New York, Ktav, 1983.

Linzer, Norman. *The Jewish Family: A Compendium*. New York: Commission on Synagogue Relations, Federation of Jewish Philanthropies of New York, 1972.

Locke, Harvey. *Predicting Adjustment in Marriage: A Comparison of a Divorced and a Happily Married Group*. New York: Holt, 1951.

Luzzatto, Moshe Hayyim. *Yalkut Yediot HaEmet*. Tel Aviv: Ahavah, 1965.

Lynch, James. *The Broken Heart: The Medical Consequences of Loneliness*. New York: Basic Books, 1979.

McCary, James. *Freedom and Growth in Marriage*. Santa Barbara, Calif.: Hamilton, 1975.

Mahoney, Michael, and Diane Arnkoff. "Cognitive and Self-Control Therapies." In *Handbook of Psychotherapy and Behavior Change: An Empirical Analysis*, ed. Sol Garfield and Allen Bergin, pp. 689–722. New York: John Wiley, 1978.

Marini, Margaret. "Dimensions of Marriage Happiness: A Research Note." *Journal of Marriage and the Family* 38, no. 3 (August 1976): 443–448.

Massarik, Fred. *Intermarriage: Facts for Planning*. New York: Council of Jewish Federations and Welfare Funds, n.d.

Masters, William, and Virginia Johnson. *Human Sexual Response*. Boston: Little, Brown, 1966.

—— and ——. *The Pleasure Bond: A New Look at Sexuality and Commitment*. Boston: Little, Brown, 1974.

May, Rollo. *Love and Will*. New York: Norton, 1969.

Meichenbaum, Donald. *Cognitive Behavior Modification*. Morristown, N.J.: General Learning Press, 1974.

Mermelstein, Jacob. "Halachic Values and the Clinical Practice of Psychotherapy." *Intercom* 16, no. 2 (1976): 4–9.

Mitchell, Juliet. *Psychoanalysis and Feminism*. New York: Random House, 1974.

Montagu, Ashley. *The Natural Superiority of Women*. New York: Macmillan, 1971.

Naftali, G. *Iggeret LeḤatan V'Hadrakhah LeNasuy*. Jerusalem: HaOsher Press, 1983.

Neriah, Rachel. *Happiness in Married Life*. Jerusalem: Central Committee for Taharat Hamishpaḥah in Israel, n.d.

——. "Likrat HaNisuin." In *El HaMekorot*, vol. 1, pp. 228–233. Bnai Brak, 1982.

Neubauer, Ruth. "The Changing Background of Pre-Marital Counseling." In *Pre-Marital Counseling: A Guide for Rabbis*, ed. David Feldman, pp. 12–18. New York: Commission on Synagogue Relations, Federation of Jewish Philanthropies of New York, 1974.

O'Neill, George, and Nena O'Neill. *Open Marriage: A New Lifestyle for Couples*. New York: Evans, 1972.

O'Neill, Nena. *The Marriage Premise*. New York: Evans, 1977.

Ostrov, Stewart. "Problems Confronting the Orthodox Jewish Family in America." *Intercom* 16, no. 3 (June 1977): 20–25.

Patai, Raphael. *The Jewish Mind*. New York: Scribner's, 1977.

Pliskin, Zelig. *Gateway to Happiness*. Monsey, N.Y.: Jewish Learning Exchange, 1983.

Raz, Simcha. *A Tzaddik in Our Time: The Life of Rabbi Aryeh Levin*. Jerusalem: Philipp Feldheim, 1978.

Reik, Theodor. *Jewish Wit*. New York: Gamut Press, 1962.

——. *A Psychologist Looks at Love*. New York: Grove Press, 1944.

Reiss, Ira. *Family Systems in America*. New York: Holt, Rinehart & Winston, 1980.

Rosenberg, Morris. *Society and the Adolescent Self-Image*. Princeton, N.J.: Princeton University Press, 1965.

Rosenfeld, Ben Zion, ed. *HaIshah V'Hinukhah*. Kfar Saba: Amanah, 1980.

Rosner, Fred, and J. David Bleich, eds. *Jewish Bioethics*. New York: Sanhedrin Press, 1979.

Saxton, Lloyd. *The Individual, Marriage and the Family*. Belmont: Calif.: Wadsworth, 1968.

Scanzoni, John. *Opportunity and the Family*. New York: Free Press, 1970.

Schachter, Herschel. "Halachic Aspects of Family Planning." *Journal of Halacha and Contemporary Society* 6 (Fall 1982): 5–32.

Schindler, Ruben. "Counseling Hassidic Couples: The Cultural Dimension." *Journal of Psychology and Judaism* 8, no. 1 (Fall–Winter 1983): 52–61.

Schlesinger, Benjamin. "The Jewish Family in the 1980's." *Viewpoints: The Canadian Jewish Monthly* 12, no. 2 (March 1983): 4–5.

———. "Reflections on Family Breakdown Among Jewish Families." *Journal of Psychology and Judaism* 1, no. 1 (Fall 1976): 45–53.

Schwartz, Yoel. *Ish V'Re'eyhu*, Jerusalem: Dvar Yerushalayim, 1981.

Shapiro, David. "Be Fruitful and Multiply." *In Jewish Bioethics*, ed. Fred Rosner and J. David Bleich, pp. 59–79. New York: Sanhedrin Press, 1979.

Shereshevsky, Ben Zion. *Dinay Mishpahah*. Jerusalem: Rubin Mass, n.d.

Shope, David, and Calfred Broderick. "Level of Sexual Experience and Predicted Adjustment in Marriage." *Journal of Marriage and the Family* 29, no. 3 (August 1967): 424–427.

Spero, Moshe HaLevi. *Judaism and Psychology: Halakhic Perspectives*. New York: Ktav and Yeshiva University Press, 1980.

———. "On the Relationship between Psychotherapy and Judaism." *Journal of Psychology and Judaism* 1, no. 1 (Fall 1976): 15–33.

Spero, Shubert. *Morality, Halakhah, and Jewish Tradition*. New York: Ktav and Yeshiva University Press, 1983.

Sternbuch, Moshe. *HaHalakhah B'Mishpahah*. Bnai Brak: Netivot HaTorah V'haHessed, 1981.

Taharani, Eliyahu. *Alufaynu Mesubalim*. Jerusalem: Siah Yisrael, 1980.

Tavris, Carol. *Anger: The Misunderstood Emotion*. New York: Simon & Schuster, 1984.

Travis, Tsvi. *Pirkey Hanhagat HaBayit*. Jerusalem: Privately printed, 1983.

Van Buren, Abigail. *The Best of Dear Abby*. New York: Pocket Books, 1981.

Van de Velde, Theodore. *Ideal Marriage: Its Physiology and Technique*. New York: Random House, 1930.

Waxman, Chaim. "The Threadbare Canopy: The Vicissitudes of the Jewish Family in Modern American Society." *American Behavioral Scientist* 23, no. 4 (March–April 1980): 467–486.

Weinberg, Yehiel Yaakov. "Nisuin." In *Bet Yisrael: HaMishpahah HaYehudit*, ed. Yehezkel Rottenberg, pp. 444–448. Bnai Brak: Netzah, 1981.

Weinberger, Bernard. "The Growing Rate of Divorce in Orthodox Jewish Life." *Jewish Life*, Spring 1976, pp. 9–14.

Weiner, Yosef Zvi. "Ezer K'Negdo." In *Bet Yisrael: HaMishpaḥah HaYehudit*, ed. Yeḥezkel Rottenberg, pp. 482–490. Bnai Brak: Netzaḥ, 1981.

———. *Neve HaBḥirah*. Tel Aviv: Ram, 1979.

Weiss, Robert. *Loneliness: The Study of Emotional and Social Isolation*. Cambridge, Mass.: MIT Press, 1975.

———. *Marital Separation*. New York: Basic Books, 1975.

Wolbe, Shlomoh. *Aley Shur*. Beer Yaakov, 1978.

———. *Kuntrus Hadrakhah LeKalot*. Bnai Brak: Ohr HaHayyim Seminary, 1976.

———. *Maamaray Hadrakhah LeHatanim*. Jerusalem: Bet HaMusar, 1983.

Wurzburger, Walter. "Covenantal Imperatives." In *Samuel K. Mirsky Memorial Volume: Studies in Jewish Law, Philosophy, and Literature*, ed. Gersion Appel, pp. 3–12. New York: Yeshiva University Press, 1970.

Yankelovich, Daniel. *New Rules: Searching for Self-Fulfillment in a World Turned Upside Down*. New York: Bantam Books, 1982.

Yashar, Barukh. *LeBat Yisrael B'Gil HaNisuin*. Jerusalem: Weinfeld Press, 1974.

Yellin, Avraham. *Erekh Apayim*. Jerusalem, 1963.

Zaks, Menahem, ed. *Kol Kitvey Ḥafetz Ḥayyim HaShalem*. New York: Friedman, 1952.

Zuk, Gerald. "A Therapist's Perspective on Jewish Family Values." *Journal of Marriage and Family Counseling* 4, no. 1 (January 1978): 103–110.